The Second World War in the Far East

THE SECOND WORLD WAR IN THE FAR EAST

H. P. Willmott

General Editor: John Keegan

CASSELL&CO

For FY. 1645.

Cassell & Co
Wellington House, 125 Strand
London WC2R 0BB

First published 1999
Reprinted 2000

British Library Cataloguing-in-Publication Data
A catalogue record for this book is available from the British Library.
ISBN 0-304-35247-0

Cartography: Arcadia Editions
Design: Roger Daniels
Picture research: Elaine Willis
Printed and bound in Italy by L.E.G.O. S.p.A.

Typeset in Monotype Sabon

ACKNOWLEDGEMENTS

In the preparation of this book acknowledgement must be made in four groups: first, of course, there is the debt to family: Pauline, Gaynor and Sean, and Stephen, and my sister Vivien. I trust that they will think that the effort that went into the preparation of this book was justified by the result, and for their support when I was seriously ill during its preparation I am grateful in a way that I can never fully express. In addition, and as always in my books, I would acknowledge my debts to Everton, Sherry and Kondor and trust they are at peace, and to Jamie and Suki not least for their insistence during my illness that I was fit enough to walk them every day.

Second, I would wish to thank those who, over many years whether in the form of conferences, lectures, exchange of letters or general conversation, provided me with the basis of knowledge and critical facility that made this work possible. To attempt to list these people is impossible, but they have the satisfaction of knowing that without them this book could never have been written and also that they are not responsible for the various errors that may be within its pages.

Third, I would acknowledge my debt to those of Cassell without whose patience, tact and ability this book would probably have gone the way of the Japanese merchant marine in the course of this conflict: specifically one would cite one's debts to Hilary Bird, Judith Flanders, Penny Gardiner, Alice Hunt, Caroline Knight, Judith Millidge and Elaine Willis and trust that they will accept this acknowledgement, and not try to amend it.

Fourth, a special acknowledgement has to be made to those professional colleagues and friends who provided me with support at a time of serious illness when this book was being prepared. Those people whom I would acknowledge as those to whom I owe a special debt of gratitude are Tim Bean, Matthew Bennett, David Brown, Patrick Burke, Tony Clayton, Michael Coles, Martine and Nigel de Lee, Christopher Duffy, Geoffrey Gentsch, Paddy Griffith, Paul Harris, Jane Kingdon, Andrea and Spenser Johnson, Jackie Lambourne, John Andreas Olsen and Tine Larsen, Richard Penrose, Ro Roberts, Raymond Sibbald, Jack and Gee Sweetman, Tomatsu Haruo, Manjinder Uppal, John Votaw, Sally and Steven Weingartner and Ed Yorke. I would not wish to thank one more than another, and those who helped me the most know who they are without my elaboration: to those especially, but to all who so aided me, I owe a special debt which I will discharge in due course. Finally, I would make reference to one person who, alas, is no longer with us. In the final stages of preparation, in fact the day when I started to write this section, I received notice that David Evans had joined the majority. Inevitably this meant that his name was moved from one list, only to be noted separately, sadly, and for all the wrong reasons. Very simply, he was a scholar of the first order, honourable and above all, a gentle man. Sailor, rest your oar.

H. P. WILLMOTT

Englefield Green, Egham, Surrey.

19 June 1999 (being the 55th anniversary of the Battle of the Philippine Sea).

Old Glory, Mount Suribachi, Iwo Jima, February 1945.

Contents

KEY TO MAPS

Military units – types

- infantry
- armoured
- motorized infantry
- airborne
- parachute
- artillery

Military units – size

- XXXXX army group
- XXXX army
- XXX corps
- XX division
- X brigade
- III regiment
- II battalion

Military unit colours

- Allied
- British
- Japanese
- French
- Russian
- other territory

General military symbols

- —XXXXX— army group boundary
- —XXXX— army boundary
- front line
- defensive line
- defensive line (3D maps)
- field work
- pocket or position
- field gun
- paratroop drop
- sunken ship
- airfield

Geographical symbols

- urban area
- road
- railway
- river
- seasonal river
- canal
- border
- bridge or pass

Military movements

- attack
- retreat
- air attack

Map list

Chronology

China 1937–45

1937

7 July — Lukouchiao Incident.
11 — Local truce agreed. Tokyo agrees to send five divisions to Kwantung Army.
29/30 — Massacre of Japanese (J.) population of Tungchow: J. capture town 30th, massacre population, raze town.
30 — J. secure Tientsin.
31–8 Aug — J. secure Peking.
7 Aug — J. policy of 'autonomy' for northern China.
9 — Abortive Imperial Japanese Navy (IJN) attempt to secure Hungchiao airfield at Shanghai.
11 — J. secure Nankow, subsequently secure Chuyungkuan pass.
13 — Landing of J. divisions at Shanghai.
14 — Start of fighting at Shanghai: J. clear city mid September.
14/16 — First bombing raids by J. naval air groups from Formosa and Kyushu: curtailed because lack of escorts lead to prohibitive losses. A5M Claude fighter introduced into service in Sept; instant drop of losses.
26 — J. secure Huailai.
3 Sep — J. secure Kalgan.
31 — North China Area Army activated.
13 Sep — J. secure Tatung, secure Pingtichuan 23rd, Kueisui 14 Oct, Paotow 17th and gain control of Inner Mongolia.
25 — J. defeat in Pingtichuan pass by communists.
Oct — First bombing of Nanking.
5 — J. secure Tehchow, Shihchiachuang 10th, Anyang 31st.
23 — Proclamation of Suiyan independence.
29 — Separatist government in Mongolia proclaimed.
31 — J. secure Yucheng.
5 Nov — J. landings in Hangchow Bay. Collapse of Chinese (Ch.) resistance at Shanghai: J. secure Sungkiang 8th, Paihokang 11th.
9 — J. secure Taituan.
29 — J. secure Changchow.
3 Dec — J. secure Tanyang.
4 — Lanchou, staging post for aircraft being supplied by USSR, raided by J. bombers.
12 — J. sinking of USS *Panay*.
13 — J. enter Nanking: deliberate terror over several weeks, estimated 2–300,000 dead.
14 — J. install 'provisional government' in Peking.
26 — Kuomintang (KMT) reject negotiations with Japan.

1938

10 Jan — J. secure Tsingtao.
Jan — J. army ministry proposes 'restrained policy for protracted war', consolidation of recent gains and large-scale operations in 1939–40 aimed at destruction of KMT government.
13 Feb — J. forces operating from Tauyuan and Anyang take Pingyaohsien, Singsiang 17th, Changchih 20th, Lishih 24th, Linfen 26th.
16 — Imperial Conference, confirms policy of restraint; rejected by main army commands in China and replacement of policy on 1 Mar. J. forces secure Tsinyang 21st, Yuanku 27th.
Mar — J. forces secure Hotsin 4th, Anyi 6th, Pinglu 9th, line of Yellow river and control of Shansi.
5 — J. secure Tamgtpucheng: move against Hsuchow 24th; Tierhchuang taken 8th.
14 — Start of J. offensive against Hsuchow aimed to effect a meeting of northern and central armies.
spring — First deliberate terror-bombing raid on Canton.
May — J. take Amoy, Foochow and Swatow by amphibious assault. J. secure Tsowhsien. J secure Hefei 14th, Yungcheng 18th: meeting of armies advancing on Hsuchow, taken 20th.
Jun — J. secure Kaifeng 6th, Chengchow 10th. Ch. open Yellow river dikes to prevent further J. advances. J. redeployment for offensive up Yangtse.
Jul — Preliminary moves in Yangtse offensive; main effort open in Aug. with Liuan secured 28th.
11/10 Aug — Changkufeng incident: clash between J. and Soviet forces in disputed border areas between Korea, Manchoutikuo and USSR.
16 — J. secure Shangcheng, Hwangchwan 17th.
autumn — First systematic air attacks on KMT communications with outside world: targets include Hanoi railroad, Burma Road.
Oct — J. secure Sinyang 10th, Canton 12th/21st.
25 — J. secure Hangkow, Sungfow, Yingshan, Hanyang and Wuchang 26th, Yingchen 30th. In effect end of campaign.
3 Nov — Tokyo announces 'New Order in East Asia'.
13 — Unthreatened Changsa razed by KMT.

1939

Feb — J. secure Hainan.
Mar — Burma Road opens.
18 — J. forces cross Hsiu at Tsaohsing and take Nanchang 27th.
21 Apr/8 May — KMT counter-attack at Nanchang defeated.
May — First air raids on Chungking. J. and Soviet forces clash around Nomonhan: major action Aug., conclusive J. defeat mid Sep.
27 Sep — Start of J. offensive against Changsa.
Nov — KMT offensive: desultory, though Kaifeng briefly re-taken.
15 — J. forces from Canton secure Chinhsein: amphibious assaults and subsequent capture of Pakhoi and Hopu.
23 — J. secure Nanning.

1940

2 Feb — J. secure Pinyang.
Mar — Wang Ching-wei regime installed in Nanking.
spring — Operation 101, bombing campaign against Chungking, other cities and air bases in interior intended to destroy will to resist: massed formations, as many as 120 bombers in single attacks. Little success and mounting casualties until Aug. and

appearance of A6M Zero-sen. Operation 101 involves 182 raids and 3,715 sorties.

8 May — J. secure Tsaoyang.

9/12 Jun — J. secure Yichang.

25 Jun — J. demand for right to land forces in northern French Indo-China conceded.

18 Jul — Br. closure of Burma Road on J. demand.

1 Aug — First demand by IJN within J. high command to occupy French Indo-China.

20/10 Sep — Communists' Hundred Regiments Campaign in Hopei and Shansi.

22 Sep — J. occupy northern French Indo-China.

26 — US steel embargo on Japan.

27 — J. accede to Tripartite Pact.

Oct/Dec — J. counter-offensive throughout Hopei and Shansi, reversing whatever success communist offensive commanded.

30 — J. abandon Nanning.

Nov — First 'rice raids' conducted in Hupei province, followed by raids in southern Honan new year, in north-west Kiangsi and Hupei Mar. 1941. Regular feature of J. effort 1940–44 intended to devastate areas and inflict mass starvation across areas that J. could not control.

17 — J. abandon Chinhsein.

30 — Axis recognition of Wang regime, collapse of last real J. attempt to gain negotiated settlement with KMT.

1941

4 Jan — New Fourth Army incident at Maolin: KMT forces attack communists, in effect resumption of civil war.

Mar — First Lend-Lease arrangements between US and China.

spring–summer — Operation 102, attempt to repeat 1940's bombing effort: less successful mainly because naval aircraft being withdrawn after spring in readiness for operations in Pacific and south-east Asia.

May — J. clear northern Honan, occupy Chengchow.

summer — Kill All, Burn All, Destroy All campaign by J. army in northern areas controlled by communists. In this and later operations communist base areas reduced from 44 to 25 million by mass deportations, massacre and deliberate starvation. Communists neutralized as a threat, with no major guerrilla activity in northern China for remainder of war.

21 Jul — IJN pronounce in favour of war with United States.

25 — J. proclaim Indo-China as joint French and J. protectorate: US freeze all J. assets in response 26th.

17 Sep — Start of J. offensive against Changsa, and advance to positions between Laotao and Liuyang rivers: KMT counter-attack 27th and J. beaten back.

Oct — J. secure Chengchow.

Dec/Jan 42 — Third J. attempt to secure Changsa defeated.

7 Dec — Opening of hostilities in Pacific and south-east Asia; after Jan 1942 KMT forces committed to Burma.

1942

7 Jun — J. secure Chuhsien 10th; J. effort in Chekiang, staged partly as retaliation for Doolittle Raid, continues end Jul.

15 Jul — Ferry command between India and China activated.

1943

11 Mar — 14th US Air Force activated.

16 — First offensive operation by US fighters within China theatre, first bomber operation 19th: target both occasions installations and shipping on Red river.

May/Jun — J. raid into western Hupei. Withdrawal at end portrayed as major victory, used by KMT and air power lobbies in Washington to support their respective causes.

21 Aug — Major air battles over Hangkow, Hengyang and Changsa.

25 Nov — First US air raid on Formosa; J. consideration of general offensive in central and southern China in 1944.

1944

17 Jan — J. authorization of a general offensive in China to secure Peking–Hankow, Canton–Hankow and Hunan–Kwangsi rail lines and Hengyang, Kweiling, Lingling and Liuchow airfields.

17 Apr — Start of Ichi-go offensive with J. advance into Honan: Peking–Chengchow–Hankow line secured by 9 May, Loyang secured 26th. First phase Ichi-go ends *c.* 2 Jun with J. having overrun Honan at a cost of 869 dead.

27 May — Second phase Ichi-go offensive. J. cross Yangtse below Ichang: secure Liuyang 14 Jun., Changsa 16th/18th.

5 Jun — First combat mission by B-29s from bases in India against Bangkok.

15 — First strike against J. home islands by China-based B-29s.

26 — J. advance from Liuyang area and capture of Hengyang airfield.

28 — First J. assault on Hengyang, subsequent siege: falls 8 Aug.

29 — Preparatory operations for third phase Ichi-go with movement of forces from Hengyang toward Kweilin and Liuchow airfields and forces moving north from Canton.

8 Sep — J. secured Lingling.

27 Oct — Third phase Ichi-go.

10 Nov — J. secure Liuchow and Kweilin.

24 — J. secure Nanning.

10 Dec — Juncture of J. forces from Nanning and Tonking: uninterrupted communication between Johore and Korea.

1945

29 Jan — J. secure Suichuan.

4 Feb — Arrival at Kunming of overland convoy via Bhamo.

May — Thinning and withdrawal of J. forces in southern China to meet anticipated Soviet offensive in Manchoutikuo.

8/9 Aug — Soviet declaration of war on Japan and invasion of Manchoutikuo, Inner Mongolia and Korea.

11/12 — Soviet forces through Greater Khingan Mountains.

15 — Unconditional surrender of Japan announced.

16 — Kwantung Army decision to ignore national surrender.

17 — Imperial intervention to ensure Kwantung Army's surrender.

18 — Soviets secure Chengteh and Kalgan; occupy Shumshu in Kuriles 18/23th.

19 Formal surrender of Kwantung Army at Khabarovsk.
20 Soviets secure Mukden and Changchung. ?/25: Soviets invade southern Sakhalin.
22 Soviet secure Port Arthur.
1 Sep Soviet occupation of Kumashir and Shikotan.

Hong Kong: 1941

1941

8 Dec J. assault; New Territories and Kowloon taken by 10th.
18 J. landings on Victoria Is.
25 British surrender.

Malaya and Singapore: 1941–2

1941

8 Dec J. overland invasion of Siam and landings in southern Siam and northern Malaya.
9/11 British abandon Kota Bahru and Machang.
10 Two Br. capital ships sunk in South China Sea.
11/12 Br. positions collapse at Jitra.
19 Br. abandon Penang and northern Malaya; airfields brought into J. service 20th.
22 J. cross Perak into central Malaya, secure Ipoh 28th.

1942

1/2 Jan J. capture Telok Anson.
7 Br. defeated on Slim river.
11 J. landings at Port Swettenham, secure Kuala Lumpur.
16 J. victory on Sungei Maur, occupation of Batu Pahat.
21 J. landing at Endau, collapse of Br. position in southern Malaya.
22 Collapse of Br. forces around Bakri and Bukit Pelandok.
27/28 Br. débâcle at Layang, evacuation of Johore 31st.
8 Feb J. assault across Johore Strait against Singapore.
15 Br. surrender of Singapore.

The Philippines: 1941–2

1941

8 Dec J. attack air bases, secure islands north of Luzon.
10 J. landings in northern Luzon.
12 J. secure Legaspi.
19/20 J. landings at Davao, Mindanao.
22 J. landings in Lamon Bay and Lingayen Gulf.

1942

1 Jan US withdrawal into Bataan complete.
2 J. secure Manila.
10/22 Main defence line on Bataan broken: US withdrawal to Bagac–Orion line complete 26th.
23/6 Feb J. offensive on Bagac–Orion line defeated.
3 Apr Renewed J. offensive on Bagac–Orion line.
9 US surrender on Bataan.
10 J. landings on Bohol and Cebu.
16 J. landings on Negros; surrender 3 Jun.
16/18 J. landings on Panay; surrender 20 May.
29 J. landings in south-west and northern Mindanao.
5/6 May J. attack on and US surrender of Corregidor.
26 J. landings at Tacloban. Surrender of Leyte.
9 Jun Surrender of Samar.

The Indies: 1941–5

1941

15 Dec J. secure Miri.
24 J. secure Jolo, Kuching on 25th.

1942

1 Jan J. secure Labuan, Jesselton 8th, Tarakan 10/12th.
11 J. secure Manado, Kendari and Sandakan 17th.
23 J. landing at Balikpapan, naval action 24th.
24 J. landings at Kendari.
29 J. capture of Pontianak.
31/3 Feb J. secure Amboina.
8 Feb J. landings at Macassar.
10 J. capture of Bandjermasin.
14/17 J. secure Palembang.
18/19 Lombok Strait action.
19 J. carrier raid on Darwin.
19 J. landings on Bali.
20 J. landings on Timor.
27/28 Battle of Java Sea.
28/1 Mar J. landings on Java. Sunda Strait action.
5 Mar J. secure Batavia.
9 Allied surrender in Dutch East Indies.
12 J. secure Medan.
7 Apr J. secure Ternate.

1944

15 Sep US landings on Morotai.
15 Nov US landings on Pegun Is.

1945

2 May Australian landings at Tarakan: secure 24 Jun.
10 Jun Australian landings in Brunei Bay: landing · at Labuan 20th, secure Miri.
1 Jul Australian landings at Balikpapan:three minor landings staged between 3rd and 9th.
4 + 13 Aug US fighter sweeps over Singapore from bases in Indies.

Central Pacific: 1941–5

1941

7 Jan Memorandum advocating a surprise attack on Pearl Harbor by Yamamoto.
7 Dec J. attack on US Pacific Fleet at Pearl Harbor.
9/11 J. secure Guam.
10 J. secure Makin.
11 J. assault on Wake defeated.
23 J. secure Wake.

1942

1 Feb US carrier raid on Marshalls and Gilberts.
24 US carrier raid on Wake.
4 Mar US carrier raid on Marcus.
18 Apr Doolittle Raid.
4/7 Jun Battle of Midway.
23 Aug J. secure Nauru.
26 J. secure Ocean Island.

1943

31 Aug US carrier raid on Manus.
17/19 Sep Raids on Gilberts by US land-based aircraft and carrier force.
5/6 Oct US carrier raid on Wake.
21 Nov US landings in Gilberts: Makin secured 23rd, Tarawa 28th.
4 Dec US carrier raid on Kwajalein.

1944

Jan Withdrawal of last naval units from Rabaul to Truk.
31 US landings on Kwajalein; atoll secured 8 Feb.
17/18 Feb US carrier raid on Truk.
17/21 US secure Eniwetok.
30 Mar/1 Apr US carrier raids against Palaus and Woleai.
30 Apr/1 May US carrier raid on Truk.
19/23 May US carrier raids on Marcus and Wake.
11/14 Jun Massed US carrier attacks on Marianas.
15 US landings on Saipan.
15/17 US carrier raids on Bonins.
19/20 Battle of Philippine Sea.

- 24 — US carrier raid on Bonins.
- 13 Jul — Saipan declared secure.
- 21 — US landings on Guam, secured 8 Aug.
- 24 — US landings on Tinian, secured 1 Aug.
- 25/27 — US carrier raid on Palaus.
- 31 Aug/2 Sep — US carrier raid on Bonins.
- 6/8 Sep — US carrier raid on Palaus.
- 9/14 — US carrier raids on southern, central Philippines.
- 15 — US landings on Morotai. US landings on Peleliu, secured 12 Oct: last resistance Dec.
- 17 — US landings on Angaur, Palau Islands, island secured by 23 Oct.
- 22/24 — US secure Ulithi.
- 10/11 Oct — US carrier raids on Formosa, Ryukyus and northern Philippines, on Formosa 12/14th.
- 16 — US landings on Ngula.
- 16/19 — US carrier raids on central, southern Philippines.
- 20 — US landings on Leyte.
- 21/24 — US carrier operations over northern, central Philippines.
- 24/25 — Action in Surigao Strait.
- 25 — Action in Leyte Gulf, off Samar and east of Cape Egano.
- 26 — US follow-up strikes over central, southern Philippines.
- 29/2 Nov — US carrier force withdraws to Ulithi; 5 Nov. recommits to Philippines campaign and withdraws 23/27th.
- 27/6 Dec — Major J. counter-attack on Leyte.
- 24 — First B-29 raid on home islands from Marianas.
- 7 Dec — US landings near Ormoc.
- 14/16 — US carrier strikes on northern Philippines.
- 15 — US landings on Mindoro.

1945

- 2/3 Jan — US carrier strikes on Ryukyus, Formosa and northern Philippines; strikes continue 6/9 Jan before sortie into South China Sea.
- 9 — US landing in Lingayen Gulf.
- 21/22 — Last US carrier strikes against Formosa and Ryukyus.
- 9 Feb — US forces enter Manila.
- 15-21 — US clearing of Corrigedor.
- 19 — US landings on Iwo Jima.
- 28 — US landings on Palawan.
- 3 Mar — Manila declared secure.
- 10 — US landings at Zamboanga.
- 26 — Iwo Jima declared secure: last resistance ended in 18–20 June: US secure Panay.
- 26 — US landings on Cebu: city secured 16 Apr.
- 29 — US landings on Negros: secured 31 May.
- 1 Apr — US landings on Okinawa.
- 6/7 — First kikusu (massed kamikaze attack) and naval action off Okinawa.
- 9 — US landings on Jolo.
- 12 — US landings on Bohol.
- 13 — US forces secure northern Okinawa.
- 16/21 — US occupation of Ie Shima off Okinawa.
- 17 — First US carrier raid on Kyushu and Shikoku airfields.
- 18 — US landings in western Mindanao.
- 20 — Motobu peninsula cleared, central Okinawa secured.
- 24 — J. abandon Machinato Line on Okinawa: US repulsed on Shuri Line 28th.
- 27 — US occupy Baguio, Luzon.
- 3 May — Davao, southern Mindanao, declared secure.
- 3/4 — US landings on Santa Cruz.
- 4/5 May — J. offensive from Shuri Line defeated.
- 10 — US landings in Macajalar Bay.
- 11 — US take Cagayan as part of general offensive in northern Luzon, crumbling of J. defence: Bolete Pass taken 13th, Santa Fe 27th.
- 7 June — Aparri taken; Bayombong 21st; Kaigan taken 12 Jul.
- 11 — Start of US offensive against Shuri Line: J. abandon Line 21st.
- 12 — Start of final US offensive on Okinawa.
- 17 — Collapse of J. resistance in southern Okinawa: last actions 4 Aug.
- 20 Jul — US landings on Balut.

New Guinea and the South-West Pacific: 1942–5

1942

- 23 Jan — J. secure Rabaul and Kavieng.
- 8/9 Mar — J. occupation of Lae and Salamaua, Finchhafen 10th.
- 10 — US carrier attack on Lae and Salamaua.
- 30 — J. secure Buka and Kessa in northern Solomons.
- 31 — J. secure Shortland and Boela.
- Apr — J. move in western New Guinea and along northern coast; Fak Fak 1st; Babo 2nd; Sorong 4th.
- 7 — J. secure Lorengau, Manus. Continuation of J. coastal moves in New Guinea: secure Manokwari 12th, Moemi 15th, Seroei 17th, Nabire 18th, Sarmi and Hollandia 19th.
- 28 — J. secure Shortlands.
- 3 May — J. secure Tulagi.
- 4 — US carrier attack on Tulagi.
- 7/8 — Battle of Coral Sea.
- 22 Jul — J. capture Buna and Gona.
- 27 — J. capture Kakoda.
- 7 Aug — US landings on Guadalcanal and Tulagi.
- 9 — Battle of Savo Island.
- 22/25 — Battle of Eastern Solomons.
- 25/7 Sep — J. landings in Milne Bay, subsequent evacuation.
- 12/14 Sep — Defeat of J. assault on Bloody Ridge on Guadalcanal.
- 16 — J. capture of Ioribaiwa.
- 24 — Start of J. withdrawal on Kakoda Trail.
- 5 Oct — Allied transport of forces to Wanighela, and to Pongani on 18th.
- 9 — Allied capture of Arapara, Laruni 15th, Jaure 20th.
- 11/12 — Battle of Cape Esperance.
- 23/25 — Defeat of J. assault on Henderson Field on Guadalcanal.
- 26/27 — Battle off Santa Cruz.
- 12/13 Nov — First naval battle of Guadalcanal.
- 14/15 — Second naval battle of Guadalcanal.
- 30/1 Dec — Battle of Tassafaronga.
- 9 Dec — Australian capture of Gona.
- 31 — J. decision to abandon Guadalcanal.

1943

- 2 Jan — US capture of Buna.
- 10 — Start of US offensive on Guadalcanal.
- 11 — J. offensive from Mobu area against Wau.
- 21/2 Feb — Defeat of J. offensive at Wau.
- 1/7 Feb — J. evacuation of Guadalcanal.
- 21 — US secure Russells.
- 2/4 Mar — Bismarck Sea action.
- 6 — Action off Kula Gulf.
- 7/18 Apr — J. air offensive over Solomons and eastern New Guinea.
- 5 Jun — Major air battle over Russells.
- 16 — Annihilation of J. air attack on Guadalcanal.

21 US landings on New Georgia: on Woodlark Island 23/24; on Kiriwan 28/29; and on Rendova, near Salamaua, on Woodlark and Trobriand Is. and Nassau Bay 30th.
2 Jul US landings on New Georgia.
4/5 US and J. landings in Kula Gulf.
6 Battle of Kula Gulf.
13 Battle of Kolombangara.
5 Aug US capture Munda airfield, New Georgia.
6/7 Battle of Vella Gulf.
15 US landings on Vella Lavella.
27 US landings on Arundel Island.
3/4 Sep Australian landings at Lae.
6 US airborne landings at Nadzab.
12 US secure Salamaua.
16 Allies secure Lae.
20 J. evacuation of Vella Lavella and Arundel.
22 Australian landings at Finchhaven repulse J. counter-attack 26th, capture of Finchhaven 2 Oct. Series of attacks on Finchhaven until 25 Oct when J. admit defeat and evacuate area.
23/2 Oct J. evacuation of Kolombangara.
6 Oct US landings on Kolombangara.
6 Battle of Vella Lavella.
12 Start US land-based air campaign aimed at neutralizing and isolating Rabaul.
27 Allied landings in Treasury Islands.
1/2 Nov US carrier raids over Upper Solomons; US landings on Bougainville and battle of Empress Augusta Bay.
5 and 11 US carrier raids on Rabaul.
12 J. withdrawal of fleet units from Rabaul.
26 Battle of Cape St George.
26 Dec US landings on Cape Gloucester.

1944
2 Jan US landings at Saidor.
15/20 Feb NZ secured Green Islands.
29 US landings at Los Negros.
6/29 Mar J. attacks on Bougainville air base defeated.
15/25 US secured Manus.
20 US occupied Emirau.
25 Australian forces secured Madang.
22 Apr US landings at Aitape and Hollandia. Hollandia secured 27th, Aitape 4 May.
17/18 May US landings at Arare and Wakde. Wakde secured 22nd.
17/26 US raids on Marshalls.
27 US landings on Biak: island secured 20 Aug.
10/11 Jun J. attempt to relieve Biak abandoned as result of US operations in Marianas.
2 Jul US landings at Noemfoor.
5 Defeat of only major J. counter-attack at Noemfoor.
10/17 Aug Series of actions around Aitape, J. defeat.
28 July End of organized J. resistance on Biak.
30 US landings on Vogelkop peninsula and on Amsterdam and Middleburg: landing near Sansapur 31st.
4 Aug End of last major J. effort against Allied positions at Aitape; area secured 1 Sep, US handover to Australians 27 Nov.
15 Sep US landings on Morotai.
15 Nov US landings on Pegun.

1945
29 Apr US landings on Los Negros.
11 May Initial Australian landing at Wewak, New Guinea: main landings on 14th: end of organized resistance 23rd.

North Pacific: 1942–3

1942
7 Jun J. secure Attu and Kiska.
27/16 Sep J. abandon Attu and reinforce Kiska.
26 Oct First sinking of J. ship by a submarine operating from Dutch Harbor.
29 J. reoccupy Attu.

1943
16 Feb Last J. raid on Amchitka.
27 Mar Battle of Kommandorskii Islands.
11 May US landings on Attu, island secured 31st.
8 Jun J. decision to abandon Kiska.
10 Jul First US raid on Kuriles by medium bombers staging through Attu from Adak; last such raid 13 Aug. 1945.
28 J. complete evacuation of Kiska in Aleutians.
15 Aug Allied landings on Kiska.

Burma and the Indian Ocean: 1941–5

1941
16 Dec J. forces cross into Burma, secure Victoria Point airfield.
23 First air raids on Rangoon.

1942
Jan Ch. forces move into eastern Burma.
19 J. forces capture Tavoy.
22 Br. decision to transfer logistics from Rangoon to Mandalay.
24 J. secureMergui.
30/31 J. capture Moulmein.
16/20 Feb Br. worsted in battle on Bilin.
18/23 Battle of Sittang and destruction of Br. force in front of Rangoon. 15th Army decision to capture Rangoon and not move directly into central Burma.
7/8 Mar Br. forces escape encirclement and J. capture of Rangoon.
19/30 J. destoy Ch. forces around Kyungon and Toungoo.
21/27 J. air strikes on Akyab and Magwe.
23 J. secure Andamans.
1/2 Apr Br. outfought around Prome and Hmawza; subsequent defeat on Minha–Loikaw line.
5/9 J. carrier offensive in Bay of Bengal.
10/19 J. capture Yenangyaung.
18/23 Battle of Loikaw.
29 J. capture Kehsi Mansam and Lashio in eastern Burma.
30 J. reach Chindwin at Monywa.
31 J. capture Mandalay.
8 May J. secure Bhamo and Myitkyina.
10/14 J. capture of Kalewa: in effect ends 1942 campaign.
Dec Br. offensive in Arakan: halts short of Akyab in Jan 1943.

1943
18 Feb Start of first Chindit operation; temporary interruption of communications between Mandalay and Myitkyina.
13/17 Mar J. successful counter-offensive at Akyab.
18 Chindit withdrawal to India under intense pressure.
23 Oct Start of Ch. offensive in Hukawng valley; advances halted by Nov–Dec counter-attack.
30 Nov Start of Br. offensive in Arakan; halts in front of Maungdaw.

1944

Jan/Feb	Successful defensive battle staged by J. in Hukawng valley and frustration of Ch. advance.
10	Br. secure Maungdaw.
4 Feb	Start of J. offensive into north-east India with diversionary attack in Arakan.
12	Encirclement of Br. formations around Maungdaw: Br. counter-attacks break J. forces 13th/24th.
3/7 Mar	Defeat of J. around Maingkwan in Hukawng valley: Sino-US aim to clear Hukawng valley with offensive into Mogaung and Irrawaddy valleys.
4/6	Start of J. offensive into north-east India with crossing of Chindwin, not detected until 12th.
5	Start of second Chindit operation.
21	Br. defeat at Sheldon's Corner and Ukhrul.
28/8 Apr	Sino–US forces checked around Nhpum Ga, but J. forces in area spent.
2/3 Apr	Start of siege of Imphal.
4	J. forces reach Kohima.
18/20	Br. relief of Kohima.
17 May	Sino–US forces take Myitkyina airfield: siege of town after 18th.
5 Jun	Start of J. withdrawal from Kohima. First combat mission flown by B-29s from bases in India against Bangkok.
16	Ch. forces take Kamaing.
19/20	Ch. forces on Salween secure Ku-feng and Chiang-chu.
22	Br. relief of Imphal.
26	Br.-Ch. forces take Mogaung. Ch. forces encircle Teng-chung, 8 Jul.
16 Jul	J. counter-offensive on Salween; Lun-ling taken 25th.
3 Aug	Allied forces take Myitkyina.
28	Br. forces take Pinbaw.
14 Sep	Ch. forces take Teng-chung.
15 Oct	Start of Ch. offensive against Bhamo.
14 Nov/ 15 Dec	Ch. siege and capture of Bhamo.
12 Dec	Start of Br. offensive in Arakan.

1945

2 Jan	Br. secure Akyab.
11/14	Br. bridgeheads over Irrawaddy at Thabeikkyin and Kyaukmyaung established.
18 /22 Feb	Br. secure Ramree.
22/17 Feb	Br. secure Kangaw.
13/21 Feb	Br. bridgehead over Irrawaddy at Nyaungu established.
14	Br. bridgehead over Irrawaddy at Ngazun established.
20/21 Mar	Battle for Mandalay.
21	Battle for Meiktila: taken by Br. on 4 Mar.
2 Mar	Last US bombing raid on Singapore.
7	Ch. capture of Lashio, Hsipaw on 15th.
26	J. acceptance of defeat at Meiktila; withdrawal 28th.
4/5 Apr	Last Br. operations in Arakan.
15	J. decision to abandon Arakan; completed by 30th.
23	J. begin their evacuation of Rangoon: completed 29th/30th.
2 May	Br. landings at Rangoon, secured 3rd.
6	Juncture west of Hlegu of Br. forces from central Burma and Rangoon.
15/16	Off Penang, only surface action involving fleet units fought in Indian Ocean during war.

The Japanese home islands and strategic bombing raids: 1944–5

1944

15 Jun	First B-29 raid on home islands from China.
24 Nov	First B-29 raid from Marianas.
16/17 Feb 45	Tokyo attacked by US carrier task force.

1945

10/11 Mar	Tokyo raided.
11/12	Nagoya raided.
13/14	Osaka raided.
16/17	Kobe raided.
18/19	Nagoya raided.
27/28	Start of Operation Starvation.
13/14 Apr	Tokyo raided.
14/15	Nagoya raided.
15/16	Tokyo, Yokohama and Kawasaki raided.
19/20	Hamamatsu raided.
23/24	Tokyo raided: largest single-target attack by B-29s during campaign.
25/26	Tokyo raided.
29/30	Yokohama raided.
17/18 May	Nagoya raided.
1/2 Jun	Osaka raided.
5/6	Kobe raided.
7/8	Osaka raided.
15/16	Osaka raided.
17/18	Kagoshima, Omuta, Hamamatsu and Yokaichi raided.
19/20	Fukuoka, Shizuoka and Toyohashi raided.
28/29	Sasebo, Okayama, Moji and Nobeoka raided.
1/2 Jul	Kure, Kukamoto, Shimonoseki and Ube raided.
3/4	Tokushima, Takamatsu, Kochi and Himeji raided.
6/7	Kofu, Chiba, Akashi, Shimizu raided.
9/10	Sendai, Wakayama, Sakai and Gifu raided.
11/12	First B-29 operation against Korean ports.
12/13	Utsunomiya, Ichinomiya, Tsuruga and Uwajima raided.
16/17	Oita, Namazu, Kuwana and Hiratsuka raided.
19/20	Fukui, Okazaki, Hitachi and Choshi raided.
24/25	Tsu and Kawana raided.
26/27	Omuta, Matsuyama and Tokuyama raided.
28/29	Aomori, Ichinomiya, Tsu, Ogaki, Uji-Yamada and Uwajima raided.
1/2 Aug	Toyama, Nagaoka, Mito and Hachioji raided.
5/6	Nishinomiya, Maebashi, Imabari and Saga raided.
6	Attack on Hiroshima using atomic weapon.
8/9	Yawata and Fukuyama raided.
9	Attack on Nagasaki using atomic weapon.
14/15	Kumagaya and Isezaki raided.
15	Announcement of unconditional surrender of Japan.
2 Sep	Formal surrender of Japan to representatives of United Nations in US battleship anchored in Tokyo Bay.

INTRODUCTION

PERSPECTIVES

OUTSIDE THE HOME ISLANDS and as a result of the US strategic bombing campaign, the Japanese war is not noted for urban devastation. But many Chinese cities and well as such places as Manila were devastated in the course of the Second World War: here, how victory appeared to a US marine at Naha, chief city of Okinawa and the Ryukyu Islands, April 1945.

PERSPECTIVES

FROM A WESTERN perspective the story of the Japanese war is told in terms of a journey marked by signposts which, over decades of repetition, have become all but very familiar friends. Coral Sea and Midway, Kakoda, Guadalcanal and Tarawa, the Great Marianas Turkey Shoot, Leyte Gulf and Luzon, Iwo Jima and Mount Suribachi, Okinawa and Sugar Loaf, and finally the razing of the cities of the home islands mark a well-trodden route, irrespective of whether the tale that is told is related in terms of nations, services or individuals. This is right because the ultimate determinant in war is armed force even though force is but one element of power and power is but one element in the process by which states arrange their affairs.

But in terms of perspective we are further in time from the outbreak of the Second World War than people in 1939 were from Grant's presidency and the death of Gordon at Khartoum. It behoves one to pause and consider, when contemplating yet another screed upon the subject of Japan and the Second World War, time's passing and the demand that should be placed upon the historian: to provide explanation, not mere description, of events. There have been histories of the Second World War that have moved beyond description, but one would suggest that there have been too many by authors who laboured under the illusion that they explained the events they described. As the decades have slipped by there has been a movement towards perspective, but there have also been two other factors at work. The first has been the detail that has become available, mainly from official records, that allowed a somewhat unfortunate development. There have been exhaustive, sometimes exhausting, studies of individual episodes or aspects of this conflict that have not aided reflection and perspective. An obvious example, drawn from the European war, is signals intelligence. One is tempted to conclude that Stephen Roskill, whose official histories were written when such matters as ULTRA remained highly secret, none the less managed to write a better balanced account of the Battle of the Atlantic than some historians who seemed incapable of writing about it except in terms of ULTRA.

The second is perhaps more serious and unfortunate. The power of image is not to be underestimated, and the Second World War was the first cinema war. Television has recognized this to an extent that some might suggest was unhealthy: cable and satellite channels repeat Second World War documentaries *ad nauseam*. Whether British or American, the Second World War has an image and appeal that cannot be denied. It was an age of heroic certainty, the triumph of good over wicked depravity. In Britain's case there is perhaps another dimension: if 1940 was indeed Britain's finest hour then what has followed is an anti-climax, hence the appeal of the Second World War. This works against the process of re-evaluation – the lifeblood of History. The process of critical examination, detailed scrutiny of events, in pursuit of that most elusive of substances, incontrovertible historical truth, cannot rest alongside a popular portrayal of known truths, long-settled and which permit no questioning.

The Second World War in the East is part of a series and at the same time complete in its own right. It attempts to set out the record of this conflict, but seeks to avoid mere description in an attempt to provide explanation of events. Inevitably, no single book could ever provide more than partial explanation, but in the case of the Japanese war the writer is confronted by a more profound historiographical problem: there are few things more difficult to explain than an inevitable defeat. It is relatively easy to deal with Germany's defeat in the Second World War precisely because at certain times her victory seemed assured: in the case of Japan, however, there was never any chance of her avoiding defeat in the war she initiated in 1941. Herein lies another problem that confronts the would-be explanation: the process by which Japan initiated a war with the only power that could defeat her. States as mismatched as were Japan and the United States seldom fight one another: even more seldom do they fight wars initiated by the weaker. Herein lies a problem of interpretation to vex perception: the process whereby Japan, from a position of local superiority and safeguarded by provisions of naval limitation upon potential enemies, ranged against herself an alliance that included the world's most populous state, greatest empire, most powerful single state and greatest military power. By any standard, the conjuring of such a coalition against herself was a remarkable achievement, however unintended: how to explain it is quite another matter.

Two more aspects of this conflict demand address. First, the Pacific war was very unusual in that the nature of naval power and warfare changed. Uniquely, the Pacific war was the only occasion in history when ownership of the trident changed hands without war between possessor and successor, and it was a war in which the relationship between supremacy and victory changed. Before late 1943 in the Pacific supremacy was the product of victories: thereafter victories were the product of supremacy. Between May 1942 and November 1943 the US Navy fought for and won the initiative with a pre-war fleet: thereafter its victories were the product of a supremacy based upon a fleet that was a wartime creation. Second, that latter was part of an awesome achievement. In the course of the Second World War the United States, which raised a hundred divisions, supplied its allies with equipment, food and raw materials the cash value of which would have been enough to have raised 2,000 infantry divisions. In one month her slips whispered adieu to 140 merchant hulls and one yard launched its fiftieth escort carrier one year and one day after launching its first. It was industrial power in depth that was the basis of America's victory, yet, in the space allowed in this work, this is a story to which only passing reference may be made. Herein are matters that form the framework of this book and which provide explanation at its end, but it is its start, and the origins of this war, that presently invite the attention of the reader.

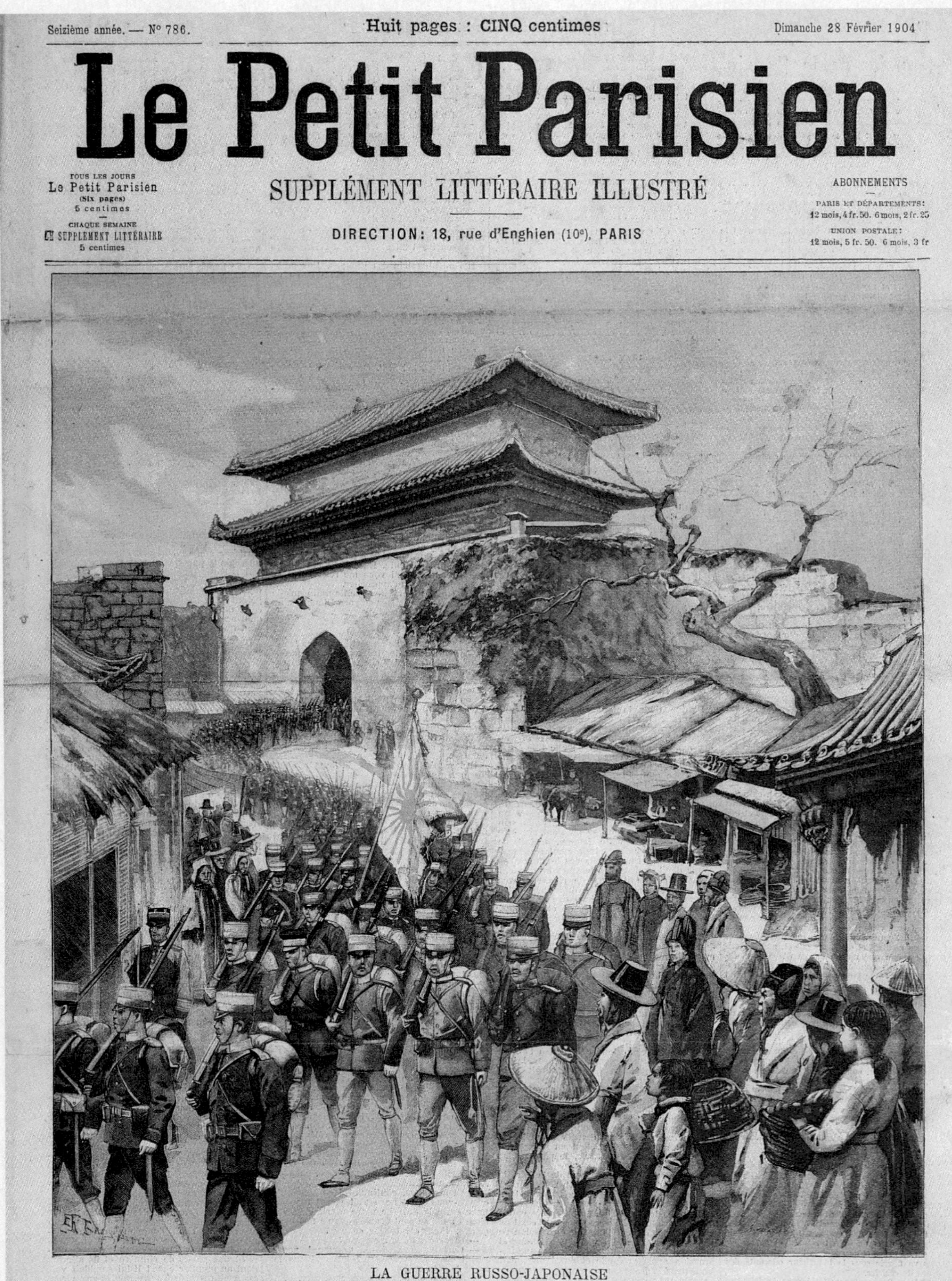

Seizième année. — N° 786. Huit pages : CINQ centimes Dimanche 28 Février 1904

Le Petit Parisien

TOUS LES JOURS
Le Petit Parisien
(Six pages)
5 centimes

CHAQUE SEMAINE
LE SUPPLÉMENT LITTÉRAIRE
5 centimes

SUPPLÉMENT LITTÉRAIRE ILLUSTRÉ

DIRECTION : 18, rue d'Enghien (10e), PARIS

ABONNEMENTS
PARIS ET DÉPARTEMENTS :
12 mois, 4 fr. 50. 6 mois, 2 fr. 25
UNION POSTALE :
12 mois, 5 fr. 50. 6 mois, 3 fr

LA GUERRE RUSSO-JAPONAISE
OCCUPATION DE SÉOUL PAR L'ARMÉE JAPONAISE

CHAPTER ONE

THE ROAD TO WAR

CONTEMPORARY REPRESENTATION of the Japanese occupation of Seoul on 11 February 1904 in the course of the Russo-Japanese war. Previously occupied during the Chinese war of 1894–5 and a battlefield for part of the later war, Korea was annexed by Japan in 1910. Throughout the period when Korea was part of the Empire, Japanese policy was ruthlessly exploitive and repressive.

THE ROAD TO WAR

WARS USUALLY lend themselves readily to historical shorthand. Even if the parties to a war differ in terms of when they entered or left the lists, wars generally have easily identifiable dates and hence duration, and normally, with the advantage of hindsight and a sense of inevitability, the road to war is well marked and can be discerned without undue difficulty. The Second World War in Europe provides obvious examples on all counts. It is given dates of September 1939 and May 1945, and the immediate origins lie in the period 1933–9 and are synonymous with the person and policies of Adolf Hitler. If longer term causes are sought, historical examination invariably does not reach beyond the Versailles Treaty of 28 June 1919.

Such historical shorthand can be simplistic, but in any event does not preclude genuine historical argument on any number of aspects of the war under examination. Civil wars, however, need not necessarily lend themselves to such summary: invariably, by their very nature their causes are complicated, while their origins, very often, are veiled and sometimes deliberately shrouded in heroic myths that obscure rather than enlighten. And there are some wars which defy these general rules of presentation.

The Second World War in the Far East is such a war. To westerners the dates of this conflict are simple enough. It began on 7/8 December 1941 with the Japanese attack on Pearl Harbor and landings in southern Siam and northern Malaya, and it ended either on 15 August 1945, when Japan announced her willingness to accept the terms of the Potsdam Declaration that demanded her unconditional surrender, or on 2 September 1945, when the instrument of surrender was signed in the

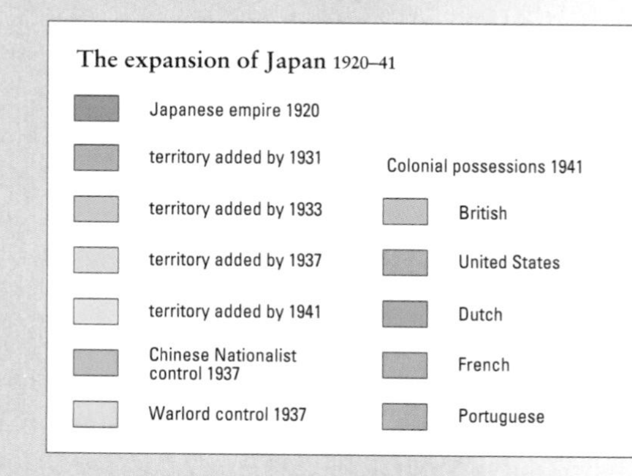

EASTERN ASIA AND THE WESTERN PACIFIC

By summer 1941 the Japanese position in the Far East by virtue of her conquests in Manchuria and China and holdings in the central Pacific gave the impression of strength in depth. The reality of Japan's position was somewhat different. Her population of 72.75 million provided a work force of 34.1 million: the comparative figures for the US were 141.94 and 52.8million. Comparative production figures were steel production (1937) 5.8 to 28.8 million tons: coal production (1938) 53.7 to 354.5 million tons: electricity production, 35 to 116.6 million mrd Kwh. In terms of the percentage share of world manufacturing output Japan's 3.5 compared to the 32.2 of the United States.

US battleship *Missouri* in Tokyo Bay. But such chronological exactitude ignores the obvious: the Second World War in the Far East was not one war but two, and the war that is identifiable in terms of the 1941–5 time frame – a war fought primarily in the Pacific and south-east Asia and between Japan and western powers – may have been the most important single part of this conflict, but it was not the first part of this war.

What Japan had dubbed a 'special undeclared war' had been in existence since July 1937 in the form of 'the China Incident'. The major fighting in this conflict had taken place between July 1937 and November 1938 and had brought under Japanese control much of northern China and the Yangtse valley as far as

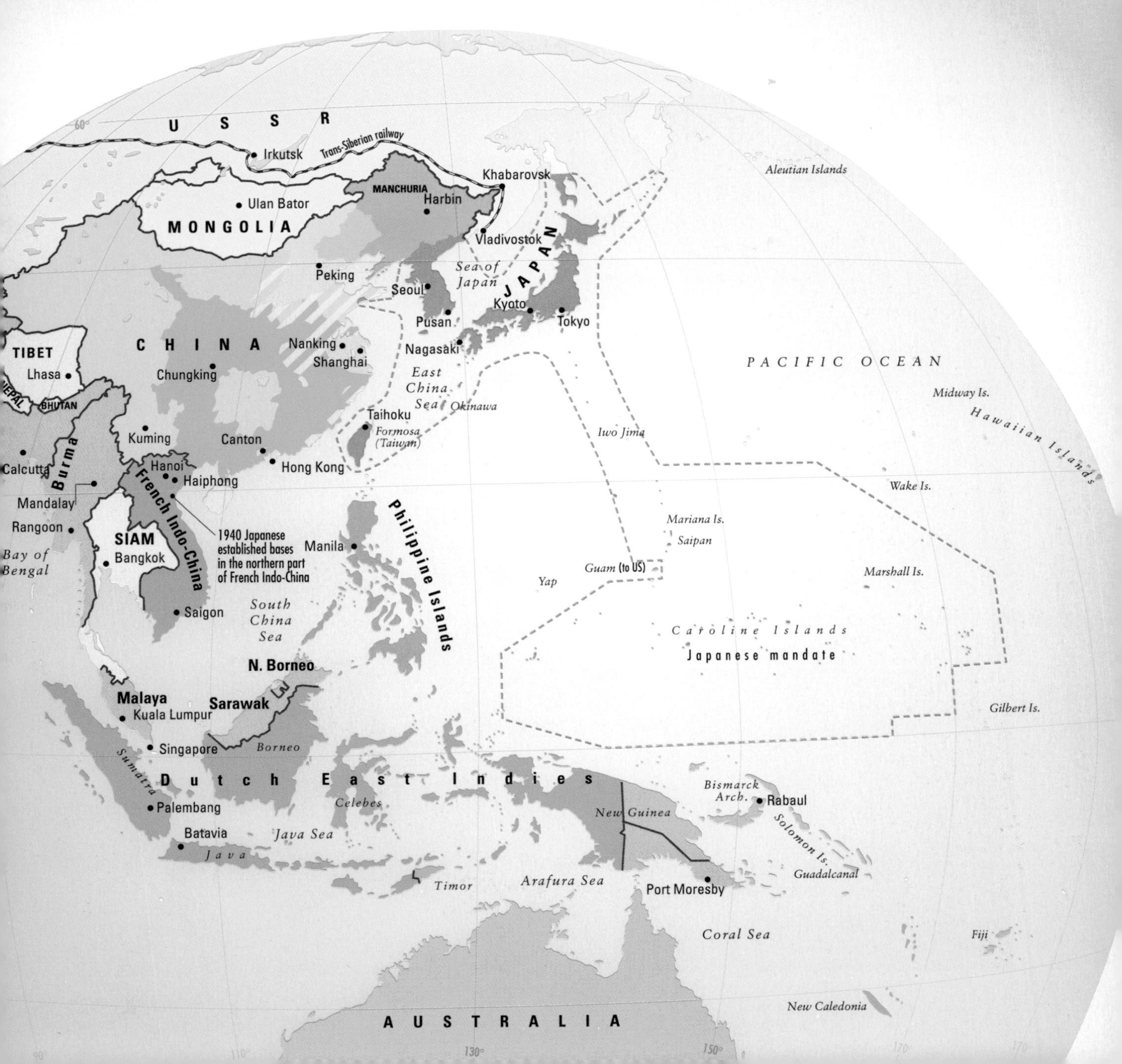

the Wuhan cities. Japan's subsequent inability to end this war by either military or political means bestowed a lingering legacy of open-ended commitment and alienation from the western powers. This lay at the heart of the crisis of July–November 1941 which was resolved by Japanese offensive operations against Britain and the United States. Nevertheless, the Japanese official histories of the Second World War begin not with 1941, not even with 1937, but in September 1931, with the invasion and occupation of three of Manchuria's four provinces, and if the path between 1931 and 1937 is both difficult and indirect no-one should doubt its existence. The link between 1931 and 1937 cannot be gainsaid, and it is as real as the link between 1937 and 1941. But to suggest that the situation of 1941 stemmed directly from 1931 would be contentious, and would bestow upon events a determinism that contains paradox: few would deny such

a link, but few would accept a linear cause-and-effect relationship between the two sets of events. In any event, most people would see the 1931–1937–1941 or Manchuria–China–Pacific relationship as only one of many factors that were at work in the making of a conflict between 1941 and 1945 that was fought on land over 60 degrees of latitude and the sinking of Japanese warships over 218 degrees of longitude.

The definition of this struggle, therefore, is beset with problems: the western terms of reference, 1941–5, do not adequately define the parameters of this war, most certainly not for the Japanese, and even less so for the Chinese whose (conservatively estimated) 13 million dead exceeded the combined number of fatalities incurred by all the other parties to this conflict. Historical accuracy demands full and proper acknowledgement of the Asian dimension of this war,

Contemporary woodcut depicting the diversionary attack of 11th and 21st Infantry Regiments of Major General Oshima's Mixed Brigade across the pontoon bridge over the Taedong during the battle for Pyongyang, 15 September 1894. Japanese success here and in the naval battle at the mouth of the Yalu on the 17th ended serious Chinese resistance in Korea: thereafter the Japanese took the war into China, securing Port Arthur and Wei-hei-wei.

and it is here one encounters numerous difficulties in seeking to trace the road to war. Where was the start line, crossed unknowingly by all concerned, in the process that was to lead to such a terrible conflagration throughout eastern and south-east Asia and the Pacific in the second quarter of the twentieth century?

There is no obvious answer to this question, though there is one set of events and one date that, perhaps more than most, helps to explain the events of the 1930s and 1940s. The date is 1868 and the set of events is the end of the shogunate, the Meiji Restoration, when after centuries of self-imposed and all but total exclusion from the rest of the world, Japan accepted the reality of western intrusion and set about the adoption of western technology and systems in order to secure for herself a place in the international order that accorded with national mythology and ethic. Clearly, however, such an answer, with its

Seemingly not too much to celebrate: the parade of 15 November 1935 to mark the visit of the US Secretary of State George Dern and the passing of the power of autonomy to the Philippines. The United States conceded the principle of Philippine independence in 1934: the flag of the new commonwealth was publicly displayed for the first time at this parade.

implication of a determinism spread over seven decades, is likely to provoke a few questions of its own, yet in one very obvious sense the arrangements that Japan crafted for herself at this time were critical in one aspect of her conduct of war in the period 1937–45. Japan, by a very large margin, was the least organized of the major combatants of the Second World War, and when one notes the competition for such a title that achievement is awesome. The incoherence of the Japanese decision-making process in very large measure stemmed from the system of government adopted in the Meiji era.

One cannot identify the road to war without acknowledging the significance of 1868 and what Japan brought with her, in terms of governmental organization and attitude, to the international community. Yet one would suggest that other events and dates, even if these in their turn can trace back their origins to 1868 and the new Japan, represent more obvious and pertinent points of departure in the process of examining the road to war. Perhaps the most obvious of these was the Washington Conference of 1921–2 when, for the first time, Japan and the United States measured themselves against one another directly, albeit in a way that imposed limitations on their naval forces. In a sense this was merely an official acknowledgement of a process that was already some fifteen years old. During that time Japan had identified the US as the 'budgetary enemy' with a defence expenditure that she would be obliged to shadow. For a similar period, US naval planning had devoted inordinate attention to the prosecution of a war in the Pacific against Japan. But if one examines American–Japanese estrangement as critical in the process that was to lead to war, then the American acquisition of the Philippines in 1898 is clearly important, since it brought the very different American and Japanese interests into relief for the first time. With the American acquisition of empire in the Far East, the element of political distance that could have enabled Japan and the United States to resolve differences by means other than war was lessened.

But in 1934 the United States conceded the principle of independence for the Philippines and therefore 1898, like any date or set of events, can explain only one part of a process of emerging hostility that paved the way for general war. Likewise, the events and dates that mark the Japanese acquisition of empire

in the Far East can provide only similar, partial, explanation: Japan's war with China in 1894; the war with Russia, 1904–5; the rapprochement with Russia in 1910 that resulted in the division of Manchuria into spheres of influence inimical to American interests and wishes. The United States viewed the Far East, specifically China, as an area in which she had a very special and disinterested role, and if these concerns stemmed from a somewhat ethnocentric view and a role in the world that was self-inflicted, then she was not alone among the great powers in harbouring such beliefs and sentiments regarding her own worth. Her belief in American values as having universal relevance, specifically with respect to a somewhat bemused China, was unsought, but none the less real, though the responsibilities that were attached were never very evident in the various crises of the 1930s. However, the basis of this self-imposed burden – a special American interest in the Far East that could not be negotiated away – did lie at the heart of American policy in the period before 1941.

The problems that associate themselves with such a line of enquiry as conducted in the preceding paragraphs are twofold and obvious: first, in seeking to explain, the narrative merely recounts on the basis of events of which the reader may not be aware; second, the narrative may possess a cleverness and plausibility that is as misplaced as it is irritating. It behoves the writer, therefore, to stop, and to make choices, and to seek to explain properly and in full from a given perspective, subject to the caveat that no single account can provide comprehensive explanation, that all knowledge is imperfect. Therefore one looks to two sets of events wherein lie the origins of the Second World War in the Far East – errors and omissions excepted.

Contemporary Japanese representation of the battle fleet in action during the Russo-Japanese war. The last ship in the line appears to be a member of the Shikishima class, and the action depicted is probably that on 9 February 1904 when Japanese warships bombarded Port Arthur rather than the fleet action of 13 April.

There are two sets of events that are critical factors on Japan's path to war: the First World War, and the economic depression of the 1930s. The consequences of the First World War were many and profound in the Far East, not least in removing from the area powers and influences critical in shaping the affairs of the region over the previous seventy or eighty years. Russia, in effect, was eliminated as a power in the Far East for at least a decade, and when she re-appeared she did so in an ideological garb that ensured Japanese enmity. The various European powers were removed entirely or their positions, specifically their military positions, were gravely compromised. In effect, the First World War brought Japan a local supremacy in the Far East that was all but unchallengeable except by full-scale war. Peace after 1919 confirmed this position when Japan acquired German concessions in China and colonial possessions in the Pacific north of the Equator. No less importantly, the First World War strengthened Japan immeasurably in terms of trade and industry since the appetite of her allies meant that she emerged from this war as a credit nation with an industrial base and a merchant marine far greater than she could ever have acquired by normal processes. Other than various operations in 1914 that resulted in the elimination of Germany's holdings in the Far East and the Pacific, plus the deployment of light naval forces to the eastern Mediterranean in 1917, Japan was spared the cost of war.

At the same time the distraction of the great powers during 1914–18 provided Japan with opportunity. The elimination of any power that might check Japan in the Far East after 1914 left her in a position of potentially overwhelming advantage, specifically in dealing with a China that in 1911–12 divested herself of her imperial identity and that, after 1916, set about the process of collapse, disintegration and civil war with single-minded determination. The fact that Japan overplayed her hand in 1915 with the infamous 'Twenty-One Demands' by which she sought to establish herself as China's overlord did not affect the situation one way or another. In 1915 her main demands were deflected by the efforts of her allies and a neutral United States, but the concessions that she none the less obtained were very substantial and provided her with a considerable position of privilege and power relative to China. Moreover, as China's divisions deepened, as local warlords created private domains for themselves and the country very literally fell apart under the impact of a series of civil wars, so Japan's position was strengthened still further, though at a price. China's difficulties presented a Japan intent on establishing her leadership of eastern Asia and crafting for herself a position of pre-eminence within China with the dilemmas of choice.

The incoherence of the Japanese decision-making process combined with three sets of influences and resulted in an inability to devise, implement and supervise any single consistent line of action towards China. The first of these influences was the belief in Japanese national uniqueness, and a mythology that stressed a heaven-granted mandate to assume the leadership of eastern Asia. The second was a view of Manchuria and northern China as natural areas of economic interest for Japan in terms of investment, raw materials, markets and colonization. The third was an inordinate concern with the physical occupation of space as the basis of national security: for Japan there could be no question of security ever being provided by an agreed border between friendly neighbours.

With the onset of China's civil wars and fragmentation came a basic need for Japan to define one thing: whether or not her interests in China were best served by Chinese weakness and division. To this was attached a second, and in a sense more immediate, problem: which, if any, of the various warring parties in China should be supported, and for what purpose. On the one side, the position of Japan's influence in China – indeed the position of privilege of all the powers in China – was dependent on Chinese weakness, yet a certain

Japanese officers look over the harbour at Port Arthur after the fall of the fortress and naval base on 15 January 1905. In the harbour lie (left to right) the battleship Pobyeda, *the protected cruiser* Pallada *(both sunk on 7 December) and the battleship* Retvizan *(sunk 6 December 1904).*

stability and order had to be maintained as a guarantee of privilege. For Japan there was the basic choice of whether to seek to preserve central government as the basis of future co-operation, or to seek to encourage fragmentation, and to rely upon local influences and Japanese force in order to sustain Japan's interests and investments. But underlying this basic problem was an inescapable reality: the position of leadership that Japan assigned for herself in eastern Asia precluded genuine co-operation on the basis of equality with any other authority. And to this there was added another problem: Japan sought physical control of resources as the best means of ensuring their availability. There was no question for the Japanese of allowing a relatively backward China, racked by corruption and inefficiency and lacking the advanced skills of a sophisticated capitalist economy, to share control of resources: Japanese ideas of leadership and co-operation were very clear in terms of leader and led.

At the heart of this dilemma was a force of nationalism that produced inconsistency: Japan recognized the force of nationalism – her own – but not the force of nationalism of any of her Asian neighbours. And just as in Korea she had ruthlessly suppressed Korean nationalist aspirations, so she could not accept Chinese nationalist resurgence as the basis of future co-operation lest it become directed against herself. Thus in China's civil wars an irresolute Japan was caught between conflicting choices, while Japanese military forces in Manchuria and various parts of northern and central China reacted locally and with no clear guidance. In the process they learnt a lesson of local initiative, which permitted no repudiation on the part of nominal authorities in Tokyo, that was to have disastrous consequences in the 1930s.

The second set of events critical to the origins of the Second World War in the Far East was the impact of the Great Depression that followed in the wake of the Wall Street Crash of October 1929. In relating the Great Depression to the Far East, specifically to Japan, three matters need be noted, namely the economic devastation caused by the Depression which struck Japan (a relatively 'young' industrial nation) early; the rise of anti-democratic and authoritarian sentiments with which Japan identified herself in terms of her choice of European associates, and the twin urges for autarky and expansion as the means of resolving the financial, industrial and economic crises wrought by the Depression.

The two world wars have been described as the mountain ranges of twentieth-century history and, without disputing this, one would add the obvious rider. Mountain ridges are separated by low ground, and the Great Depression was arguably as important in shaping the history of the twentieth century as the two world wars. Certainly the rise of Hitler, and the general emergence of totalitarian tendencies in Europe in the course of the 1930s, were the direct products of the Great Depression, as was (at least in part) the enfeeblement of the Democracies in the face of the challenge presented by the new authoritarian states. In the case of Japan, the hardship imposed by the

Depression bore heavily both upon the countryside and upon an army very conscious of rural distress in the home islands. The obvious failure of economic liberalism served to discredit political liberalism, and under the impact of the Depression, representative and responsible government, a somewhat delicate bloom in even the most benevolent times in Japan, became nothing more than a condemned man under sentence.

These products of the Depression began to come together with the Manchurian campaign of September 1931 to March 1932. The initiative for this campaign came not from the government, but from the Kwantung Army, the Japanese army of occupation in southern Manchuria, and was the direct response to the desperation that gripped the home islands in the wake of the Depression. The inability of the government to control the Kwantung Army, and the widespread and fanatical support within Japan that the conquest of Manchuria created, amounted to a death sentence for political liberalism in Japan, and over the next five years 'government-by-assassination' established itself as successive governments fell and a number of senior politicians were assassinated. 'Government-by-assassination' was both personal and physical, but more importantly, it was also institutional, a result of the structure of the state as arranged in the Meiji era. In the Japan that emerged from centuries of self-exclusion, the principle of civilian primacy, the subordination of the military to the political and the principle of denial of systematic opposition, had been observed not because these were institutionalized or incorporated into the body politic, but because these features were understood and observed by the closely-knit associates who ruled Japanese society. By the 1930s these men had passed from the scene and, under the impact of recession, these principles suffered the same fate, as government was reduced to a position of *minor inter pares* relative to the army and the navy.

The means by which government was reduced to a position of impotence relative to the armed services was simple. The constitution provided for service ministers who were serving officers, and by refusing to appoint ministers or by the threat or reality of resignation, the armed services were able to reduce government and hence national policy to a position of dependence upon their own will. In the course of the 1930s the services demonstrated an ever-increasing willingness to use what amounted to the power of veto in their own interests. The simplicity of this statement belies the complexity of the events that witnessed and resulted in a process whereby the armed forces came to dominate the affairs of state. However, it neither explains why this happened, nor does it acknowledge that the armed services worked to very different agendas and pursued aims that were as often as not diametrically opposed to one another.

At work within the military in the 1930s, and to a lesser extent in the 1920s, was what can only be described as a culture of insubordination, with regard to government and within the services themselves. No less importantly, under the impact of events, factions within the services identified their own aims and

intentions with those of their service and the state: in a process of transposition that all but defies belief, the armed services effectively reduced state and society to positions of subordination to themselves. The natural bonds of discipline that should have ensured order and obedience within the army and navy, and their proper subordination to government, dissolved for different reasons and to different ends within the two services, but with one result: the devising of national policy, and the ordering of national priorities, became all but impossible.

The indiscipline within the two services recalls Lamartine's famous comment on seeing a mob in the street – 'I must follow them because I am their leader' – since the *gekokujo* phenomenon was to involve the dictation of policy

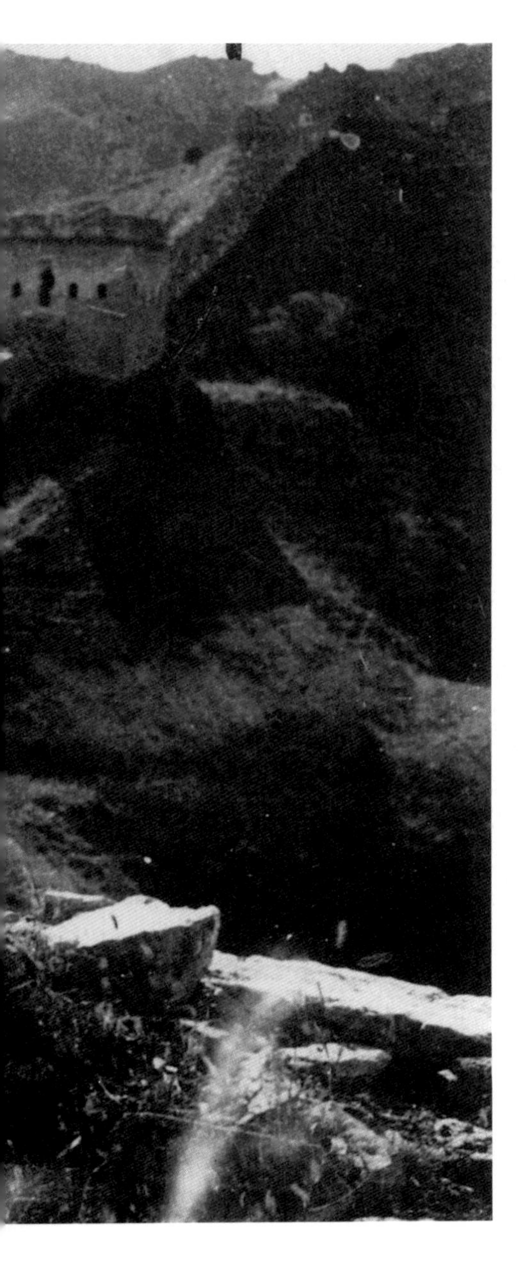

by juniors to those ostensibly in superior command. In the navy this was built around resistance to naval limitation. The principle established at Washington in 1922 and restated at London in 1930 was bitterly resisted for professional reasons as well as being a reflection of nationalist patriotic resentment. The navy believed that Japan had been afforded second-class status in relation to Britain and the US, and only agreed to accept the London treaty on condition that future limitation would be resisted. The navy's attitude, therefore, ensured that after 1936 Japan was certain to cast aside the security afforded by restrictions placed upon American naval construction, with all that that entailed for relations between the two countries, but there was an additional dimension to the navy's waywardness. As the junior service, the navy was very conscious of its weakness in relation to the army and it was also very well aware of its institutional and budgetary vulnerability should the army secure unchallenged control of the political process. Within the army, divisions ran deeper and were even more bitterly fought than in the navy, but in one sense this was predictable: the issues between factions within the army centred upon the state itself, the control of society and the direction of the nation's foreign policy.

Obviously for public consumption and symbolic value: machine-gun position of the Chinese 8th Army on the Great Wall. Japanese encroachments over the previous five years, positions inside the Wall and control of the sea meant that the Great Wall formed no real obstacle to an advance and had no real strategic significance by July 1937.

The period of fratricidal strife within the army and simultaneously increasing military encroachment on the policy-making process was notable for three developments that led to war itself. These were the army's negotiation of the Anti-Comintern Pact with Germany and Italy in November 1936; the institution of the Miyazaki Plan of 1936–7 that involved the expansion of heavy industry with a view to enabling Japan to wage total war for three years; and the start of Japan's 'special undeclared war' with China. Obviously the first and third of these developments possessed singular significance, but arguably it was the various unsought consequences of the second that proved the most significant milestone along the road to war.

Japan's ever-closer identification with Germany and Italy in the course of the 1930s was of symbolic rather than practical value: Japan's hope that the Treaty would serve to check the Soviet Union was to prove stillborn. The significance of Japan's association with Germany and Italy was not missed, but in the event this need not have been significant. What was far more significant was the outbreak of war in China following a clash between Chinese and Japanese forces outside Peking on 7 July 1937. At first this encounter did not seem unduly important: there was every possibility that it could be resolved by the Japanese in exactly the same way that numerous incidents in northern China had been resolved over the four previous years. After overrunning Manchuria in 1931–2 the Japanese had set about a deliberate encroachment on Chinese territory: Jehol was invaded and occupied in January–February 1933 and the Chinese squeezed from Hopei in June 1935 and from Charar in the following month.

In the aftermath of the clash of July 1937 the Japanese, by their standards, were restrained, confining themselves to the occupation of Tientsin and Peking. There was good and obvious reason for such restraint, not least the paucity of Japanese forces in northern China, but in the event the determination of the Kwantung Army in Manchuria to further its ambitions in Inner Mongolia and the outbreak of fighting in Shanghai on 13 August pushed Japan towards general war: by the end of September the Japanese Army had dispatched ten divisions to northern China and another five to Shanghai, primarily to rescue the naval formations which had provoked the August clash in an attempt to ensure that the army did not steal a march on its sister service in matters Chinese.

In reality, deeper forces were at work in producing Japan's 'special undeclared war' with China, specifically China's attempts after December 1936 to resolve her civil wars in order to present a united front to future Japanese aggression. Within the Japanese high command, therefore, there were elements that sought to forestall such a development, and with the spread of war, and the inability of Tokyo either to contain the conflict or to end it by negotiation, Japanese operations quickly assumed their own momentum. Within four months of the outbreak of general war, the Kwantung Army had secured Inner Mongolia and installed a puppet regime at Kueisui while by the end of 1937 much of China north of the Yellow River – considered by some of the Japanese military to be the minimum sphere of influence that was acceptable – had been overrun. It was in central China, however, that the main story unfolded, specifically the Japanese capture of Shanghai in November and Nanking, amid scenes of mass murder, rape, torture and pillage, in December.

In the course of 1938 Japanese forces in northern China cleared Shansi and Shantung and advanced to the Pinglu-Kaifeng-Hsüchow-Taierhchwang line, while from their positions on the lower Yangtse the Japanese were able to develop offensives that cleared Anhwei north of the river and moved into the

The old and the new: the Japanese capture of Hsüchow, Honan province, 1 July 1938. Representation of a light tank invites the suggestion that it was the only tank available to the Japanese in this operation: the fact was that the Imperial Army was wholly under-invested in armour and mechanized–motorized forces, as the Soviet Army demonstrated one year later.

Wuhan cities, the Chinese having ceded the middle Yangtse in order to withdraw into the fastness of Kweichow and Hunan. With the simultaneous seizure of Canton, Japanese success in the course of 1938 was impressive, yet it represented failure, and for obvious reason: the basic dilemmas which had proved so intractable during the Chinese civil wars of the 1920s presented themselves anew. The Japanese were confronted by the basic question of whether to seek to destroy the Nationalist regime of Chiang Kai-shek or to preserve it as the only authority that might deliver a negotiated settlement. They also faced the related problem of whether to sponsor rival regimes in an attempt to put pressure on the Nationalists to come to a settlement, or as genuine alternatives to the Nationalist government in Chungking. But either and both of these sets of alternatives concealed the real problem. Japan did not embark upon the conquest of northern and central China in order to provide alternatives to her own rule: Japan sought to secure the power of decision exclusively for herself, and certainly never understood any force of nationalist aspiration other than her own.

Moreover, success in the field merely confirmed the truth of the Clausewitzian observation that it is easy to conquer but hard to occupy. In the vastness of China it was impossible to force a military victory, while by the

A sign of change: Japanese troops disembarking at the Shanghai bund, for long the physical manifestation of western power in China, in November 1937 in readiness for the move against Soochow (abandoned by the Chinese on the 19th) and thence against Nanking.

beginning of 1938 guerrilla warfare had taken hold in many areas nominally under Japanese control, even as banditry revived inside Manchuria as a result of the reduction of the Japanese garrisons in order to provide for operations in China. With the Nationalists having opted for 'a sustained strategy of attrition' that in the end the Japanese could never counter, 1938 also saw clashes with the Soviets, which in turn presented another conundrum: whether operations in China were to be curtailed in order to ensure the security of Manchuria or developed without reference to the distinct possibility of further, serious clashes with the Soviet Union.

In such a situation, and unable to force battle upon the Chinese Nationalist armies in the wastes of Szechwan, Kweichow and Yunnan, the Japanese undertook the first strategic air campaign in history. Douhet, Mitchell and Trenchard are always paraded as the high priests of air power, specifically strategic bombing, but interestingly the first person to have committed to paper the idea of breaking an enemy's will to resist by a bombing campaign directed against a civilian population was a Japanese naval officer, Nakajima Chikuhei, in 1915. The first such employment of air power came as early as August 1937, and in summer 1938 the Japanese undertook a terror bombing campaign against Canton; in May 1939 the Japanese launched their first attacks on Chungking.

In spring–summer 1940, however, the Japanese launched Operation 101, a systematic campaign against Chinese cities in the interior, primarily Chungking, with a view to breaking Chinese morale. A year later, in spring–summer 1941, the Japanese renewed their attempt with Operation 102, but this was a halting affair as Japanese naval aircraft were in the process of being withdrawn from China in readiness for operations in south-east Asia and the Pacific.

The two offensives produced interesting results, although not the ones that the Japanese sought. Chinese cities, on account of their massive concentrations of people and generally flimsy construction, were peculiarly vulnerable to bombing, and a number of them, most obviously Chungking, were all but razed. With their populations either driven out or underground, Chinese morale faltered under the initial blows, but it did not break. Moreover, the Japanese were to find that the effectiveness of their raids was directly dependent upon fighters first having secured air superiority: before August 1940 and the commitment of the A6M Zero-sen long-range fighter to the battle, Japanese losses were all but prohibitive. As it was, both Operation 101 and Operation 102 were conducted on a scale that was too small to have realistic chances of success – the total effort involved in Operation 101 was less in terms of aircraft sorties and bomb load than those directed against Dresden in February 1945 – and, critically, this last-resort option failed. The army and navy air forces were not able to record a result that the Japanese military could not achieve on the ground, and the China war remained thereafter, as it had been since 1937, unwinnable by military means.

Representation of the Japanese entry into Nanking, allegedly in November 1937. In reality, Japanese forces occupied the city on 13 December and subjected its inhabitants to infamous treatment that still casts its shadow in both China and Japan to the present time.

No less seriously, and in 1937–8 of more immediate importance, the China war in effect wrecked the Miyazaki Plan: Japan could have her plan or her war, but not both. But by 1938 Japanese industrial ambitions were beginning to fall apart in any case. The idea of developing heavy industry and the resources of Manchuria and northern China in order to ensure self-sufficiency had the twin results of restricting merchant fleet development by ensuring its concentration on short-haul trade and increasing Japanese dependence on foreign finished products and credits without which major plant development was not possible. By 1939, given Europe's movement towards war, such credit was increasingly scarce and expensive, as was the foreign shipping required to carry the raw materials that Japan needed for her very existence. What made Japan's position even worse was the fact that while the China war cost a staggering $5 million a day, her holdings on the mainland and resultant pattern of trade had the effect of warping her trade balances. By 1939 something like 75–80 per cent of all Japanese trade was directed to her so-called partners within the newly created 'Yen Bloc', but the credits that she earned by a ruthless manipulation of exchange rates could not provide the hard cash she needed in order to pay for her real needs – the purchase of industrial goods and raw materials from the outside world – and Japan could not afford the investment essential to develop her own resources and those of her conquered territories.

Moreover, by 1939 another problem was emerging in the form of the naval rearmament programme initiated in 1937 with the ending of limitation treaties. It was not that Japan could not fulfil her own programme, but that the limitations of her shipyards had a triple consequence: she could not meet the demands of naval and merchant shipping programmes simultaneously, at least not on a scale sufficient for her requirements; the demands of building meant that Japan could not undertake the rate of maintenance needed to keep the merchant fleet fully operational; and the congestion of shipyards imposed massive delays on the completion of even the most important fleet units. Moreover, in the summer of 1939 Japanese forces in Mongolia were quite literally taken apart by their Soviet opposite numbers in battle at Nomonhan, and in the middle of these proceedings Germany chose to conclude a non-aggression pact with the Soviets preparatory to her attack on Poland and the start of general war in Europe.

Comprehensive defeat, disillusionment with Germany, and a new-found respect for the Democracies that at last showed the will to resist Hitler, caused a chastened Japan to make for the sidelines after September 1939, to wait upon events, even though her basic problems remained unresolved. In spring 1940 one set of uncertainties ended: Germany's victory over the Democracies rekindled admiration and support for the Reich within Japan, specifically within the army, and Japan's adherence to the Tripartite Pact followed in September 1940. By this action Japan committed herself irreversibly to the new order that was in the process of reshaping the international community, and perhaps this was inevitable: the defeat of France in spring 1940 removed, in the form of French Indo-China, the European colonial empires' first line of defence in south-east Asia, thus providing Japan with maximum temptation with apparently little risk to herself. Within weeks of the French defeat, Japan had forced the French authorities in Indo-China and the British in Burma to close down supply routes to the Chungking regime. In so doing Japan initiated a process that was to end one year later with the crisis that provoked general war throughout the Pacific and south-east Asia in December 1941. But in reality two other matters arising from the events of June–July 1940 contributed in full to this process.

The first is well known: the passing of the Two-Ocean Naval Expansion Act by the US Congress. The Maginot Line had been the first line of defence of both France and French Indo-China, but it had also been the first line of defence of the United States. The fall of France, and the overwhelming likelihood of Britain's defeat and surrender, forced the US to look to her own defences with the result that Congress authorized a building programme on such a scale that all other navies would be reduced to positions of impotent irrelevance by the time it was completed. The short-term implication of this development was largely lost upon the United States, but not upon the Imperial Japanese Navy, and herein lies the second matter.

In June 1940 the Imperial Navy reacted to American shipbuilding by ordering full mobilization, a process that needed eighteen months to implement. What in June 1940 the Imperial Navy expected to happen in December 1941 or thereabouts has never been fully explained. Nor has there ever been a full account of the eighteen-month refitting and modernization programme which left just one single ship, a destroyer, *not* in service on 7 December 1941. But if the Imperial Navy's 1940 expectations have never been properly explained, one fact is obvious: the Imperial Navy could not remain at full mobilization if only because of the massive inroads made into the strength of a merchant fleet already inadequate to the task of fulfilling national import requirements. The fact of the matter was, simply, that while the American rearmament programme was provoked by the German victory in north-west Europe, it also marked the point when the United States in effect picked up the challenge that Japan had presented over the previous decade. And as the Imperial Navy checked its sums one matter was clear: with the provisions of its 1937 construction programme more or less complete by the end of 1941 and the Americans at least two or three years from the completion of the first major fleet units authorized by the Two-Ocean Act, at the end of 1941 the Imperial Navy would stand at the peak of its strength relative to the United States. Indeed, in December 1941 the Imperial Japanese Navy possessed clear superiority of numbers in every type of fleet unit over the US Pacific and Asiatic fleets.

In a very obvious sense, what was to follow (the conclusion of a non-aggression treaty with the Soviet Union in April 1941; the decision to occupy French Indo-China even at the risk of a breach with the United States; the occupation of Indo-China and the American imposition of sanctions; the futility of subsequent American–Japanese diplomatic negotiations and Japan's final decision for war) represents the final playing-out of a script, written in, if not before, June 1940. Admittedly, this interpretation of events is something of a simplification, and it does not explain the one point about what happened. States as mismatched in terms of area, population size, resources and military strength as Japan and the United States very seldom fight one another, and even more rarely do they fight wars initiated by the weaker side. The process whereby Japan induced war in December 1941 has all the hallmarks of a national kamikaze effort and provokes incredulity matched only by the detail of the process and Japan's final decision. In summer 1941 the Japanese leadership accepted the prospect of war with the United States as the price of a move against British and Dutch possessions in south-east Asia, and thereby embarked upon a war with the only power in the world that could defeat Japan. In the process, Japan provided the United States with a *casus belli* that she could never have provided for herself.

In setting out the story of the road to war, one war in 1937 and another in 1941, this chapter has sought to explain rather than describe events. But in so doing it has incorporated two weaknesses. It has followed Japanese decisions and actions, and it has done so on the basis that the road to war was primarily marked by milestones bearing *kanji* not Roman script. It does not follow, however, that other powers were merely passive onlookers, that their actions, or lack of action, did not contribute to the denouement of 1941: the estrangement of Japan and past associates involved a journey on a two-way not one-way street. Certainly the contribution of the United States to the process of alienation was very real, most obviously in terms of the racist denigration to which Japan was subjected within the United States, and the discriminatory trade practices adopted by that country against Japan in the course of the 1930s. But the basic historiographical point is correct: the story of the drift to war is best related in terms of Japan's power of decision which, more than any other factor, shaped and directed events.

The second weakness is one that besets the writing of history: an inability on the part of the historian to take proper account of two phenomena, namely the march of events and irrationality. Of course some historical works have left themselves open to the charge that they have provided more than a little evidence of the latter, and while one hopes that such a charge cannot be levelled at this particular work one would note that these two commodities were present in full measure in the events leading to the Second World War in the Far East. The idea of the inevitability of war between Japan and the United States pervaded the whole of the inter-war period, and certainly the events of 1940–41 seem to have acquired their own momentum. It is certainly possible to see the Japanese choice of 'go-now-or-never' in terms of a decision dictated by circumstances: no less certainly, it is possible to portray the decision for war in autumn 1941 as one forced upon the Japanese high command. The American demands in summer 1941 for a withdrawal of Japanese forces from Indo-China, China and Manchuria as the price of a resumption of normal trade was an impossible one for the Japanese high command, and acceptance would have triggered civil war, if indeed anyone in Japan would have fought for a government that was prepared to accept such humiliation. Moreover, in the crisis of summer 1941 it was impossible for the Imperial Navy, after all the care and money lavished upon it, to admit its powerlessness in face of the Two-Ocean Naval Expansion Act, or to accept that its demands for an end of naval limitation had resulted in its inability to resist relegation to second or third class status. Yet this line of argument, which must have some validity, invites two questions. Why was it that in 1941 the Japanese undertook no new drilling for oil either in the home islands or in any of their overseas possessions? And what significance attaches itself to the fact that even without the American trade embargo of July 1941 Japan would have exhausted her currency reserves in spring 1942 and would have been unable to continue to trade after that time? Clearly, the line of argument that places momentum or inevitability of events at the heart of explanation cannot provide all the answers to the questions that have to be asked about these developments.

Thus one turns to irrationality for explanation, though perhaps a better term might be either misplaced hope or wishful thinking. Herein, perhaps, lies

The prelude to war: Japanese soldiers outside Saigon in October 1941. Japan's occupation of southern Indo-China in summer 1941 represented the ne plus ultra *for Washington: the imposition of sanctions initiated the process that led to general war in December at a time of Japan's, not America's, choosing.*

1. THE AKATSUKI-CLASS FLEET DESTROYER *Inazuma*

2. THE SHUMUSHU-CLASS GENERAL-PURPOSE *Shumushu*

5. THE KONGO-CLASS FAST BATTLESHIP *Kirishima*

6. THE ATAGO-CLASS HEAVY CRUISER *Takao*

explanation. The Japanese leadership that guided, or misguided, the nation's affairs in the 1930s consisted of individuals no more gifted or stupid than those of other national leaderships, and every nation, at some time or another, has arranged its affairs in a manner and to an end not dissimilar to that of Japan in the period under consideration, even if to not so rapid and so disastrous a conclusion as the one achieved by Tokyo. But certainly the Japanese leadership in 1940–41 was thoroughly mendacious in terms of its 'situating the appreciation', arranging hard evidence to wish away reality and to support conclusions based upon hope, particularly in relation to the Miyazaki Plan. Its aims had never been realized and originally it had set provision for a war with the Soviet Union, but by 1941 it had become an article of faith within the Japanese high command that the country could sustain a total war for three years against the United States, and projections of oil production estimates were altered to prove it. And in this process explanation, at least partial explanation, for what would otherwise be incomprehensible might exist in the shape of four sets of circumstances.

The first, and by far the most important, is a perspective of the time that has been lost when set against the reality of American national power over the last six decades. The world has become familiar with this power, a power that did not exist in 1941. Second, a nation with no experience of defeat over a history that reached back over thousands of years could not imagine defeat: a people that believed itself to be protected and ruled by the gods, and mandated by Heaven to assume its proper place in the world, could not envisage failure. Third, the Japanese military, specifically the navy, did not understand the nature of war, specifically the nature of the war that it began in 1941. It did not understand the difference between war and *a* war, between a war and a

3. THE ASASHIO-CLASS FLEET DESTROYER *Asagumo*

4. THE ATAGO-CLASS HEAVY CRUISER *Atago*

7. THE REBUILT KONGO-CLASS FAST BATTLESHIP *Haruna*, 1936

8. THE TYPE B-1 CRUISER–SUBMARINE *I-26*

campaign, between a campaign and a battle, and it did not understand that a war in the Pacific would involve a naval war – between fleets and formations and endowed with an amphibious dimension – as well as a maritime war in defence of shipping. All its attention was geared to battle, an obsession that over time obscured the distinction between battle and the other elements that relate to the nature and conduct of war. And here lies the basis of the fourth and last matter: the Imperial Navy, as a basic rule of thumb, knew that it could not defeat the Americans, but hoped that its success in battle would ultimately be translated into American acceptance of a new arrangement to Japanese advantage.

Hope is a poor basis of a plan, and such hope as the one that the Imperial Navy entertained was wholly unrealistic – at least in retrospect – because the basic premise was flawed: the terms of reference of a Pacific war were not Japan's to determine. The alternative to Japan's victory in a limited war in the Pacific was not defeat in a limited war in the Pacific, but defeat in a total war in the Pacific. All this, however, was very far from obvious in the opening weeks of the war which Japan initiated with her attack on the US Pacific Fleet at its base at Pearl Harbor on the morning of Sunday, 7 December 1941.

AFTERTHOUGHT

In setting out this account, specifically the account of Japanese naval programmes, the author has deliberately made no reference to one matter: the problem of block obsolescence. At the outbreak of the Pacific war the Imperial Navy was owner of 111 destroyers. Of this total thirty – the twelve Minekaze-class members of the 1917, 1918, 1919 and 1920 programmes, three Momi-class members of the 1918 and 1920 programmes, six Wakatake-class members of the

JAPANESE WARSHIPS IN THE INTERWAR PERIOD

1. *The* Inazuma, *as rebuilt: six 5-inch guns, nine 24-inch torpedo tubes, 34 knots.*
2. *The* Shumushu*: three 4.7-inch guns, six depth charges.*
3. *The* Asagumo*: six 5-inch DP guns, eight 24-inch torpedo tubes, 38 knots.*
4. *The* Atago*: ten 8-inch guns, sixteen 24-inch torpedo tubes, three aircraft.*
5. *The* Kirishima*: her pre-1914 origins are revealed by the distinctive layout of her X and Y turrets.*
6. *The* Takao*: ten 8-inch guns, sixteen 24-inch torpedo tubes, three aircraft.*
7. *The* Haruna*, after second reconstruction in 1936: eight 14-inch guns, 30.5 knots.*
8. *The* I-26*: 2,589 tons maximum displacement: six 21-inch torpedo tubes, seventeen torpedoes, one 5.5-inch gun, one floatplane.*

1921 programme, and nine members of the Kamikaze-class 1921 programme – belonged to either complete classes or classes with lead ships laid down before or in December 1921. A total of thirty-one destroyers – the twelve members of the Mutsuki-class 1923 programme and nineteen surviving members of the Fubuki-class of the 1923, 1926 and 1927 programmes – possessed a similar pedigree reference December 1926, and ten units – the four members of the Akatsuki-class of the 1927 programme and the six units of the Hatsuharu-class of the 1931 programme – reference December 1931. Thus in December 1941 no fewer than seventy-one of the Imperial Navy's 111 destroyers were in the second half of their service lives, and, by the least exacting standard, thirty units were at or even beyond their sell-by dates: lest this be doubted, the Imperial Navy had nineteen other ships drawn from pre-December 1921 classes in service, but these had been relegated to secondary or tertiary duties and did not serve as destroyers.

It would appear, therefore, that for all its efforts in the inter-war period, by 1940 the Imperial Navy was threatened with a massive erosion of its front line strength over the next few years. The twenty-eight-strong Yugumo class and the sixteen-strong Akizuki class, ordered under the 1939 and 1941 programmes, would have ameliorated but could not have forestalled a decline in real numbers: on completion these would have replaced units being phased out and would not have added to strength. In this there was obvious irony. Throughout the inter-war period the Imperial Navy sought qualitative superiority to make good its lack of numbers, and its destroyers were superior in design and capabilities to their contemporaries in foreign service. But by 1940 the qualitative advantage enjoyed by each successive class was exhausted, in part because of lack of numbers, and in part because of the pace of change in the 1930s. In real terms, anything before the Mutsuki and Fubuki classes

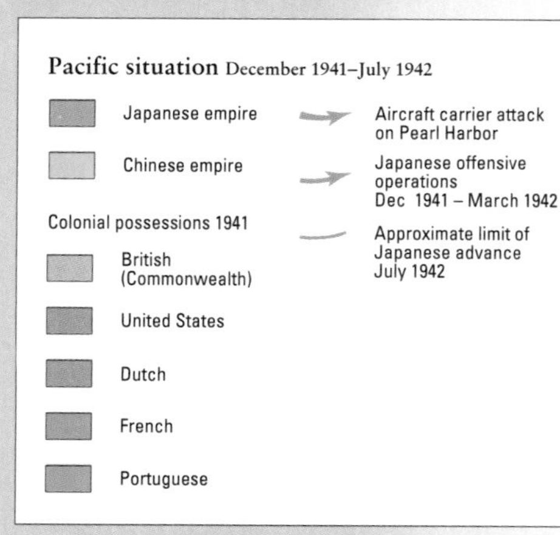

and an armament that included 24-inch torpedoes was of very limited usefulness, and arguably the Mutsukis, as members of the first class with this armament, were of marginal value by 1941.

This long tail of ageing ships and Japan's declining strategic position, especially when set against the difficulties experienced with the 1939 programme and the provisions of the Two-Ocean Naval Expansion Act, would seem to add extra measure to the 'go-now-or-never' thesis, but the author's inability to provide evidence of linkage on this score led to the argument not being employed in the account of proceedings given in this opening chapter. The reality is noted herein, for what it is worth.

THE OPENING JAPANESE OFFENSIVES

Beginning with attacks across a distance of 6,000 miles, the Japanese offensives that opened the Pacific war were characterized by an impressive synchronization and economy of effort: in every sector the Japanese brought a local superiority to bear and inflicted successive humiliating defeats on their various enemies.

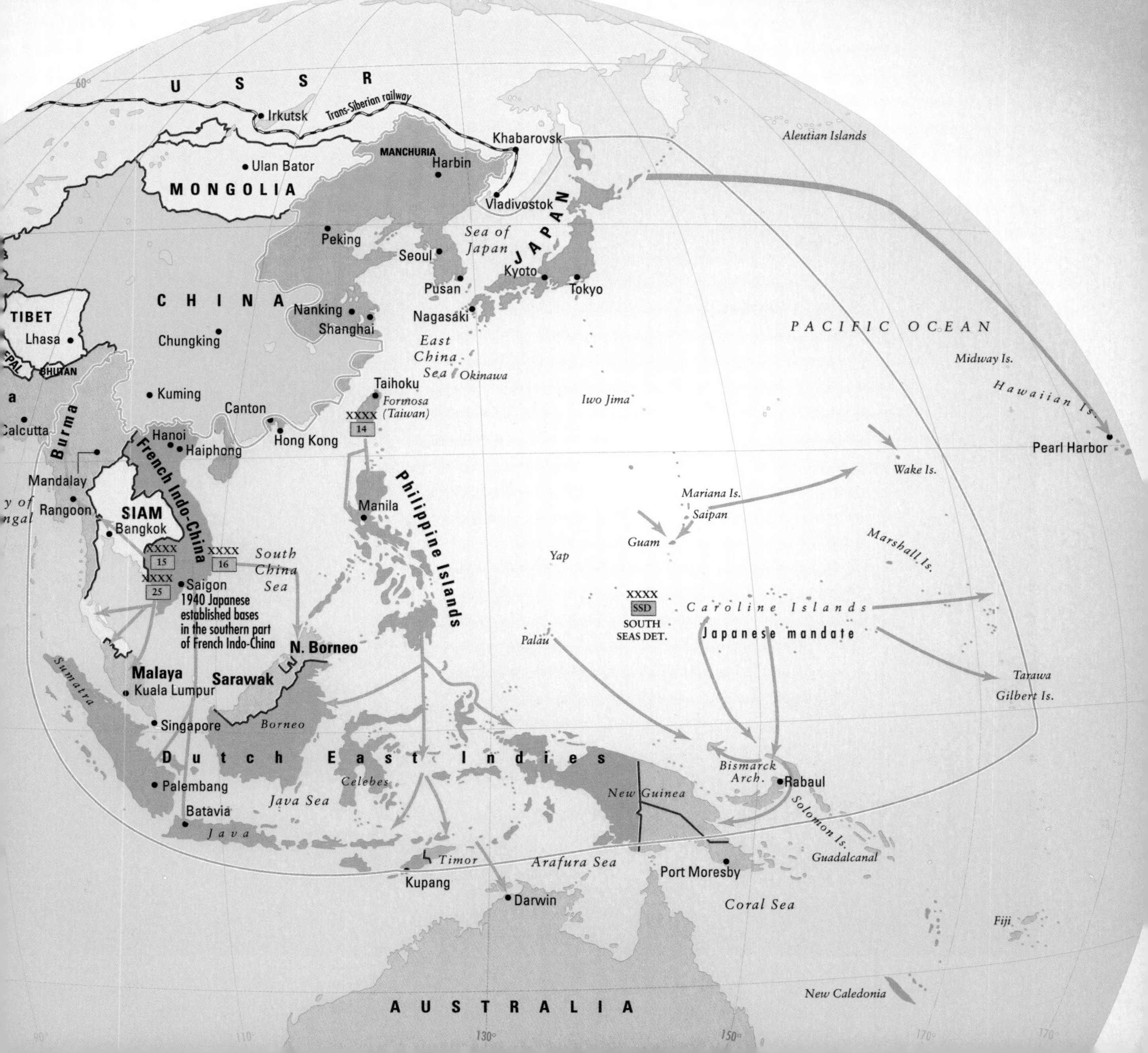

CHAPTER TWO

THE FIRST MILESTONE: SUCCESS AND VICTORY

DECEMBER 1941 – APRIL 1942

WITH ONE BOAT RESCUING a sailor in the water, the battleship West Virginia *lies burning as token of Japanese success on 'the day of infamy'. In the company of two other battleships that were lost on 7 December 1941, she was raised and modernized to such effect that she fought in the Surigao Strait action during the battle of Leyte Gulf and off Iwo Jima and Okinawa.*

THE FIRST MILESTONE: SUCCESS AND VICTORY

ON 27 APRIL 1898 an American cruiser squadron sailed from Hong Kong and four days later fought in Manila Bay an action that reached over sixteen square miles and bought the United States an empire in the Far East. Between 7 December 1941 and 5 April 1942 Japanese forces conducted fleet operations over 58 degrees of latitude and 123 degrees of longitude, and in so doing inflicted upon four imperial powers defeats that were stunning in impact and, for the victor, incomplete in nature and disastrous in consequence.

The story of the Pacific war can be told in a number of different ways, but inevitably must begin with the five months of Japanese triumph that resulted in the conquest of Burma, Malaya, the East Indies, Hong Kong and the Philippines and various island groups in the western-central Pacific. In this period the Japanese were able to secure the various outposts on which they intended to build a perimeter defence and on which the Imperial Navy intended to conduct a defensive war while drawing upon the riches of the 'southern resources area'. It was a four-month campaign with few, if any, parallels in history, both in terms of the scale and range of operations and the extent of conquest, and it was conducted by Japanese forces with only a bare margin of numerical superiority over their enemies. To defeat the single British divisions in Burma and Hong Kong, the two Dutch divisions in the Indies, the three British divisions in Malaya and Singapore and nominally four American divisions in the Philippines, the Imperial Army, after its commitments in Korea, Manchoutikuo, China, Indo-China, the home islands and in the Pacific were discounted, was able to free the equivalent of just eleven divisions for offensive purposes. At sea the Imperial Navy possessed no significant margin of superiority over its intended prey other than in one single, crucial type of warship, the aircraft carrier, while the narrowness of the administrative margins on which Japanese forces were obliged to work can be gauged by the fact that something like 3.6 million tons of merchant shipping was all that was available to support military and naval undertakings. With shipping allowances for the transportation of troops set at five tons per man in the tropics and three tons elsewhere, the shipping requisitioned by the Imperial Army in readiness for the offensives in the south represented little more than minimum requirement.

Japanese success in this opening phase of hostilities in south-east Asia and the Pacific was fairly bought in terms of planning and preparation. The

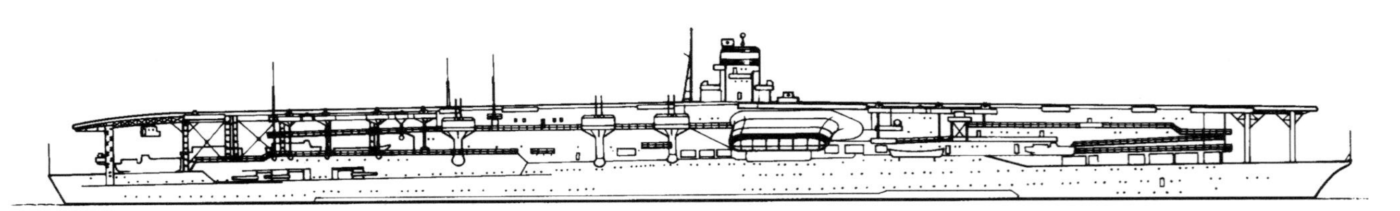

THE *AKAGI*

The fleet carrier Akagi. *41,300 tons (normal load): ninety-one aircraft, six 8-inch, twelve 4.7-inch and twenty-eight 25-mm guns, 31.25 knots. With the* Kaga *the mainstay of Japanese inter-war carrier aviation, the* Akagi *saw service in China, Pearl Harbor, Rabaul, Darwin, south of Java, Ceylon and finally Midway.*

campaign that unfolded in south-east Asia and along the Malay Barrier was brilliantly conceived. Its opening operations were orchestrated across the International Date Line and no fewer than seven time zones, and almost possessed an aesthetic quality in terms of its synchronized, successive movements which were distinguished by impressive economy of effort. But Japanese success was also the product of other factors that were on the scales at this particular time.

The Japanese chose when to begin hostilities, which gave their armed forces a potentially overwhelming advantage in terms of the initiative, and this single asset was compounded by three further benefits which were matched by Allied handicaps. With the start of hostilities the Japanese were endowed with the benefits that accrue to a concentrated attacker: Japan's enemies, in contrast, were divided by geography and everywhere were defensively dispersed; in virtually every theatre the Japanese possessed numerical advantage. The Japanese possessed the advantage of single-nation status: Japan's enemies were ill-assorted, the co-operation between them halting and ineffective, and their difference of interest very marked. Japanese forces were very well trained and equipped, especially in the air: Allied forces, particularly in south-east Asia, were, at very best, of somewhat uneven quality. To these Japanese advantages must be added another: the element of surprise which, in this first phase of operations, took several forms. The American and British high commands had never contemplated a Japanese ability to move across the whole of the Pacific and its adjoining seas from Pearl Harbor to the Gulf of Siam in a single opening offensive, and seriously underestimated the quality of the forces and the equipment with which they found themselves at war.

The Japanese Triumph

The first Japanese moves in a war that was to last forty-five months involved two operations separated by 6,000 miles, namely landings by formations of the 25th Army in southern Siam and northern Malaya in the early hours of 8 December and, some thirty minutes later (across the International Date Line), on the morning of 7 December, the attack by carrier aircraft on the US Pacific fleet at its base in Pearl Harbor. The latter, involving six fleet carriers and 460 aircraft, resulted in the destruction or crippling of eighteen US warships, including five battleships, and here, for a world still accustomed to measuring naval power in terms of dreadnoughts, lay the immediate impact of the Japanese attack. In fact the real significance of this attack was not in what

Vice Admiral Nagumo Chuichi. In some four months the commander of a carrier strike force that attacked Pearl Harbor, Darwin in Australia and Ceylon: in another six months he was largely discredited as a result of failures at Midway, Eastern Solomons and Santa Cruz.

PEARL HARBOR

First wave attack
7 December 1941.

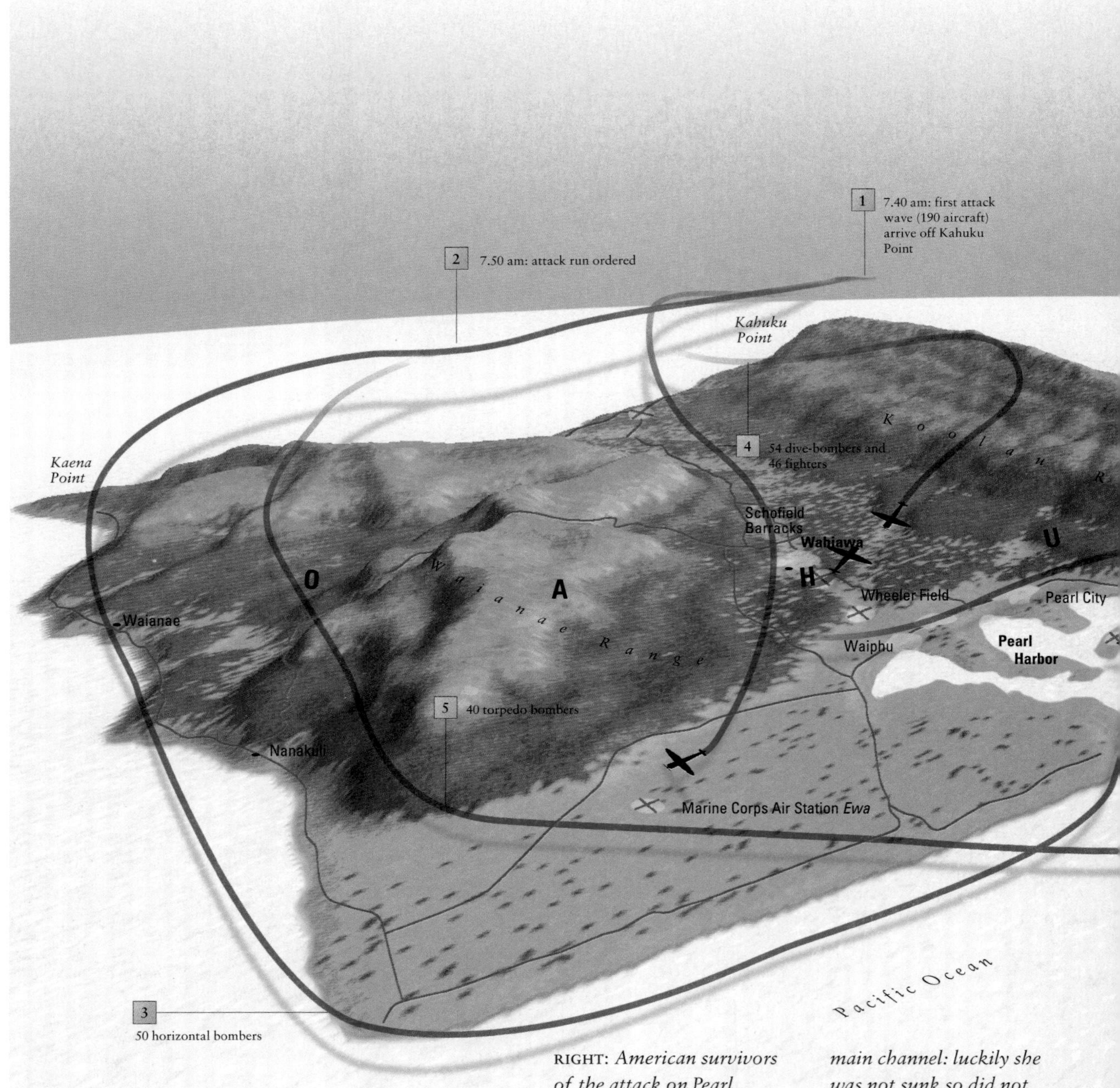

RIGHT: *American survivors of the attack on Pearl Harbor have testified that one of the most inspiring sights was the* Nevada, *the only American battleship to get under way, seeking the main channel: luckily she was not sunk so did not block the harbour. She was run aground, raised and updated and fought off Normandy, southern France, Iwo Jima and Okinawa.*

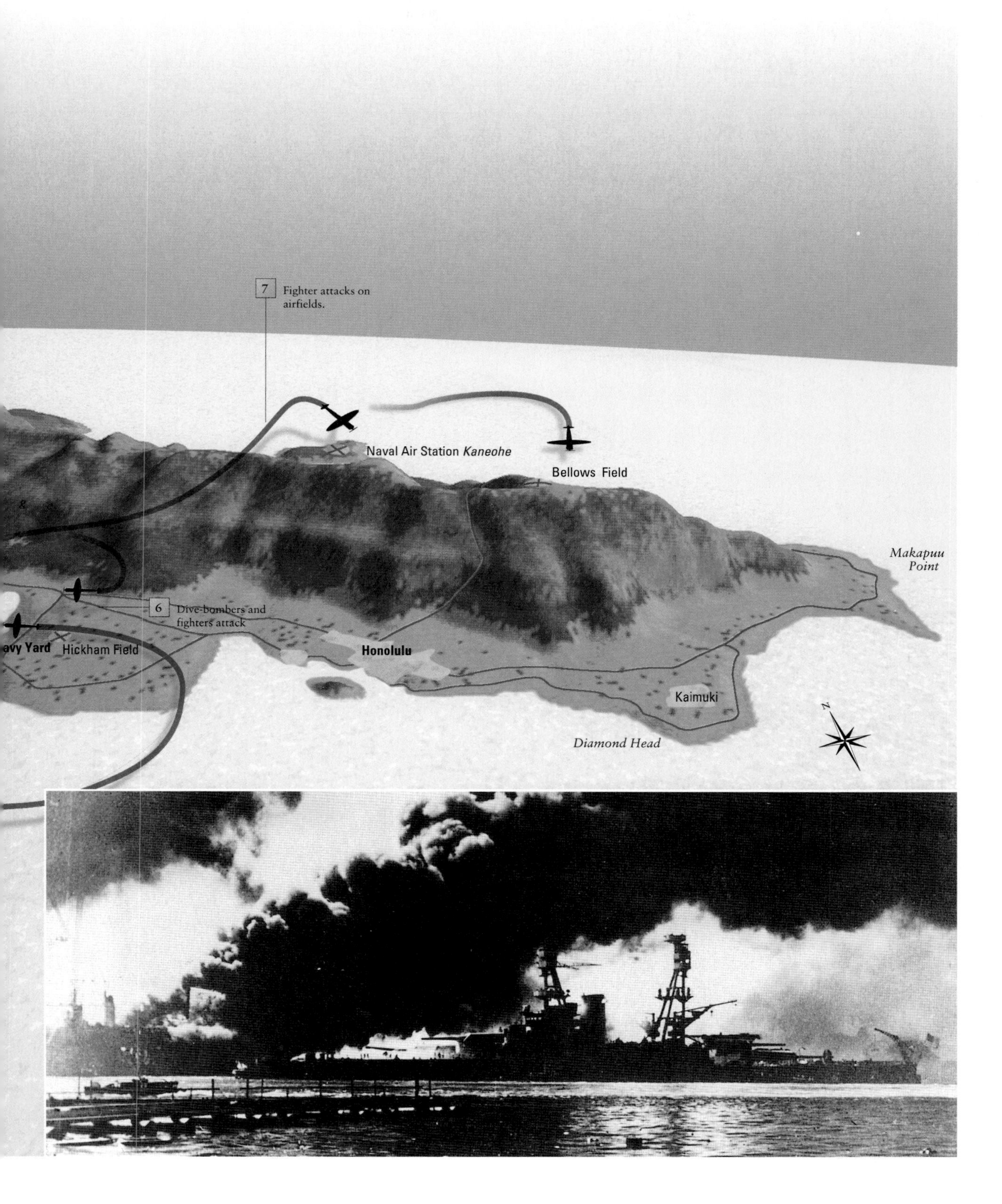
7 Fighter attacks on airfields.
Naval Air Station *Kaneohe*
Bellows Field
Makapuu Point
6 Dive-bombers and fighters attack
avy Yard
Hickham Field
Honolulu
Kaimuki
Diamond Head
N

Pearl Harbor

Second wave attack
7 December 1941.

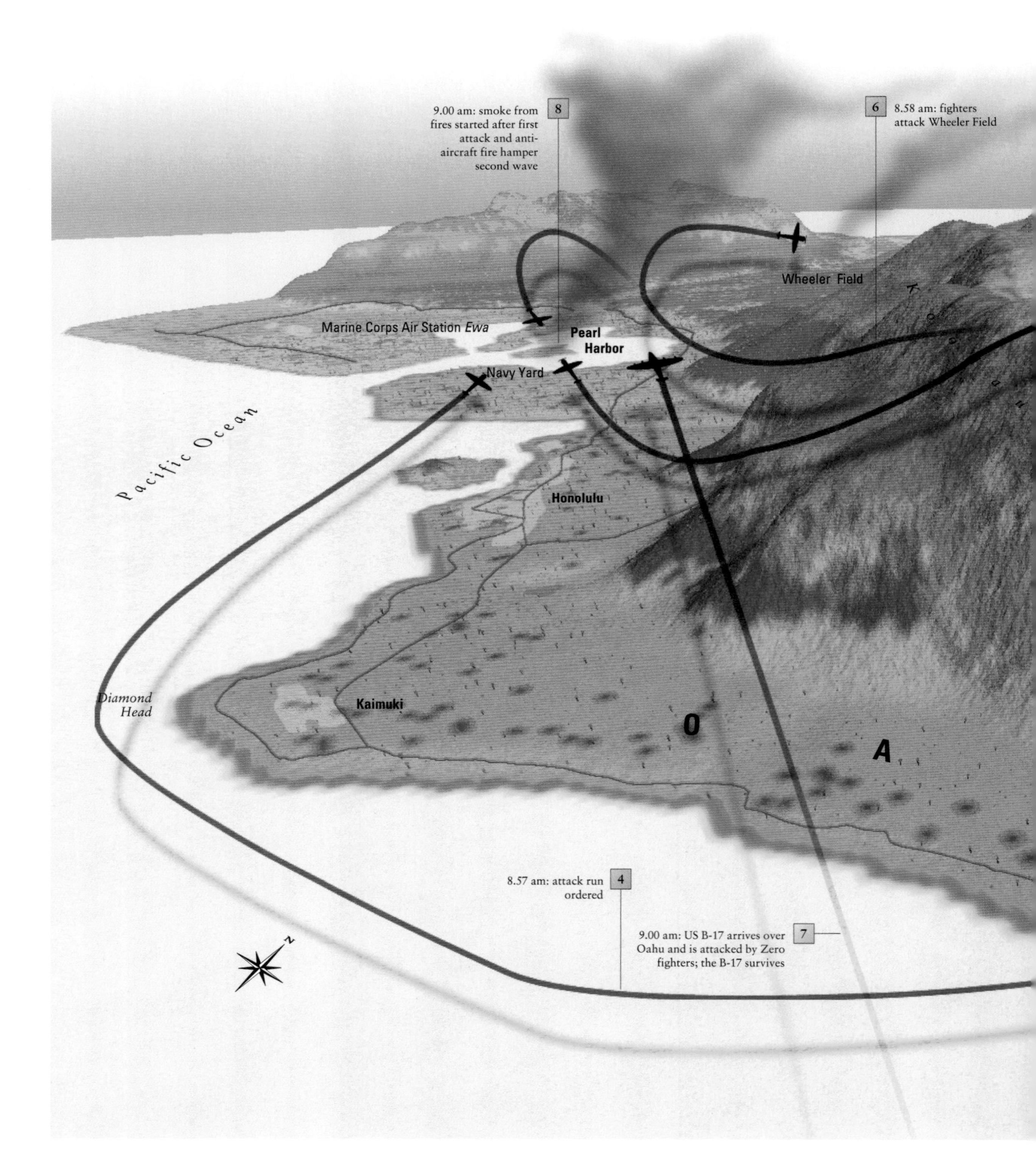

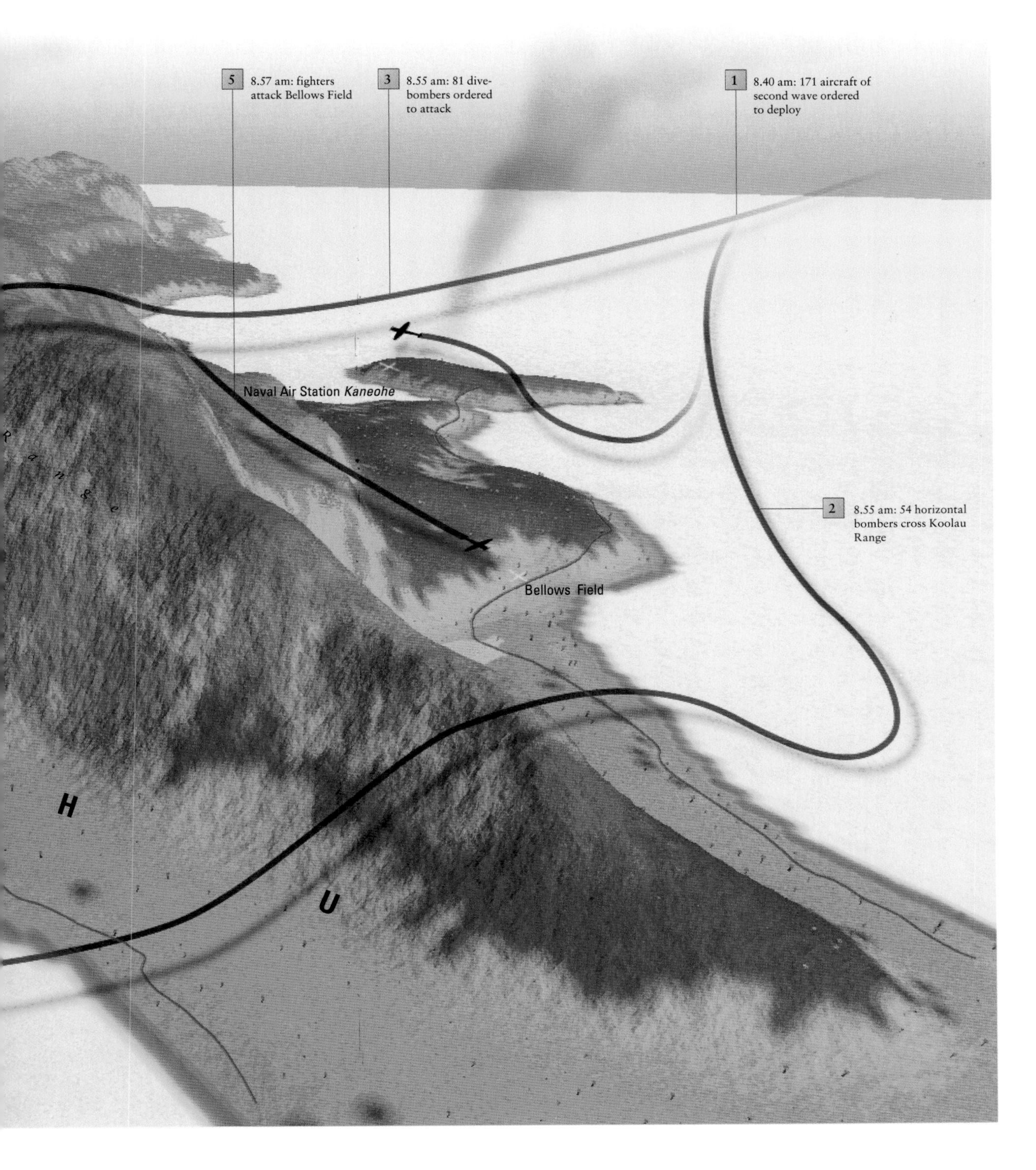
5 8.57 am: fighters attack Bellows Field
3 8.55 am: 81 dive-bombers ordered to attack
1 8.40 am: 171 aircraft of second wave ordered to deploy
Naval Air Station Kaneohe
2 8.55 am: 54 horizontal bombers cross Koolau Range
Bellows Field
H
U

'We flew through and over the thick clouds, which were at two thousand metres, up to where day was ready to dawn. And the clouds began gradually to brighten below us after the brilliant sun burst into the eastern sky. I opened the cockpit canopy and looked back at large formations of planes. The wings glittered in the bright morning sunlight.'

CAPTAIN MITSUO FUCHIDA, 7 DECEMBER 1941.

8.05 am: 64 level bombers drop 360 plus bombs on main anchorage

it either destroyed or missed, but in its scale and distance. Though the *Bismarck* chase in the North Atlantic of May 1941 had involved three carriers, the greatest single strike by carrier aircraft before Pearl Harbor – at Taranto on the night of 11/12 November 1940 – involved just twenty-one of their number. The attack on Pearl Harbor was conducted by a self-sufficient task force over a distance of some four thousand miles, culminating in a two-wave attack *en masse*. It inaugurated a new era of naval warfare, but this was largely obscured by the immediacy of the situation and the elements of Japanese failure that surrounded it. Japan's action brought the United States into a war that, on account of the American temperament, could only end in either total victory or total defeat. But if the crippling of the Pacific Fleet confirmed the Japanese Navy in its possession of the initiative and a marked superiority of strength in the western and central Pacific, the attack miscarried in two vital respects: no American carrier or submarine was damaged and the base facilities at Pearl Harbor were not neutralized. Even more seriously, the shipping requirements of the south-east Asia effort had prompted the Imperial Navy's refusal to consider a landing in the Hawaiian Islands in order to occupy the only possible base for an American effort into the western Pacific: this ordering of priorities was recognized as an error almost as soon as the Pearl Harbor operation came to an end. As a result, the campaign in south-east Asia was to unfold even as the Imperial Navy turned its attention to the demands of an offensive campaign in the central Pacific.

The conduct of amphibious operations that reached back to the Sino-Japanese war had equipped Japan with a doctrine that sought out weakness, a concept of operations that accepted natural obstacles in order to avoid contact with major enemy forces during the most vulnerable phase of landing operations. Thus the opening Japanese moves in south-east Asia involved the overland entry into and occupation of Siam from French Indo-China, landings at her ports on the Kra Isthmus from which Japanese formations were to advance into northern Malaya, and landings on the islands on the approaches to

7.55 am: 139 Val dive bombers attack various locations dropping 450 plus bombs

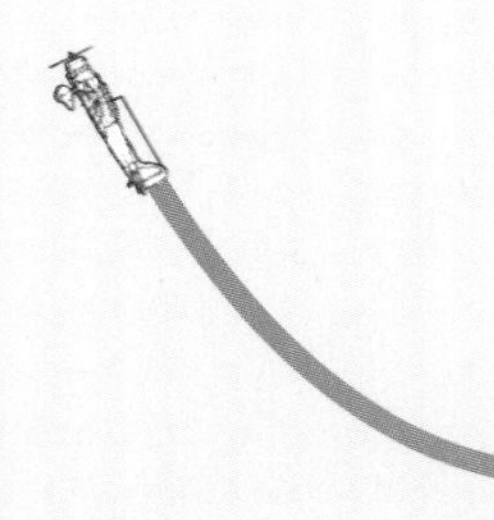

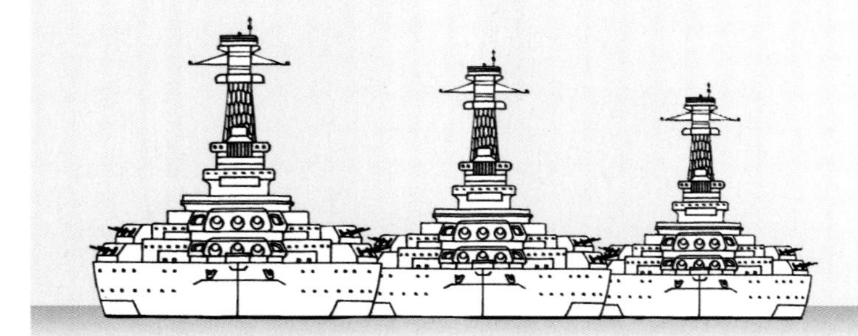

Luzon and on northern Luzon itself in the Philippines. In southern Siam and the Philippines the Japanese successfully established themselves ashore against enemies that were both surprised and dispersed and, through the separate campaigns that followed, were unable to concentrate their full forces against a numerically inferior invader. The Japanese 14th Army used positional advantage in the Philippines to conduct landings in southern Mindanao and southern Luzon to complement its initial landings in northern Luzon before making its main effort in the form of a double envelopment of Manila, with landings at Lingayen Gulf and Lamon Bay on 22 December. The next day the Americans decided to abandon Manila and withdraw into the Bataan Peninsula, and it was an admission of failure. Bataan could provide no more than temporary sanctuary followed by siege and ultimately defeat; it was not a base from which Japanese success could be contested. Japanese forces from northern and southern Luzon linked up around Manila on 2 January 1942, when the Japanese high command took the decision to release air forces and one division from the Philippines for second-phase operations in the Indies.

By this time the British position throughout south-east Asia had been similarly destroyed. With the surrender of Hong Kong on Christmas Day 1941 and Japanese landings in Brunei and Sarawak over the previous week, the last week of 1941 witnessed the rout of British forces in northern Malaya. Having landed at Singora and Patani, the Japanese struck across the border against a fragmented,

82 ZERO FIGHTER

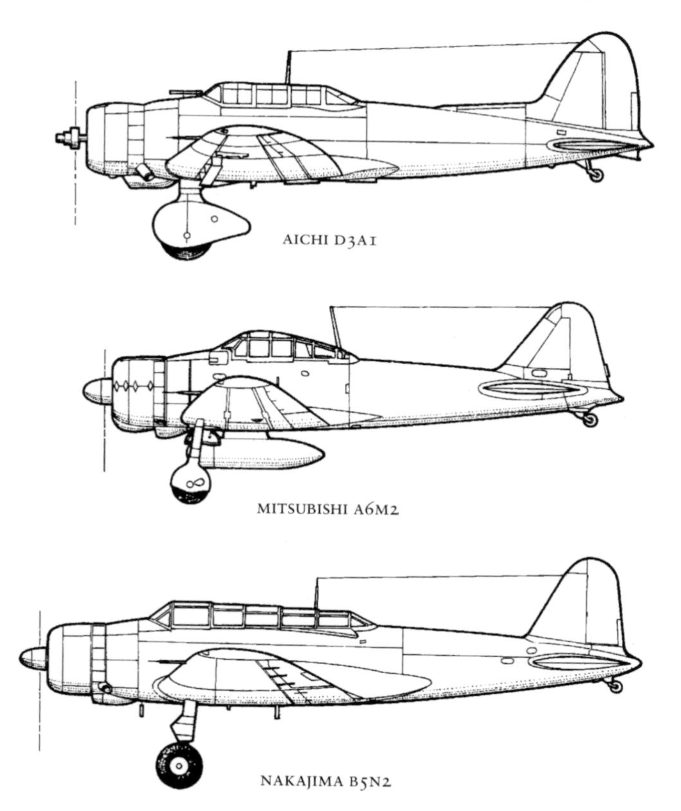

PEARL HARBOR

Attack on Battleship Row in Pearl Harbor, 7 December 1941.

7.57 am: forty torpedo bombers deliver forty long lance torpedos on Battleship Row

Lieutenant General Honma Masaharu, commander of the 14th Army, coming ashore in Lingayen Gulf on 24 December 1941. His failure to win a quick victory in the Philippines resulted in dismissal: the reality of his army's victory was the real reason for his post-war execution.

THE JAPANESE INVASION AND CONQUEST OF MALAYA AND SINGAPORE

The strength of Singapore's defences forced the Japanese to attempt an overland advance on the fortress: from beachheads in southern Siam and northern Malaya the key to success proved to be the speed of Japanese operations, outflanking movement through jungle against a road-bound enemy and local superiority, especially in the air.

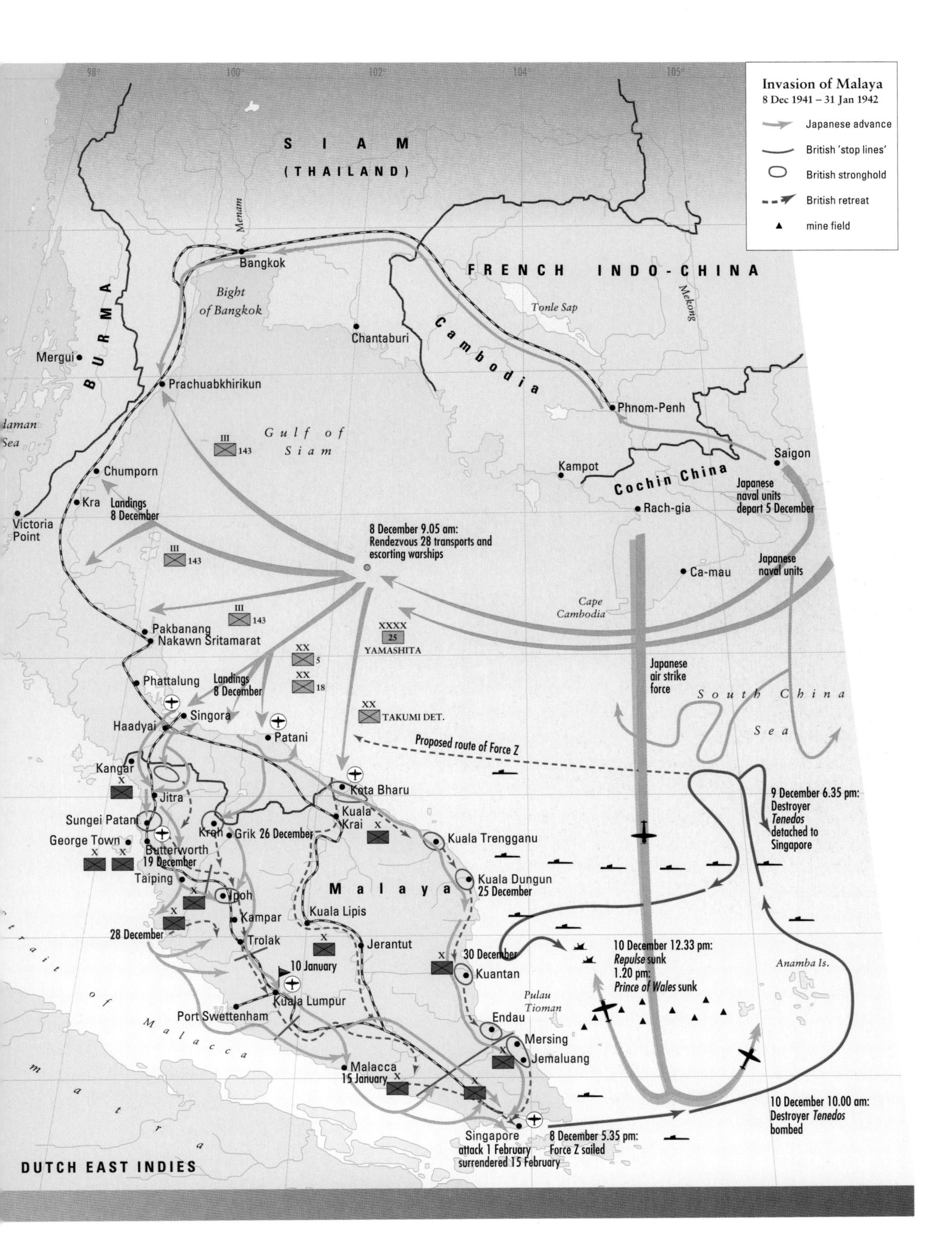
Invasion of Malaya
8 Dec 1941 – 31 Jan 1942
Japanese advance
British 'stop lines'
British stronghold
British retreat
mine field
SIAM
(THAILAND)
FRENCH INDO-CHINA
BURMA
Cambodia
Cochin China
Malaya
DUTCH EAST INDIES
Menam
Mekong
Tonle Sap
Bight of Bangkok
Gulf of Siam
South China Sea
Straits of Malacca
Sumatra
Bangkok
Chantaburi
Mergui
Prachuabkhirikun
Phnom-Penh
Saigon
Kampot
Rach-gia
Ca-mau
Cape Cambodia
Chumporn
Kra
Victoria Point
Pakbanang
Nakawn Sritamarat
Phattalung
Singora
Haadyai
Patani
Kangar
Jitra
Sungei Patani
George Town
Butterworth
19 December
Taiping
Ipoh
Kampar
Trolak
Kroh
Grik 26 December
Kota Bharu
Kuala Krai
Kuala Trengganu
Kuala Dungun
25 December
Kuala Lipis
Jerantut
30 December
Kuantan
10 January
Kuala Lumpur
Port Swettenham
28 December
Endau
Mersing
Jemaluang
Malacca
15 January
Singapore
attack 1 February
surrendered 15 February
Pulau Tioman
Anamba Is.
Landings 8 December
8 December 9.05 am: Rendezvous 28 transports and escorting warships
Japanese naval units depart 5 December
Japanese naval units
Japanese air strike force
Proposed route of Force Z
9 December 6.35 pm: Destroyer Tenedos detached to Singapore
10 December 12.33 pm: Repulse sunk
1.20 pm: Prince of Wales sunk
10 December 10.00 am: Destroyer Tenedos bombed
8 December 5.35 pm: Force Z sailed
XXXX 25 YAMASHITA
XX 5
XX 18
XX TAKUMI DET.
III 143

The Japanese advance on Bataan. MacArthur's pre-war bombast to the effect that his forces could prevent any landing in the Philippines was shown for what it was by a lightly but well-equipped Japanese army that overran Luzon and all positions of major significance in the islands with very little hindrance. In real terms the American withdrawal on to the Bataan Peninsula cost the Japanese very little.

piecemeal defence and by 19 December had forced the British to abandon Penang: within another day the abandoned British airfields at Alor Star, Sungei Patani and Butterworth had been brought into Japanese service. With forces that had landed at Kota Bharu advancing south along the coast to secure Kuantan at the end of the year, the Japanese were able to break the British intention to fight a series of delaying actions around Kuala Kangsar and on the Perak River and, with landing operations being conducted in the Malacca Strait against Kuala Sengalor and Port Swettenham, were able to rip apart an unsupported 11th Indian Division on the Slim River on 7 January. By 12 January Selangor had

been cleared and Japanese forces had moved into Negri Sembilan: at the same time formations from the 16th Army had also secured Tarakan on Borneo and Menado on Celebes in their opening moves into the Dutch East Indies.

On 24 January Japanese task groups at Tarakan and Menado moved against Balikpapan and Kendari respectively, while thirty degrees of longitude to the east (2,450 miles), Japanese forces secured Rabaul on New Britain, having captured its massive natural harbour the previous day, and Kavieng on New Ireland. At the same time, in the Philippines, a number of Japanese attempts to land behind American lines across the neck of the Bataan Peninsula resulted in defeat in 'the Battle of the Points'. Nevertheless the main American defensive effort astride Mount Natib was broken, resulting in a general American withdrawal to the Bagac–Orion line by the 26th. In Malaya the last two weeks of January 1942 saw the Japanese clear Negri Sembilan and Pahang and, with the capture of Endau, Mersing and, on the 31st, Johore Bahru, complete the clearing of the Malay Peninsula. Also on the 31st, while Japanese forces overran Amboina and thereby exposed the whole of the Lesser Sundas to attack, sister formations, drawn from the 15th Army, which had crossed the border into Burma eleven days earlier, secured Moulmein in Tenasserim. Throughout south-east Asia the Allied powers stood on the point of collapse as January gave way to February in 1942.

That collapse became reality in the course of February 1942. Singapore Island was subjected to assault on 8 February, and amid fearful scenes as

discipline and resolve disintegrated, the city was surrendered on the 15th. On the 8th Macassar was taken by forces operating from Kendari, while two days later Bandjermasin was captured by a Japanese task group from Balikpapan. On 19/20 February Japanese troops landed on Bali and Timor, while Japanese carriers struck at Darwin. Having secured Palembang on Sumatra on the 16th, the Japanese gathered around Java, and after landings in the western and central parts of the island, formal Allied resistance throughout the Indies came to an end on 9 March, even as the Japanese navy attacked shipping which was trying to reach the safety of Australian ports. In just sixty days, beginning with the seizure of Tarakan and Menado, the Japanese had overrun the greater part of the Indies: at exactly the time as the Indies were surrendered Rangoon changed hands, the British having been defeated disastrously on the Sittang on 21/22 February. In what remained of March, as Japanese forces in Burma were re-organized for an offensive that was to take them into central and upper Burma during April and May, other forces landed in northern Sumatra, secured Lae and Salamaua in north-east New Guinea and established themselves in the northern Solomons.

The Japanese victory parade at Hong Kong, headed by Lieutenant General Sakai Takashi and Vice Admiral Niimi. The small garrison was obliged to surrender on Christmas Day 1941, the Japanese success completing their control of virtually the whole of China's southern coast.

With the surrender of the American garrison on Bataan on 8 April the Japanese all but completed one of the most remarkable victories in history. The American garrison on Corregidor at the entrance to Manila Bay, and Allied units on Timor, were unreduced at this time, and the various islands of the central Philippines, plus most of Mindanao, remained to be occupied, while on 5 and 9 April Japanese carrier aircraft struck at Ceylon and eastern India in the course of an operation that accounted for the light carrier *Hermes*, two heavy cruisers, three other warships and thirty-two merchantmen in what London feared might well herald the beginning of the end of the whole of the British position on the Indian sub-continent and in the Indian Ocean. In the event, the Japanese turned for home after attacks that were never to be repeated: no Japanese carrier ever returned to the Indian Ocean after April 1942.

The New Realities

The Japanese victories in south-east Asia in the course of the first months of the Pacific war were to outlive Japan's final surrender in 1945: these victories were to inflict upon great imperial powers defeats from which, in the long term, there was to be no recovery even in the aftermath of Allied victory. After the war, the western imperial powers were to re-establish themselves in their lost colonial territories but within two decades all these possessions, with the exception of Hong Kong, were to become independent states with further wars attending each and every new birth of freedom and national self-determination. Yet in this fact, and in the very fact of Japanese conquest in 1941–2, was evidence of Japan's long-term failure, one of the many aspects of failure that, by 1945, was to be comprehensive and all-embracing. As noted elsewhere, at the heart of this failure on the part of Japan was an inability to recognize the force of any form of Asian nationalism other than her own; an inability to offer the people of her newly acquired territory anything other than a position of subservience and dependence. In every part of south-east Asia there were nationalist organizations that aspired to independence, many of which welcomed the Japanese as liberators. Yet by 1945 there were resistance movements in most south-east Asian countries, and virtually the only people who remained associated with the Japanese were those so closely implicated with a brutal, rapacious Japanese military system that they had no real choice in the matter. In terms of commanding the support of the uncommitted, being able to draw to herself the endorsement of the subjugated peoples of empire, Japan's wartime failure in south-east Asia was catholic in extent and range.

But these matters remained for the future as the Japanese conquest of south-east Asia was completed: the occupation of various little towns on the northern coast of New Guinea during April and May established the basis of the perimeter which Japan had sought to establish around her conquest and on which she sought to wage a defensive war until her enemies came to recognize

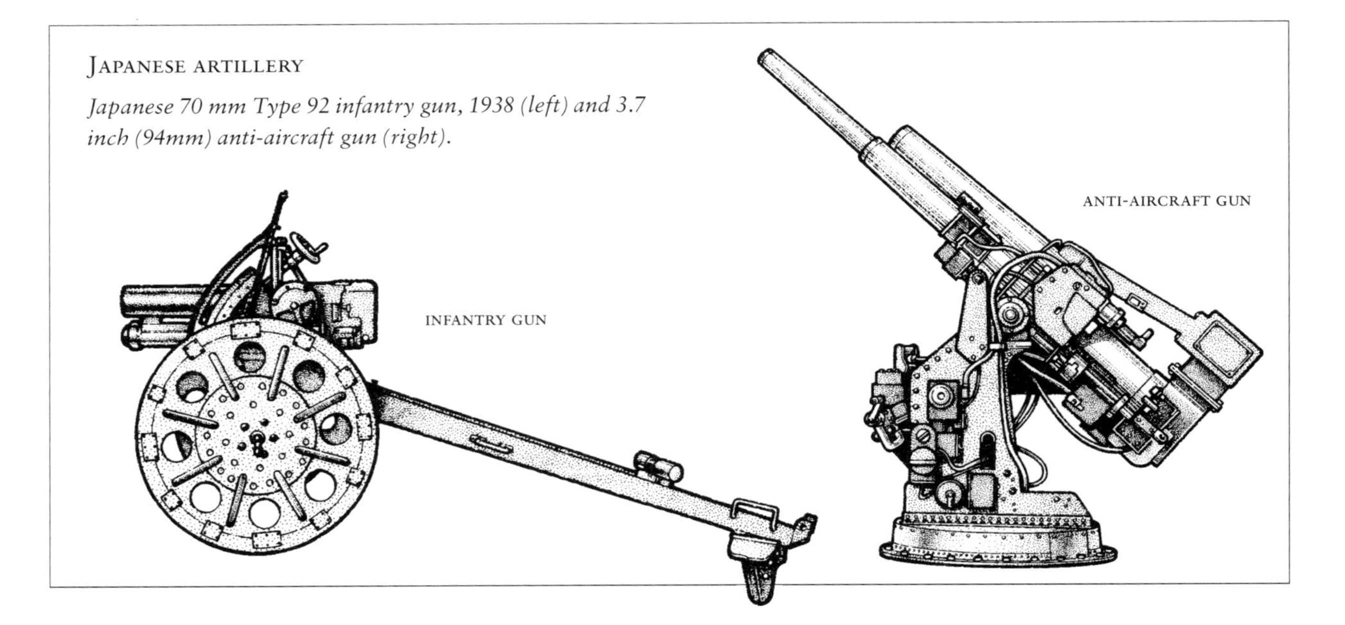

JAPANESE ARTILLERY

Japanese 70 mm Type 92 infantry gun, 1938 (left) and 3.7 inch (94mm) anti-aircraft gun (right).

her *fait accompli*. The Japanese success in this opening phase of the war was remarkable by any standard, and there were aspects of her victory, and specific operations such as the attack on Pearl Harbor and the sinking of the British capital ships *Prince of Wales* and *Repulse* in the South China Sea by land-based aircraft on 10 December 1941 that were unprecedented. What was no less significant was the ease of Japanese victories. Only in one case, at Wake Island on 11 December, did the Japanese encounter defeat, and here, after a less than inspired operation conducted by 'the second eleven' that resulted in the loss of two warships, they were able to reverse the verdict within twelve days. Elsewhere, the Japanese victories were recorded with contemptuous ease. Only off Balikpapan, between 23 and 27 January 1941, did the Japanese encounter any major losses – one destroyer-transport and six naval auxiliaries and support ships of 33,632 tons – yet even here there was to be no faltering of the pace and timing of Japanese operations. Off the Lombok and Sunda Straits, and, most obviously, in the battle of the Java Sea on 27/28 February, Japanese naval forces routed the motley collection of Allied warships pitted against them. Outnumbered Allied units, with no common communications or doctrine, were wholly outclassed by a navy that, in terms of tactical technique, was probably second to none at this stage of the war. It was probably fortunate that the exceptionally ill-advised British attempt to force a night action off Ceylon in April failed to establish contact, since there is very little doubt which way the battle would have gone had this intention been realized. As it was, the subsequent British withdrawal to East African ports was admission of the Eastern Fleet's strategic impotence.

The Japanese success in south-east Asia was bought remarkably cheaply: in the central and south-west Pacific and south-east Asia between 8 December 1941 and 30 April 1942 the Japanese lost just thirty-two warships of 61,170 tons, eighteen naval auxiliaries of 90,931 tons, thirteen army transports of 72,488 tons and seven merchant-men of 29,694 tons; these losses were more than made good by captured or salvaged Allied shipping. On the other side of the coin, the Allied defeats had virtually no redeeming features. If the Dutch in the Indies can be exempt from general criticism since the evident inability of their forces to withstand attack by a major enemy rendered their defeat a formality, the same cannot be said of their more powerful American and British allies. If the outlying British possessions were certain to fall to any Japanese move, the British defeats in Malaya and Burma contained no mitigating factors. The surrender of Singapore was among the worst and most humiliating ever incurred by British arms, and defeat in Malaya was all the more shameful because the British had anticipated virtually every aspect of the Japanese plan of campaign, yet still managed to be out-thought and out-fought at every stage of the proceedings. The only aspect of comfort was that defeat in Malaya and Singapore was so rapid and all-encompassing that the British high command was denied the opportunity to waste even more troops in the vain defence of Singapore.

Morituri te salutant.
The battleship Prince of Wales *sails from Singapore on 8 December 1941: two days later she and the battlecruiser* Repulse *became the first capital ships to be sunk at sea by aircraft when they were caught in the South China Sea by Japanese shore-based aircraft.*

THE JAPANESE CONQUEST OF BURMA

Pre-war Burma had represented Britain's nineteenth defensive priority since its defence had been vested in the Singapore base. With the Japanese occupation of Indo-China its position was compromised and with little more than a division it was unable to resist a Japanese offensive that conquered the country with embarrassing ease and that established Burma as part of Japan's defensive perimeter.

The American defeat in the Philippines was no different. Pre-war bombast to the effect that no Japanese forces could land anywhere in the archipelago was revealed on the outbreak of hostilities for what it was, while the destruction of the American air forces on the ground in the first hours of the war, and after the example of the Pearl Harbor attack was known, elicited the same post-war evasion of responsibility that attended the Singapore episode. Despite all the contemporaneous and subsequent claims to the contrary, the conduct of the defence in the Philippines was as inept as the British defence of Malaya, and was accompanied by self-advertisement and personal conduct on the part of senior American commanders in the Philippines that reached beyond the merely distasteful. The withdrawal into Bataan prolonged American resistance in the Philippines, but in no way bought time for the Allied cause anywhere else in south-east Asia and, despite American claims, did not facilitate the defence of Australia since the Japanese had no plans to take the war to that country in the form of invasion and occupation of the main centres of population.

The worst, most humiliating disaster. Singapore burning in February 1942, and the British party led by the commander, Lieutenant General Arthur Percival, going to surrender, 15 February 1942.

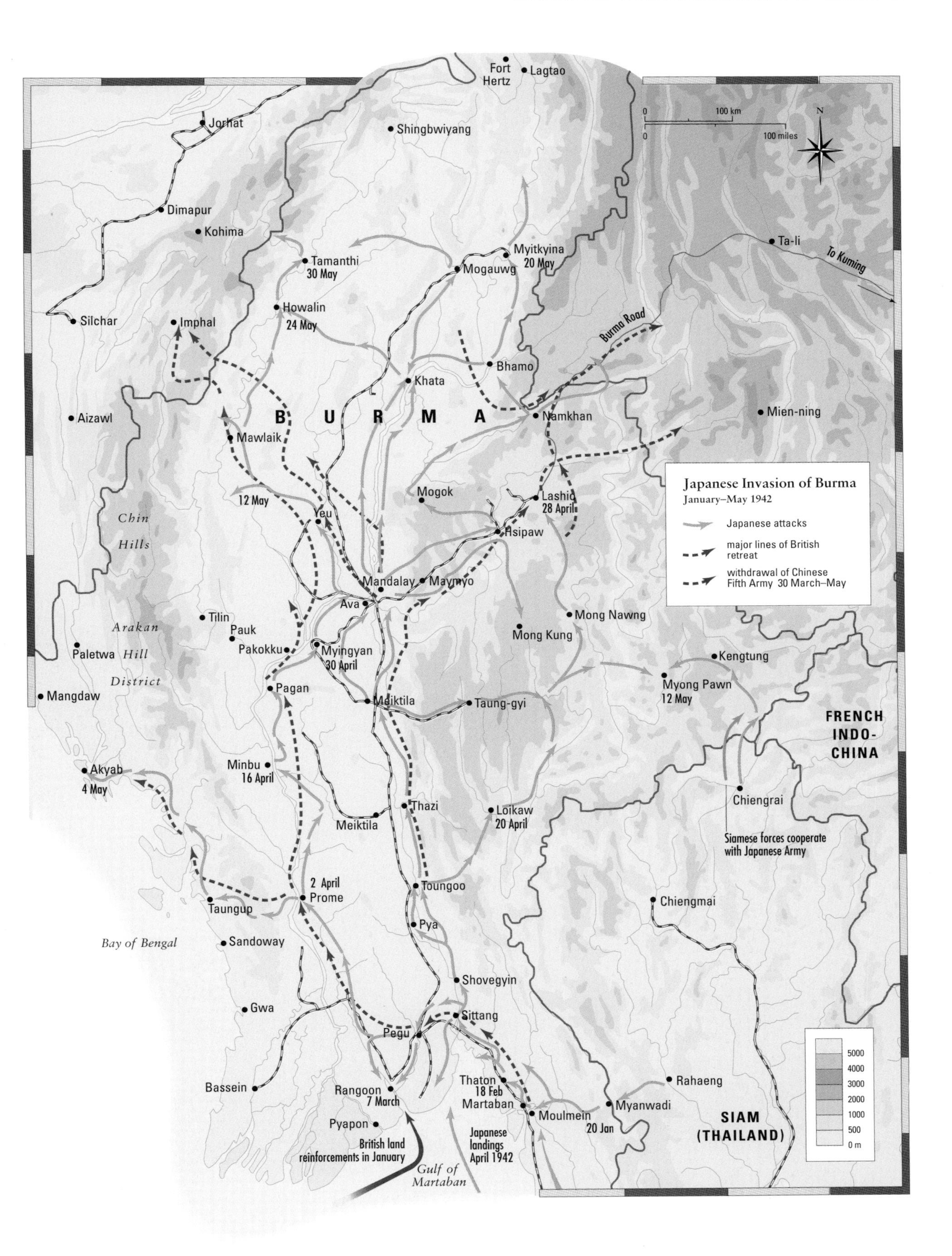
Japanese Invasion of Burma
January–May 1942
Japanese attacks
major lines of British retreat
withdrawal of Chinese Fifth Army 30 March–May
B U R M A
FRENCH INDO-CHINA
SIAM (THAILAND)
Chin Hills
Arakan Hill District
Bay of Bengal
Gulf of Martaban
Burma Road
To Kuming
Fort Hertz
Lagtao
Jorhat
Shingbwiyang
Dimapur
Kohima
Tamanthi 30 May
Myitkyina 20 May
Mogauwg
Ta-li
Silchar
Imphal
Howalin 24 May
Bhamo
Khata
Aizawl
Mawlaik
Namkhan
Mien-ning
Mogok
Lashio 28 April
12 May
Yeu
Hsipaw
Mandalay
Maymyo
Ava
Tilin
Pauk
Pakokku
Myingyan 30 April
Mong Nawng
Mong Kung
Paletwa
Kengtung
Mangdaw
Pagan
Meiktila
Taung-gyi
Myong Pawn 12 May
Akyab 4 May
Minbu 16 April
Thazi
Loikaw 20 April
Chiengrai
Siamese forces cooperate with Japanese Army
2 April Prome
Toungoo
Taungup
Chiengmai
Pya
Sandoway
Shovegyin
Gwa
Sittang
Pegu
Bassein
Rangoon 7 March
Thaton 18 Feb
Martaban
Rahaeng
Myanwadi
Moulmein 20 Jan
Pyapon
British land reinforcements in January
Japanese landings April 1942
0 100 km
0 100 miles
N
5000
4000
3000
2000
1000
500
0 m

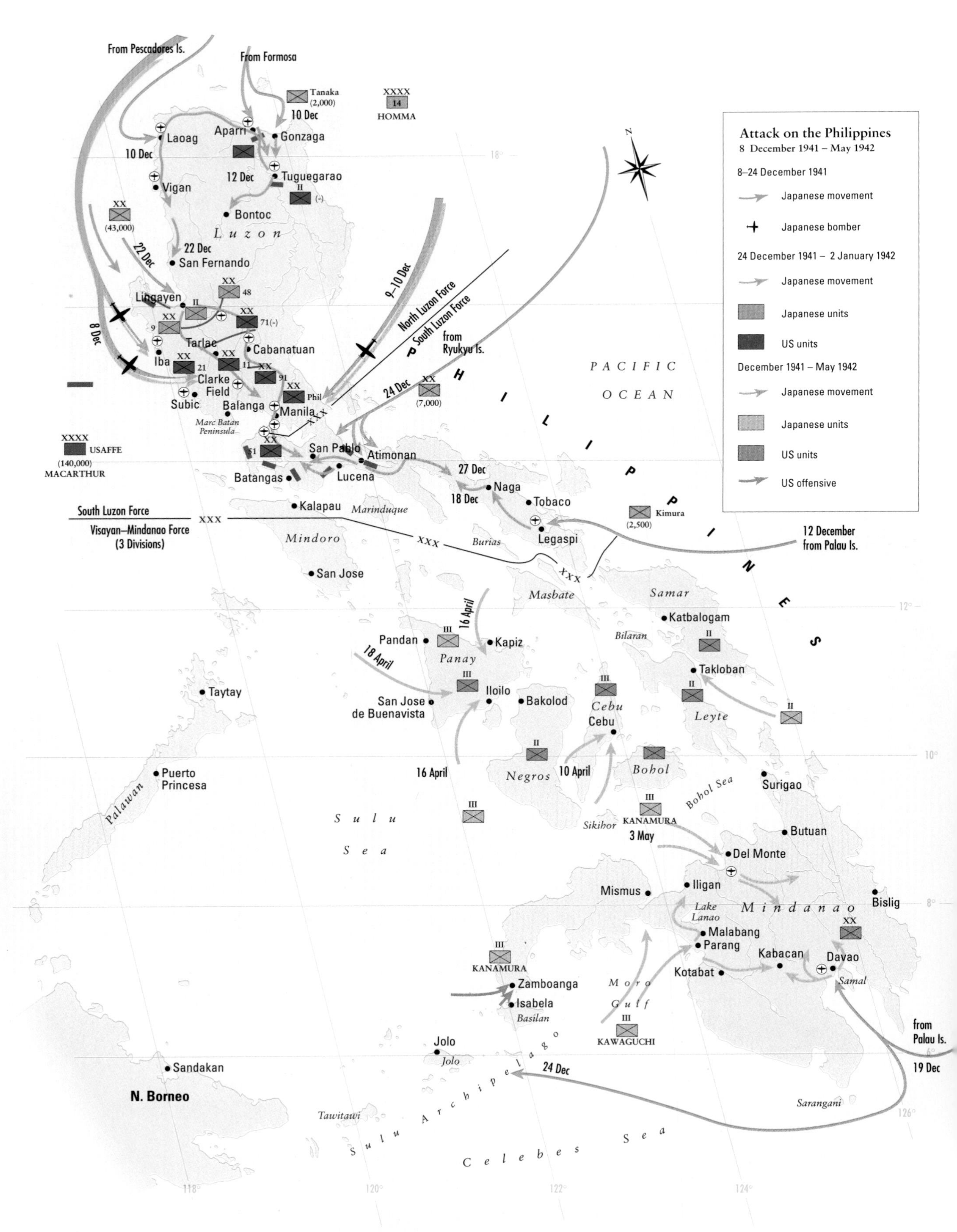
Attack on the Philippines
8 December 1941 – May 1942
8–24 December 1941
Japanese movement
Japanese bomber
24 December 1941 – 2 January 1942
Japanese movement
Japanese units
US units
December 1941 – May 1942
Japanese movement
Japanese units
US units
US offensive
From Pescadores Is.
From Formosa
Tanaka (2,000)
10 Dec
XXXX
14
HOMMA
Aparri
Gonzaga
Laoag
10 Dec
12 Dec
Tuguegarao
Vigan
Bontoc
Luzon
(43,000)
22 Dec
22 Dec
San Fernando
9–10 Dec
North Luzon Force
South Luzon Force
from Ryukyu Is.
Lingayen
48
71(-)
8 Dec
Tarlac
Cabanatuan
Iba
21
11
91
Clarke Field
Subic
Balanga
Manila
Phil
24 Dec
(7,000)
Marc Batan Peninsula
PACIFIC OCEAN
XXXX
USAFFE
(140,000)
MACARTHUR
51
San Pablo
Atimonan
Batangas
Lucena
27 Dec
Naga
18 Dec
Tobaco
Kimura
(2,500)
Legaspi
12 December from Palau Is.
South Luzon Force
Visayan–Mindanao Force (3 Divisions)
Kalapau
Marinduque
Mindoro
Burias
San Jose
Masbate
Samar
PHILIPPINES
16 April
Katbalogam
Pandan
Kapiz
18 April
Panay
Bilaran
Takloban
San Jose de Buenavista
Iloilo
Bakolod
Cebu
Cebu
Leyte
Taytay
16 April
Negros
10 April
Bohol
Bohol Sea
Surigao
Puerto Princesa
Palawan
Sulu Sea
Sikihor
KANAMURA
3 May
Butuan
Del Monte
Mismus
Iligan
Lake Lanao
Mindanao
Bislig
Malabang
Parang
Kabacan
Davao
Kotabat
Samal
KANAMURA
Zamboanga
Isabela
Basilan
Moro Gulf
KAWAGUCHI
from Palau Is.
19 Dec
Jolo
Jolo
24 Dec
Sandakan
N. Borneo
Tawitawi
Sulu Archipelago
Sarangani
Celebes Sea
118°
120°
122°
124°
126°
18°
12°
10°
8°
6°

It is sometimes very difficult to remember how disastrous were the first months of 1942 for those states that gathered themselves together and on New Year's Day proclaimed themselves as the United Nations pledged to wage war until the unconditional surrender of their enemies was achieved. In the first half of 1942, in addition to the collapse of Allied arms in the western Pacific and south-east Asia, British naval power in the eastern Mediterranean was eclipsed; British forces incurred humiliating defeat in North Africa and German U-boats ravaged the eastern seaboard of the United States. In the spring Soviet forces incurred a defeat in front of Kharkov that bared the whole of the eastern Ukraine to enemy advance. The speed with which the fortunes of war were reversed in autumn 1942 tends to diminish the extent of Allied defeats in the first six months of the year. But the fact that these defeats *were* reversed points to one matter, both general to the Axis powers and specific to Japan: that even at the period of her greatest success, basic weaknesses and flaws underlay Japan's strategic position. At work was an interplay of certain unalterable facts of time, distance, space and national resources which were to ensure her ultimate defeat.

The reality of Japan's position, even as her forces overran south-east Asia, is best summarized by the United Nations' declaration: it served notice that the Pacific war would be a total, not limited, war. Japan, therefore, had to address a basic question – how the United States was to be brought to acceptance of Japan's conquests. There was only one answer: Japan had to undertake offensive operations that would destroy the American capacity and will to wage war. But this answer produced a series of dilemmas that cut across the whole basis of pre-war planning.

THE JAPANESE CONQUEST OF THE PHILIPPINES

Japanese possessions to the north, west and east of the Philippines left the island group hopelessly vulnerable, and Japan's opening moves were against the main island, Luzon, and against Mindanao. The assault on the latter allowed for the capture of bases from which to develop operations against northern Borneo and the Indies.

JAPANESE STRATEGY

The first of these realities concerned Japan's strategic intention when she went to war. Essentially, she wished to conduct a defensive war by overrunning south-east Asia and then casting around her conquests a perimeter defence on which the Americans would expend themselves in vain. This plan was no more than a slightly modified edition of the basic idea, current throughout the 1930s, for the conduct of a defensive war in the western Pacific, and which had shaped Japanese design and construction programmes accordingly. Crucial to this was the concept of 'decisive battle', to be fought in the general area of the Marianas and Carolines against an American fleet advancing from its base in the central Pacific. The battle was to be opened off Hawaii by submarines which would conduct the attritional battle as the Americans advanced into the western Pacific. Three types of submarine were built to prepare for this: scouting submarines, equipped with seaplanes, were to find the American formations; command-submarines were then to direct cruiser-submarines to battle. The latter were endowed with a very high surface speed of 24 knots, the Japanese calculation being that such speed would allow these units to outpace an

American fleet advancing at economical cruising speed and to mount successive attacks to the limit of their torpedo capacity during the approach-to-contact phase.

These operations were to be supported, as the American fleet fought its way into the western Pacific, by shore-based aircraft, and to this end in the 1930s the Japanese developed the Betty medium bomber that in its day possessed a range and speed superior to any other medium bomber in service anywhere in the world. In addition, as the Japanese fleet closed with its enemy its fast battleships and heavy cruiser squadrons were to sweep aside the enemy screening forces and allow light cruiser and destroyer flotillas to conduct successive, massed, night torpedo attacks on the head of the American line. With midget submarines also laid across the American path in order to exact their toll upon the enemy, the Imperial Navy anticipated that these operations would cost the American fleet perhaps 30 per cent of its strength before the main action was joined. Japanese carriers would operate in independent divisions forward from the battle line, and their aircraft were expected to neutralize their opposite numbers by a series of dive-bombing attacks. With the American fleet blinded, weakened and its cohesion compromised, action would then be joined by the battle force.

The G4M (Betty) land-based medium bomber in American markings: the mainstay of Japanese shore-based naval aviation in the inter-war period and critical to Japanese plans to fight a defensive battle in the western Pacific. First in service in 1938, the Betty was easily the best medium-range bomber of her generation, but by 1941 was balancing on the edge of obsolescence.

Between the wars the Imperial Navy undertook the most comprehensive reconstruction of capital ships of any navy, stressing the importance of exceptional speed, weight of broadside and gunnery range over potential enemies. Evidence of this endeavour was the *Yamato* class with its 18.1-inch main armament, but this was to have been an interim class: with the intention of building battleships with 19.7-inch guns, the Imperial Navy sought to equip itself with a main battle force so superior to anything that the Americans could produce that its overwhelming victory in the 'decisive battle' would be assured.

Very curiously, the doctrine on which the Imperial Navy relied as the basis of its conduct of operations showed no real advance over the 'seven-stage plan of attrition' with which it had fought and won the battle of Tsushima in May 1905. In virtually every aspect, Japanese naval doctrine in 1941 was wholly unrealistic

and flawed beyond recall, but the various details of weakness tend to obscure one fundamental defect: Japan went to war without a strategic policy. The Imperial Navy had a doctrine, geared to fighting and winning one battle: it was a doctrine of battle that masqueraded as a plan of campaign, and the plan of campaign was a substitute for strategy. And it was not so much a doctrine with which the Imperial Navy went to war in 1941 as the naval equivalent of a de Dondi's timepiece, a majestic clockwork of wheels-within-wheels that represented the medieval European view of the universe: ingenious and imaginative, lovingly and beautifully crafted, hopelessly misdirected and obsolescent even as it reached the pinnacle of its achievement.

The most obvious weakness of a process whereby a vision of war became confused with a concept of operations and thereafter with a method of fighting lay in the Imperial Navy's neglect of maritime as opposed to naval requirements of trade and shipping at the expense of the fleet. But the most immediate weakness was the concept of a perimeter defence that exposed individual outposts to defeat in detail. No single base, with the possible exceptions of Truk and Rabaul, could be equipped on the scale needed to meet an enemy which was certain to possess the initiative and choice of offensive operations. The concept of perimeter defence consisted of gaps held apart by individual bases, each of which was too weak to resist the scale of attack to which they were certain to be subjected.

A second weakness, scarcely less obvious, concerned shipping resources: Japan lacked the shipping resources needed to sustain the bases in the central and south-west Pacific on which she depended for her first line of defence. A nation and navy unable to provide for the extension of their defensive zone into the Marshalls in the 1930s certainly lacked the means to sustain the new bases in the Gilberts and south-west Pacific in 1942, while the lack of heavy engineering equipment meant that plans for airfield construction in the new outposts of empire were, at best, somewhat ambitious. The extension of these responsibilities across thousands of miles of empty ocean, away from the resources of south-east Asia and the trade routes with the home islands, merely compounded Japanese difficulties.

A third weakness exacerbated the other two, namely that for the concept of 'perimeter defence' to work, the fleet had to be permanently ready to intervene

The greatest of all the dreadnoughts, the Yamato, *on trials off Sata Point, western Inland Sea, 30 October 1941. She displaced 71,659 tons full load. Armed with nine 18.1-inch, twelve 6.1-inch, twelve 5-inch guns and endowed with a maximum speed of 27.7 knots, each of her main turrets weighed more than a destroyer.*

to support any garrison that was subjected to assault. This was simply impossible. With the entire fleet in service from December 1941, sooner or later ships would have to be taken out of action for repair and refitting, which could not but undermine the fleet's state of readiness.

There were, in addition, a number of other weaknesses, not least the fact that the Imperial Navy went to war in the knowledge that its doctrine was flawed in one critical respect. In 1939 an exercise revealed that Japan's submarines could not achieve the success which was critical to overall victory. In 1940 the exercise was repeated, but even with the rules of engagement amended to assist the submarines, they were still unable to meet requirements. The force itself was too small, and a maximum speed of 24 knots did not provide its units with a sufficient margin of superiority to carry out successive attacks on an enemy fleet. But the Imperial Navy went to war in 1941 with no change of role for the submarine force, and with the assumption that its effectiveness in the process of attrition was assured. Moreover, Japanese success in this attritional process was clearly based on a certain passivity on the part of American forces: in fact, Japanese plans were based on tactical formation long abandoned by the US Navy. And, most surprising of all, the Imperial Navy's battle plan had never been subjected to a fleet exercise before the outbreak of war.

Lurking in the wings, however, were other weaknesses, some suspected and others not. Japan's very limited aircraft replacement capacity, and her equally limited aircrew training programmes, rendered the whole question of maintaining a fleet in readiness problematical. In addition, the support of a defensive perimeter had to involve prolonged operations by main fleet units, the type of operations that the US Navy began to conduct in the last quarter of 1943. The Imperial Navy could not undertake prolonged operations. Its carriers, with crews of 1,400 officers and men compared to the 2,700 embarked in American carriers, were one-shot, but even more importantly, the Imperial Navy lacked the auxiliary shipping needed to support fleet operations at the forward point of contact. In no single class of ship was this more obvious than fleet oilers, Japan having just nine at the outbreak of hostilities.

The seriousness of Japan's situation can be gauged by the fact that to make good its weakness of oiler numbers the Imperial Navy chartered at the expense of the merchant fleet, but in December 1941 Japan possessed just forty-nine tankers of 587,000 tons. By way of comparison, in 1939 Britain had 425 tankers of 2,997,000 tons and the United States 389 tankers of 2,836,000 tons. This slenderness of Japanese resources, however, was but a reflection of a general inadequacy of shipping resources, a fact both noted elsewhere and a major source of weakness in terms of Japanese strategic policy and war-making capability. Before the war Japan needed 10 million tons of merchant shipping in order to sustain herself, but with only three-fifths of this amount under her own flag she was dependent for her needs upon foreign shipping which, but for captures, was denied her with the start of hostilities. Given that the Imperial Army held 519 ships of 2,161,000 tons and the Imperial Navy 482 ships of 1,740,200 tons at the outbreak of war, plus the fact that in March 1942 some 12.61 per cent of Japanese shipping was laid up for want of routine maintenance and refitting, the Japanese shipping position in spring 1942 was a disaster waiting to happen.

But this lack of shipping was only one aspect of Japanese mercantile problems: no less serious was an inability to use what shipping was available to full effect. After the services had taken what they required, what was left to the merchant marine was not necessarily what was best suited to the demands of trade, but, critically, there was no effective means of controlling what shipping was available. The two services operated their shipping independently of one another and quite separately from civilian agencies with results that, in light of shipping shortages, were bizarre. It was not unknown for ships of different services to sail common routes together, one in ballast outward and the other in ballast on the return voyage. Such wastefulness, however, went alongside an inability to provide for the proper protection of shipping as was shown by the utter inadequacy of escort forces in terms of their numbers, their lack of organization, their technological backwardness and their lack of co-ordination with land-based air power.

The extent of Japan's weakness in these fields can be seen by the fact that in December 1941 the Imperial Navy had just four purpose-built escorts in service. None of the fourteen escorts of the Modified Type A class, ordered in the Emergency War Programme of that year, were within two months of being laid down. The total number of oceanic and local trade-protection units in commission in December 1941 was 32 escorts of all types and 26 chasers, with another 30 escorts projected and another 16 chasers either being built or about to be laid down.

Fleet Admiral Isoroku Yamamoto. The longest-serving commander of the Combined Fleet in the history of the Imperial Navy: with a reputation as a moderate in intemperate times, ostensibly he was sent to sea in 1939 in order to avoid the attention of various extremists. He served at Tsushima and presided over the Midway and Guadalcanal débâcles, but whether he deserved the favourable treatment afforded him by Clio is debatable.

In reality lack of numbers was only one aspect of Japan's problems. No less serious for the Imperial Navy was qualitative inadequacy. The only purpose-built escorts in 1941 were singularly ill-provided for escort duties. Its units initially embarked only eighteen depth charges, and it was not until autumn 1942, at a time when the British had some 2,100 ships equipped with asdic/sonar, that the class was equipped with any form of underwater detection – hydrophones. The Imperial Navy lacked any ahead-throwing weapon system, and its depth charges were wholly inadequate in terms of weight of explosive and rate of sinking. The Imperial Navy had no influence mines, or any form of airborne anti-submarine weapon other than the bomb. Moreover, it was not until autumn 1944 that Japanese escorts began to be fitted with the Type 13 search radar, and Japanese escorts were equipped with only one radio transmitter that had to work on both high and low frequencies despite the fact that escorts were often required to work on both simultaneously. At no stage of the Pacific war was the Imperial Navy able to provide escorts with the high-capacity No. 4 transmitter that was essential for long-range operations in distant waters. Such were some of the more obvious Japanese technological failings; suffice to summarize thus: that in *matériel* terms, the Imperial Navy entered the war as ill-equipped to fight a trade defence campaign in 1940 as the Italian Navy.

Such were the most serious and immediate weaknesses that beset Japan even in the moment of success: collectively they provide the basis of understanding of the events that were to unfold, specifically after November 1943. But in early 1942, as Japanese attention turned to the question of how the war was to be prosecuted, they – and other matters – began to intrude upon Japanese deliberations. The vulnerability of forward bases was demonstrated by the American carrier operation that resulted in the destruction of the entire torpedo-bomber force based at Rabaul on 20 February. Having secured Finschhafen in February, Japanese forces from Rabaul moved on 8 March to occupy Lae and Salamaua; two days later shipping still gathered in Huon Gulf was caught by American carrier aircraft and incurred such losses that the Japanese, with very little shipping in theatre, were forced to abandon further operations in eastern New Guinea and the Solomons. For the first time in the war Japanese plans and timetable were decided by something other than Japanese choice. In May, sinkings by submarines alone were greater than the monthly losses that the Japanese high command in 1941 had deemed to be tolerable. In this single month, when there was very little shipping committed to the support of operations, the Japanese lost twenty-two service auxiliaries and civilian merchantmen of 107,991 tons. The significance of such losses, incurred even before the battle of the perimeter was joined, lay in the fact that the Imperial Navy had anticipated losses of 2.7 million tons of shipping over three years, a figure that very strangely represented its estimation of national replacement capacity of 900,000 tons a year: the fact that merchant shipping output never exceeded 497,742 tons in any year between 1931 and 1941 was seemingly ignored. But in April 1942 such matters were set at nought by an intrusion, an intimation of reality.

In the immediate aftermath of the Huon Gulf action, the thoughts of the Japanese naval high command turned to the possibility of using fleet carriers to support future operations in the south-west Pacific. By this time, however, attention was also being forced back to the central Pacific, specifically to Pearl Harbor. Pecking around the periphery of conquests, American carrier activity served notice, in the form of raids on Kwajalein, Wake and Marcus, of Japanese vulnerability in the central Pacific, while the movement of American forces into the south-west Pacific and to Australia pointed to an inexorable widening of the war. Japan realized that there was little option but to take the war to the United States, to seek out and destroy American carrier forces. After bitter dispute, the Imperial Navy agreed upon the detachment of a carrier division to the south-west Pacific to cover operations in the Solomons and against Port Moresby, before the main endeavour unfolded in the form of a diversionary offensive into the Aleutians, followed by the occupation of Kure and Midway Islands at the western end of the Hawaiian chain. The capture of Midway was seen as the prelude to fighting and winning the 'decisive battle' against the American carrier formations that would be obliged to fight for these islands. Thereafter, Japanese formations were to head for Truk in readiness for a general offensive in the south-west Pacific that would result in the capture of New Caledonia, Fiji and Samoa before the resumption, in August, of operations in the central Pacific; the capture of Johnston Island was to be the prelude to the main effort against the major islands of the Hawaiian group.

This plan of campaign was settled at a time when the main Japanese carrier force was in the Indian Ocean, an interesting comment on Japanese priorities in April 1942, and just before notice of reality was served in the form of the Doolittle Raid of 18 April when American medium bombers operating from the carrier *Hornet* attacked Tokyo, Kube, Nagoya and Yokohama. The damage caused was minimal, but the humiliation inflicted upon the Imperial Navy was profound: the immediate effect was to silence the reasoned and well-justified opposition to the plan of campaign then being finalized in various naval headquarters. In truth, this plan was nonsense on a number of separate counts. Because the Japanese knew from the scale of the attack of 10 March that two American fleet carriers were operating in the south-west Pacific, the dispatch of just the fleet carriers *Shokaku* and *Zuikaku* to this theatre was neither here nor there. The forming of a submarine scouting line off Hawaii was almost useless given the fact that units were deployed at intervals beyond interlocking detection range. The plan for the occupation of Kure and Midway made little sense when the two carriers that were to transport aircraft there in readiness for main force action were the same carriers earmarked for operations in the Aleutians. The division of Japanese strength between widely separated task groups unable to offer mutual support, and the refusal of the fleet command to state whether the occupation of Midway or dealing with any American task force that sought to intervene represented the operational priority in the opening phase of this effort compounded matters. In addition, the raid on Ceylon should have provided cause for reflection. Having flown off their strikes, the Japanese found British fleet units at sea and were subjected to counter-attack by land-based aircraft. On both counts, Japanese luck held: two British heavy cruisers were dispatched and the Japanese carriers escaped unscathed, but the basic problem that had been glimpsed – inadequate reconnaissance and a division of resources between conflicting priorities – remained unaddressed and unresolved at the heart of the Midway plan. All these points were swept aside in the aftermath of the Doolittle Raid as a result of two corrupting influences: what was subsequently called 'Victory Disease', born of recent, overwhelming success but which in truth had a much longer pedigree; and the hypnotic, filter-up filter-out phenomenon so often associated with the planning of major offensives – especially in retrospect, and especially after such operations have failed.

The weakness of Japanese strategic intention: US Dauntless dive-bombers over Wake, October 1943. An island base in the defensive perimeter, Wake was attacked by aircraft from three fleet and three light fleet carriers and subjected to a cruiser bombardment. In two days and at a cost of twenty-six aircraft from a total of 738 sorties flown, the Americans effectively neutralized Wake for the remainder of the war.

ABOVE: *Lieutenant Colonel James Doolittle fastening medals to the tail fins of bombs that were to be dropped by B-25 medium bombers operating from the fleet carrier* Hornet *on 18 April 1942. By striking at a number of Japanese cities, the Doolittle Raid forced the Imperial Navy to focus its attention on the central Pacific and provided impetus for the ill-fated Midway endeavour.*

CHAPTER THREE

The Second Milestone: Problems

May 1942 – November 1943

Misplaced symbolism: the explosion of an American ammunition dump on Guadalcanal, 26 November 1942. Given the desperately narrow administrative margins on which both sides worked during the campaign for the island, the loss of such stores could have been very serious but for the fact that November 1942 saw the destruction of Japanese intentions, primarily in the naval actions fought in Ironbottom Sound.

THE SECOND MILESTONE: PROBLEMS

MILITARY HISTORY is cursed by the concepts of 'the decisive battle' and 'turning points'. In the story of the Second World War, and specifically the Second World War in the Far East, such concepts are meaningless. If Japan's defeat was assured from the time that her carriers struck Pearl Harbor, then no single battle fought in this war can be defined as decisive or the turning point of the war: the concepts of inevitability on the one hand, and of 'decisive battles' or 'turning points' on the other, are mutually exclusive. No action or battle, unless it was the attack on Pearl Harbor, marked the point where the road divided: the battles in this war were milestones, not signposts, on the road.

Decades of repetition have ensured that the battle fought off Midway Islands in June 1942 is widely regarded as the turning point of the Pacific war. This battle undoubtedly possesses singular importance, as it was the first irreversible victory won by Allied arms in the Second World War. But it was neither a decisive battle nor a turning point, even though it did mark the end of a flood tide of Japanese victories. With only slight exaggeration, before Midway the Japanese met nothing but victory, and after Midway the Americans commanded only success. The importance of Midway lies not in an interpretation of this battle as the 'decisive battle' or 'turning point' of the Pacific war, but as key to a three-fold understanding: of naval warfare; of the

The Mikuma *after having been devastated by a series of carrier aircraft strikes off Midway on 6 June 1942. The heavy cruiser was the only Japanese warship to be sunk in the final phase of the battle.*

war in the Pacific; and of the campaigns that were fought, specifically in the period between May 1942 and February 1943, but more generally between May 1942 and November 1943. These three matters provide the basis of this and following chapters.

Any consideration of naval warfare necessarily involves the examination of the relationship between victory and supremacy. In any consideration of British naval mastery the conventional wisdom holds that supremacy was the result of victory. In reality, though individual victories have to be won; victory was the product of supremacy. The Pacific war is very unusual: it was a war in which the relationship between victory and supremacy changed. In the first two years of the Pacific war two inter-war navies fought one another for possession of the initiative and for supremacy, and in the process the US Navy secured the initiative. Its success, however, was neither the product of, nor did it provide supremacy. After November 1943 a fleet that was very largely a wartime creation exercised a supremacy that provided victories. Lest the point be doubted, of the 111 units in the task groups that raided the Tokyo area in February 1945 just four were in commission before the raid on Pearl Harbor, and the havoc wrought by Allied action in the seas that washed the island empire in the last weeks of the war was not the cause of victory but the product of supremacy. This is the key to an understanding of this conflict, a war that ended in November 1943 in terms of the certainty of decision. By the time that the Americans gathered off the Gilberts a force that was assured of success, the issue of victory and defeat, both specifically in the Gilberts but more generally in the war as a whole, had been resolved: thereafter the only questions that remained to be answered were the method and timing of Japan's final defeat, and the cost that would be exacted in the process.

The defeat that Japan incurred in the Pacific had two dimensions, namely the defeat of her armed forces in and among the various island groups of the south-west and central Pacific, and the destruction of her seaborne trade. Herein lies paradox: Japan could have been brought to defeat as a result of the destruction of the Imperial Navy but which left her merchant marine intact, and Japan could have been brought to defeat as a result of the destruction of her merchant marine but which left the Imperial Navy untouched. But the two elements of defeat did not unfold simultaneously, and Japanese shipping losses before November 1943 were not of the order that ensured defeat. But Japan was brought to final defeat, and Japan could only have been brought to assured defeat, by the parallel destruction of the Imperial Navy and the merchant fleet and Japan's seaborne lines of communication. In this context, the two elements of Japan's defeat in the Pacific, naval and maritime, were properly complementary.

Herein lay the significance of such battles as the one fought off Midway in June 1942 which cost the Imperial Navy four fleet carriers and a heavy cruiser. Midway was the most important single battle fought between the outbreak of the Pacific war and the battle of the Philippine Sea in June 1944, but its

OVERLEAF: *The ubiquitous SBD Dauntless on the flight deck of an Essex-class carrier. Only in the years immediately before the outbreak of the Second World War did the dive-bomber emerge as potentially the decisive instrument in carrier warfare, and in most carrier battles it was the Dauntless in its scouting and attack roles that was at the forefront of American endeavours.*

importance lies in its being one of a series of battles, fought between May 1942 and February 1943, that formed the watershed of the Pacific war and which resulted in the Americans winning the initiative throughout the Pacific.

This watershed of the Pacific war consisted of two battles, the Coral Sea and Midway Islands, as well as the campaigns in eastern New Guinea and the lower Solomons. The two campaigns were very different, the one primarily fought on land and the other primarily at sea and in the air, but in one critical respect they shared a common characteristic. Both developed more from the momentum of events rather than from deliberate choice, as the two main parties to the war were obliged to take the war as they found it in the summer of 1942 rather than as they would have wished.

The first US carrier loss of the Pacific war: the Lexington *at Coral Sea, 8 May 1942. At 12.47 p.m., over an hour after last contact with the enemy, the first explosion destroyed most of her communications and killed many of her damage control personnel. Without power her pumps would not work, and a series of internal explosions progressively devastated her.*

The Battle of the Coral Sea

In May 1942 the Japanese renewed their effort in eastern New Guinea which had been halted by the American carrier raid on Lae and Salamaua in March. Even with a carrier division in support, this second effort was frustrated at the battle of the Coral Sea. The Imperial Navy's attempt to secure bases in the lower Solomons and on the eastern approaches to Port Moresby, and to move against these objectives with divided forces that were unable to support one another, left its formations liable to defeat in detail. After scattering Japanese units in the lower Solomons on 4 May, the single American carrier task force deployed to oppose Japanese moves in this theatre sank the light carrier *Shoho* on the 7th and forced the formation bound for Port Moresby to retire. On the 8th, in the

The Lexington's *engine room was abandoned at 4.30 p.m. and the final order to abandon ship was given at 5.07 p.m.: recovery of survivors was completed at 6.53 p.m. The* coup de grace *was administered by a destroyer and she sank at 7.52 p.m. with an explosion felt fourteen miles away.*

The Indies and south-west Pacific

The Japanese drive into the Indies took the form of successive operations through the northern and central Indies: the battle of the Java Sea completed a Japanese victory that was assured by the time the battle was fought; the battle of the Coral Sea was the first battle in history when ships of the opposing forces never saw one another.

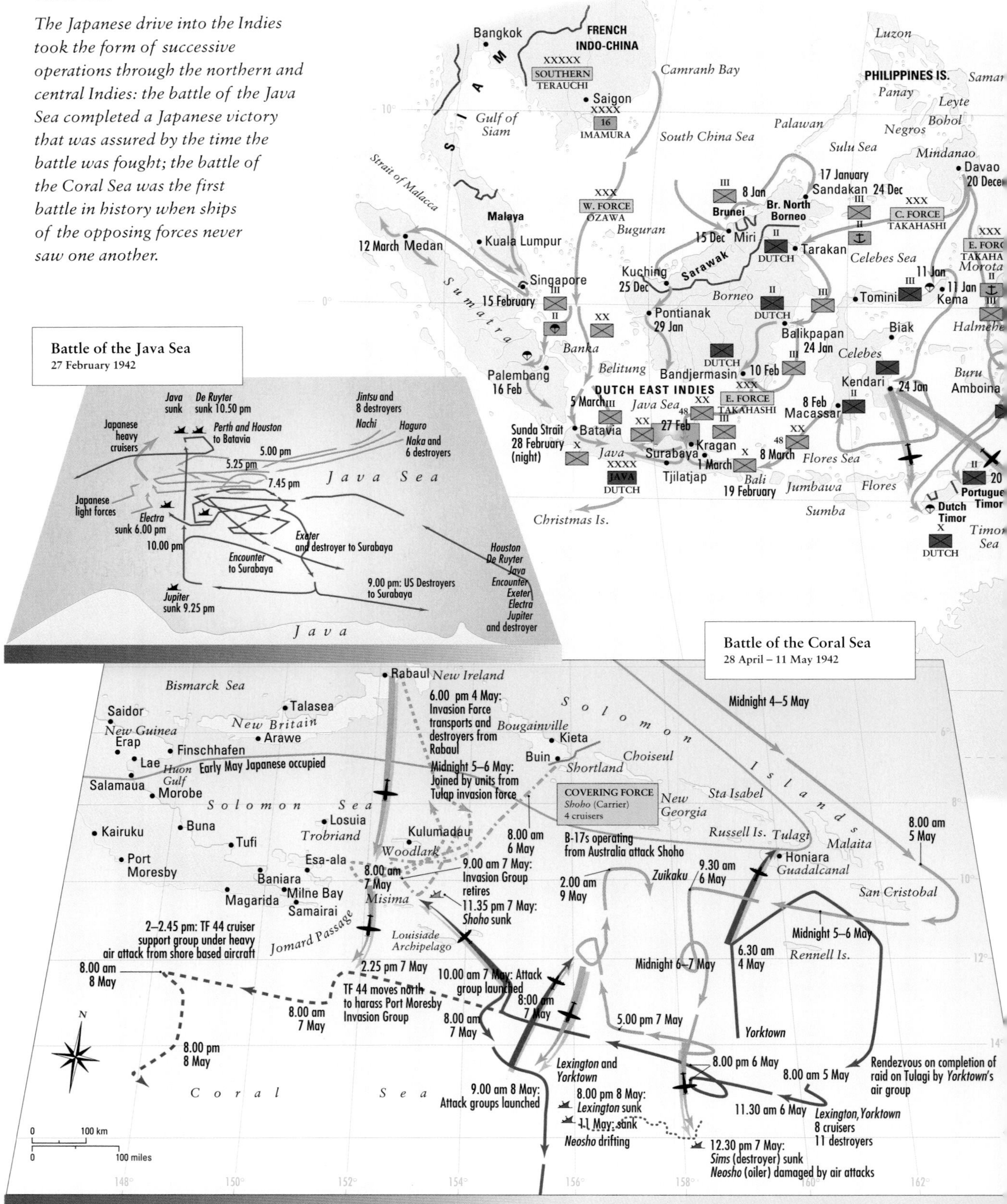

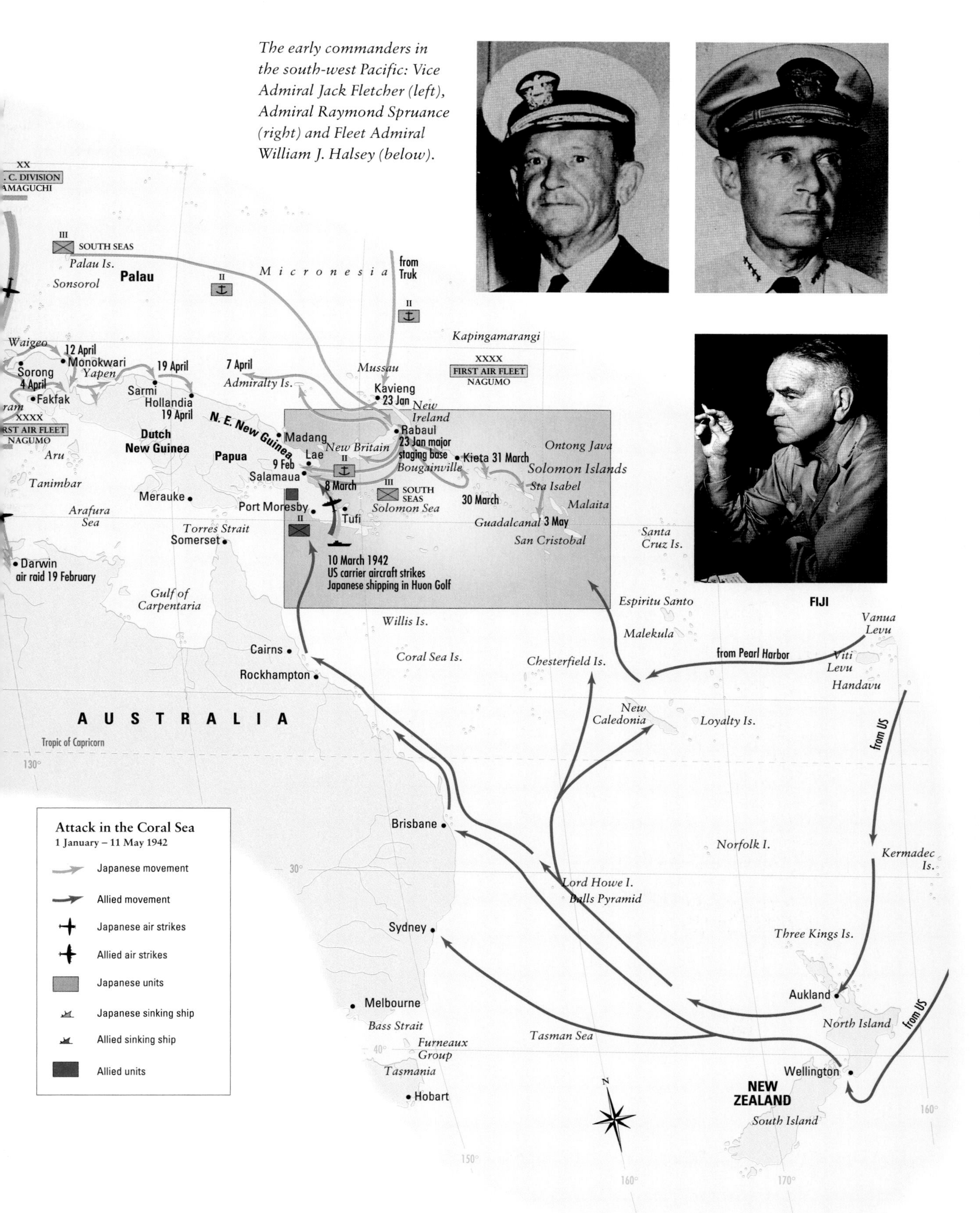

The early commanders in the south-west Pacific: Vice Admiral Jack Fletcher (left), Admiral Raymond Spruance (right) and Fleet Admiral William J. Halsey (below).

first naval battle in which surface units did not come into contact with one another, this American formation lost the fleet carrier *Lexington*, one destroyer and one oiler, but extensively damaged the *Shokaku* and rendered the *Zuikaku*'s air group *hors de combat*. Tactically a draw, the battle of the Coral Sea was strategically a clear Allied victory because the Japanese attempt to secure Port Moresby by seaborne assault was forestalled, never to be renewed. Even more importantly, the battle cost the Imperial Navy two of the six fleet carriers required for the Midway operation as well as 75 per cent of their bomber pilots and planes.

MIDWAY

Arguably Japanese losses in the Coral Sea were a major factor in the Japanese defeat off Midway in the following month: without the *Shokaku* and *Zuikaku* the main Japanese carrier formation committed to the Midway operation possessed no margin of superiority over the two American task groups that

THE BATTLE OF MIDWAY

The Japanese planned to secure Midway and then fight and win a battle against American forces obliged to offer battle because of Japanese possession of these islands. Their deployment was flawed on three counts: the various task forces could not support one another, the carrier force had few reconnaissance aircraft, and American reading of Japanese signals allowed a deployment of submarines and carriers to contest the Japanese attempt to secure Midway.

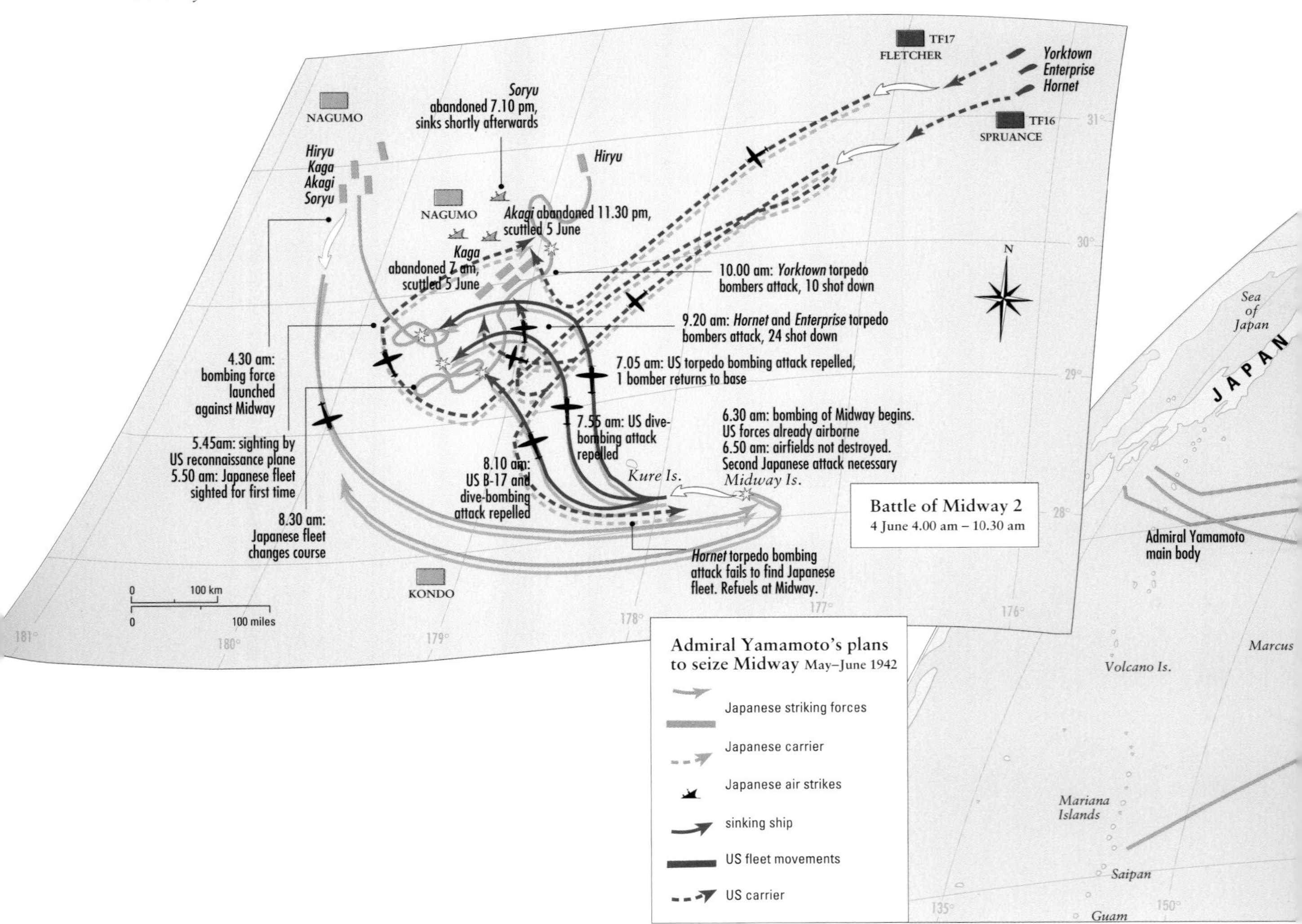

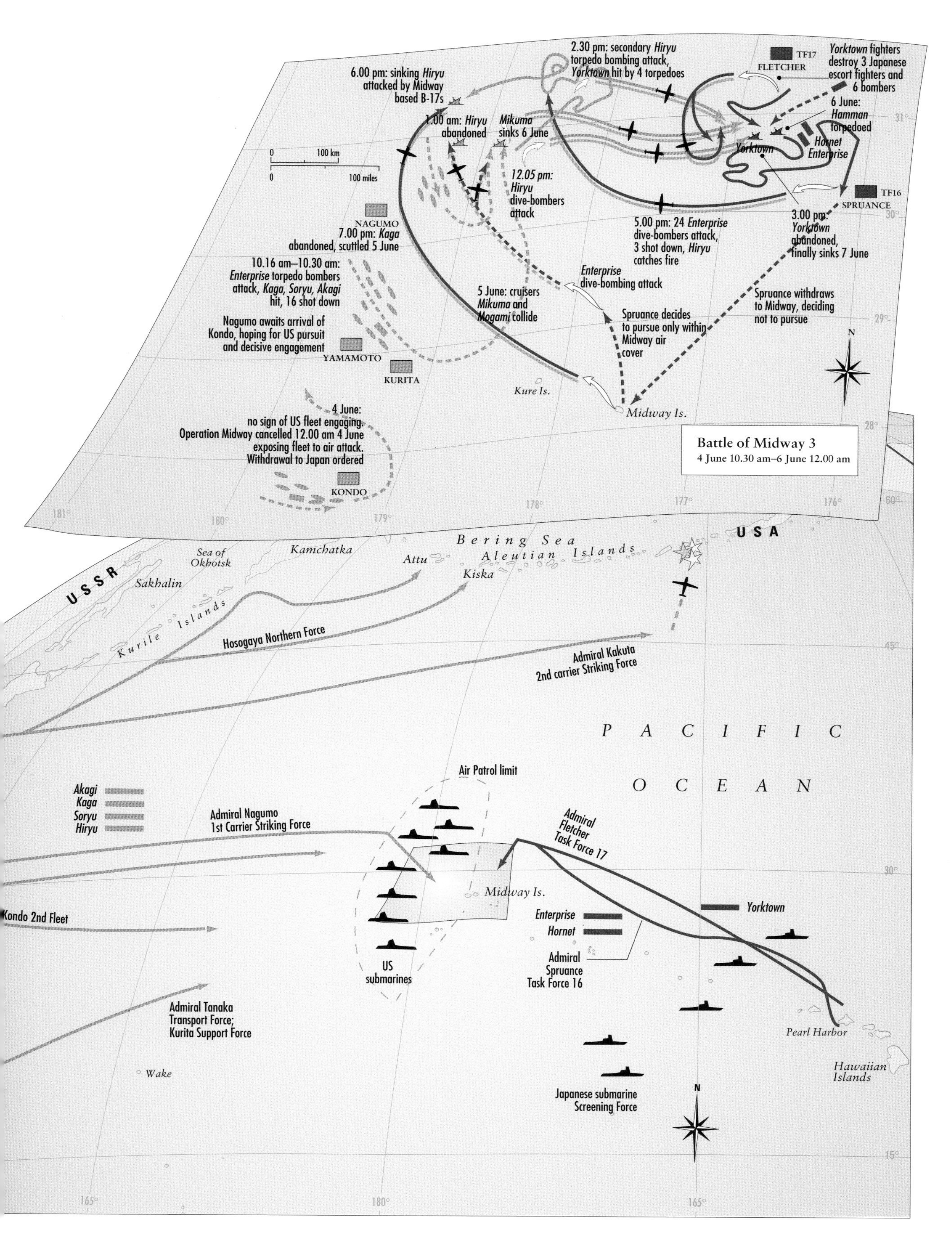

Battle of Midway 3
4 June 10.30 am–6 June 12.00 am
2.30 pm: secondary Hiryu torpedo bombing attack, Yorktown hit by 4 torpedoes
TF17
FLETCHER
Yorktown fighters destroy 3 Japanese escort fighters and 6 bombers
6.00 pm: sinking Hiryu attacked by Midway based B-17s
6 June: Hamman torpedoed
1.00 am: Hiryu abandoned
Mikuma sinks 6 June
Hornet
Enterprise
Yorktown
0
100 km
100 miles
12.05 pm: Hiryu dive-bombers attack
TF16
SPRUANCE
NAGUMO
7.00 pm: Kaga abandoned, scuttled 5 June
5.00 pm: 24 Enterprise dive-bombers attack, 3 shot down, Hiryu catches fire
3.00 pm: Yorktown abandoned, finally sinks 7 June
10.16 am–10.30 am: Enterprise torpedo bombers attack, Kaga, Soryu, Akagi hit, 16 shot down
Enterprise dive-bombing attack
5 June: cruisers Mikuma and Mogami collide
Spruance withdraws to Midway, deciding not to pursue
Spruance decides to pursue only within Midway air cover
Nagumo awaits arrival of Kondo, hoping for US pursuit and decisive engagement
YAMAMOTO
KURITA
Kure Is.
Midway Is.
N
4 June: no sign of US fleet engaging. Operation Midway cancelled 12.00 am 4 June exposing fleet to air attack. Withdrawal to Japan ordered
KONDO
31°
30°
29°
28°
181°
180°
179°
178°
177°
176°
USSR
Sea of Okhotsk
Kamchatka
Bering Sea
Aleutian Islands
USA
Attu
Kiska
Sakhalin
Kurile Islands
Hosogaya Northern Force
Admiral Kakuta 2nd carrier Striking Force
PACIFIC
OCEAN
60°
45°
30°
15°
Air Patrol limit
Akagi
Kaga
Soryu
Hiryu
Admiral Nagumo 1st Carrier Striking Force
Admiral Fletcher Task Force 17
Midway Is.
Kondo 2nd Fleet
Enterprise
Hornet
Yorktown
Admiral Spruance Task Force 16
US submarines
Admiral Tanaka Transport Force; Kurita Support Force
Pearl Harbor
Hawaiian Islands
Wake
Japanese submarine Screening Force
N
165°
180°
165°

opposed it. In reality, however, a number of other factors were also at work in deciding the outcome of the battle of Midway. The division of Japanese forces between two strategic objectives – the western Hawaiian Islands and the Aleutians – and recourse to separated formations that could not provide mutual support was critically important in ensuring Japanese failure and defeat off Midway. Moreover, the carrier force's lack of adequate strength with which to deal with two operational objectives – the suppression of Midway's air groups and the destruction of American carrier groups – and the inadequate reconnaissance provision of the Japanese carrier force were no less important in settling the outcome of this action. But with second-line carrier aircraft embarked because of an inability to replace earlier losses, the whole Japanese undertaking in the central Pacific hung on a thread, no more obviously than with the Japanese plan of campaign.

The Imperial Navy planned to secure Midway and to fight and win a battle off the islands, but the only battle that it could have won was the battle it planned to fight. The fact that the battle did not unfold in accordance with Japanese plans left the leading carrier formation exposed to crushing defeat without other formations being able to intervene. If this was perhaps one of the most important single causes in the Japanese defeat off Midway, then the reason why the battle did not develop along the lines that had been planned – the Americans' ability to offer battle as a result of their capacity to read Japanese signals – was no less important, as was outrageous good fortune which favoured the American carrier groups on the morning of 4 June. Off Midway the full measure of Japanese failure in terms of manifest deficiencies of planning and conduct of operations can be gauged by one simple fact: that despite committing eight carriers, eleven battleships, twelve heavy and nine light cruisers, sixty-four destroyers, eighteen submarines and 433 aircraft to this enterprise, only one American warship was attacked in the course of the battle of Midway. And in common with so many of their efforts, the Japanese perversely managed to sink two American warships, the fleet carrier *Yorktown* and the destroyer *Hammann* - the latter by a torpedo that had been aimed at the carrier.

The Campaign in the Solomon Islands

In the aftermath of Midway a lull was imposed on the Pacific war as both sides reorganized in readiness for the next phase of operations. Abandoning any attempt to carry the war deeper into the south-west Pacific, the Japanese planned to consolidate their present holdings and to develop their bases in the lower Solomons and eastern New Guinea. In the vastness of their conquest was an apparent assurance of security, especially as the Japanese had calculated that the United States would not be able to undertake any major offensive in the south-west Pacific until the second quarter of 1943, a view shared by American planning staffs. The Japanese high command assumed that it still retained a

The abandoned Japanese fleet carrier Hiryu *on the morning of 5 June 1942 off Midway Islands. After the crippling of three carriers on the previous day the* Hiryu *had attempted to continue the battle against three US carriers and her aircraft attacked the* Yorktown *on two separate occasions before she was overwhelmed.*

local initiative in this theatre and therefore had time to attend to the requirements of its perimeter bases and garrisons.

The American position was somewhat different, but not markedly so. The Midway victory brought a halt to months of defeat and humiliation, but the priority afforded the European war ensured that only very limited offensive commitments could be accepted in summer 1942. A lack of assault and support shipping, as well as combat-ready formations, precluded any significant undertaking in the central Pacific. But the American high command was determined to exploit the advantage gained at Midway. With a single division available for offensive purposes, its attention was directed to the lower Solomons at the very time when Japanese concentration was fixed upon eastern New Guinea, specifically to the task of securing Port Moresby to prevent a gathering of Allied strength in this area. Thus the main battlefields of the next six to eight months were marked out, and with them the sequence of events that was to result in the breaking of Japanese naval power.

Interdependence and victory: Hell's Corner, Guadalcanal. The critical elements in the American victory in this campaign were the defensive – not offensive – victories won around Henderson Field and the ability of aircraft, primarily naval aircraft, based on the airfield to deny Japanese warships use of the waters of the lower Solomons.

These two campaigns were to unfold at the same time, and operations in the Solomons and New Guinea were to continue until the very end of the war. The main part of both campaigns, however, was over by February 1943, by which time the Japanese had been forced to evacuate their surviving troops from Guadalcanal, their forces had been annihilated on the Kakoda Trail, and checked around Wau, the Allies being left free to develop their offensive into and beyond Huon Gulf. In the event, and despite the annihilation of a Japanese military convoy in the Bismarck Sea in March 1943 that dissuaded the Japanese high command from attempting the direct supply of its formations in Huon Gulf after that time, it was not until September 1943 that Allied forces moved to secure Lae and Salamaua and to move into the Markham Valley and beyond Cape Cretin. It was in the following month, October 1943, that Allied forces, after a slow six-month struggle in the central Solomons, were able to move into the upper Solomons. The American carrier raids on Rabaul on 5 and 11 November, plus the actions fought by light forces in the northern Solomons that same month, closed this second phase of the Pacific war, at the end of which the Japanese position across the whole of the south-west Pacific had been compromised. Despite a recasting of plans with the inauguration of the so-called New Operational Policy in September, the Japanese outer line of defence in the south-west and central Pacific stood on the brink of collapse.

The American intention was to move to secure the Japanese positions on Tulagi and Guadalcanal in the Solomons in early August and to occupy the Dobodura area by an overland advance from Port Moresby that was to begin in the middle of that same month. But by occupying Buna and Gona on 21/22 July the Japanese forestalled the Allies, swept aside feeble Australian resistance around the beachheads and pressured rapidly inland to secure Kakoda on the 27th. Thereafter Japanese progress faltered, and for four reasons. First, before their landings the Japanese fondly believed that the Kakoda Trail was a motor track over the forbidding Owen Stanley mountain range, but in fact it was no more than a jungle trail which the Japanese could not hope to negotiate with their available forces and logistics. Second, the Japanese plan to support their move through the mountains by landings in Milne Bay miscarried, and their forces were landed in the middle of an Allied base. Despite being heavily outnumbered, the Japanese none the less inflicted on their opponents a series of defeats that varied between the outrageous and farcical, though in the end only one outcome was possible. The Japanese recognized this and evacuated their surviving forces, with pride on both sides severely dented (25 August/6 September). Third, Australian resistance on the Trail came together very quickly after a series of small but disastrous actions once raw formations were steadied by the arrival of battle-experienced forces from the Middle East. The Japanese were able to advance to the Ioribaiwa Ridge, within sight of Port Moresby, on 14 September, but on the 24th began to withdraw down the Trail. By mid October the Japanese had withdrawn to positions in front of Kakoda, but at this stage

Australian troops passing knocked-out Japanese light tanks at Milne Bay, August–September 1942. In an attempt to renew their offensive against Port Moresby after Midway the Japanese unknowingly landed in an Allied base in Milne Bay on the eastern tip of New Guinea. In a battle that lasted two weeks, Japan's last amphibious offensive in the south-west Pacific was broken.

were in very real danger of being overwhelmed as their enemies sought to outflank their positions by an advance up the Minami Valley and by airlifting forces from Milne Bay and Port Moresby to positions on the north coast from which to move against Buna and Gona. By the end of November the Japanese forces, approximately 5,500 men, had been restricted to two separate areas both less than a mile in depth within the beachhead. While Australian formations cleared Gona by 18 December, it was not until 22 January 1943 that Japanese resistance at Buna came to an end. Within another three weeks the Japanese attempt to overrun the Australian positions around Wau was defeated, the Allied ability to airlift forces to the Wau–Mobu area being critical to the defeat of a much superior Japanese formation.

The fourth reason for the Japanese defeat in eastern New Guinea in the second half of 1942 was that after 7/8 August, Japanese attention and resources within the south-west Pacific were divided as a result of the American occupation of Tulagi and Henderson Field on Guadalcanal. As battle was joined in the lower Solomons, the campaign in eastern New Guinea assumed secondary status for the Japanese, with the result that their defeat along the Kakoda Trail, given the Allies' local superiority of resources, was assured. The fact was that the Japanese lacked the means to support two efforts in theatre, and as events unfolded they were shown to lack the means to support even one effort to full effect.

The basis of this weakness, and the basis of an understanding of what was to happen in the lower Solomons over the next six months, lies in recognition of one reality of naval warfare. A fleet's vulnerability is never greater than when obliged to operate in direct support of ground forces, when its freedom of action is restricted. The greatest danger exists not when the battle on land is fluid, but when there is

The final scene at Buna on 2 January 1943 when American troops finally completed the destruction of Japanese forces that had been committed to the overland offensive against Port Moresby. Japanese forces trapped on Huon Gulf fought literally to annihilation.

deadlock ashore. In the lower Solomons campaign these terms of reference applied to both sides. The Imperial Navy was obliged to try to reduce what amounted to an American fortress: the commitment of American forces ashore to a defensive battle around one airfield imposed upon Allied naval formations a lingering commitment 'in harm's way'. Though not appreciated at the time, the issue of victory and defeat was resolved very quickly by the Americans bringing Henderson Field into service, and securing local air superiority that became increasingly marked with the passing of time. Without any forward bases, and obliged to operate aircraft from Rabaul at the very limit of their endurance, the Japanese effort between August and November 1942 very slowly unravelled in the face of this local but ever-growing American advantage in the air. The defeat of successive offensives against Henderson Field and the loss of balance and organization of their naval formations both reflected and compounded this basic failure.

Over fifty actions involving warships from one or both sides were fought in the course of the Guadalcanal campaign, which was the first test of the Japanese concept of perimeter defence, but for one fact. Possession of the island base was in enemy hands, and the obligations of defensive and offensive action were directly contrary to what the Japanese had intended. There were, moreover, two other points of difference between what the Imperial Navy had anticipated and reality, namely the speed of decision and the timely intervention of Japanese battle forces in support of their formations ashore. Initially, the situation seemed to suggest that these two matters were of small account: the battle off Savo Island (9/10 August) saw a Japanese cruiser formation overwhelm part of the Allied force off Guadalcanal, sinking four heavy cruisers. Critically, however, fear of being caught in the area at dawn by enemy aircraft meant that the Japanese formation withdrew without setting about the assault shipping gathered off Guadalcanal. This omission was crucial because the Americans were then able to establish themselves securely ashore, annihilate a Japanese detachment put ashore on 18/19 August and fly fighters into Henderson Field on the 20th without interference from the Japanese battle forces. With its main forces in the Inland Sea at the time of the American landings in the lower Solomons, it was not until the third week after the American occupation of Henderson Field that the Imperial Navy was able to deploy carrier forces in theatre. The battle of the Eastern Solomons, 23/25 August, again witnessed the Imperial Navy's use of dispersed formations, and again with the same result as Coral Sea and Midway. The Japanese light cruiser *Ryujo* and a destroyer were sunk, and the Japanese fleet carriers were eliminated from further proceedings as a result of the losses incurred by their air groups: one American fleet carrier was lightly damaged.

Over the next weeks the Imperial Navy was to correct the imbalance of losses with its submarines badly damaging the *Saratoga* (31 August) and sinking the *Wasp* (15 September). It also succeeded in taking Henderson Field under fire

GUADALCANAL

Guadalcanal covered an area of some 2,060 square miles but the struggle for its possession concerned itself with some 20 or so square miles of coastal plain on the northern coast. The interior of the island, through which Japanese forces had to move against the US position astride the Lunga, consisted of heavily eroded ridges covered by thick tropical forest. The campaign's outcome was largely decided by American defensive success along the southern perimeter, specifically in breaking the offensives of 12/14 September and 24/25 and 25/26 October. With the Japanese unable to overrun or even neutralize Henderson Field, their long-term failure in the campaign was assured: their defeat became reality with the American victories in the first and second naval battles of Guadalcanal in mid November. Only in the very last phase of the campaign did US forces move beyond the Matanikau.

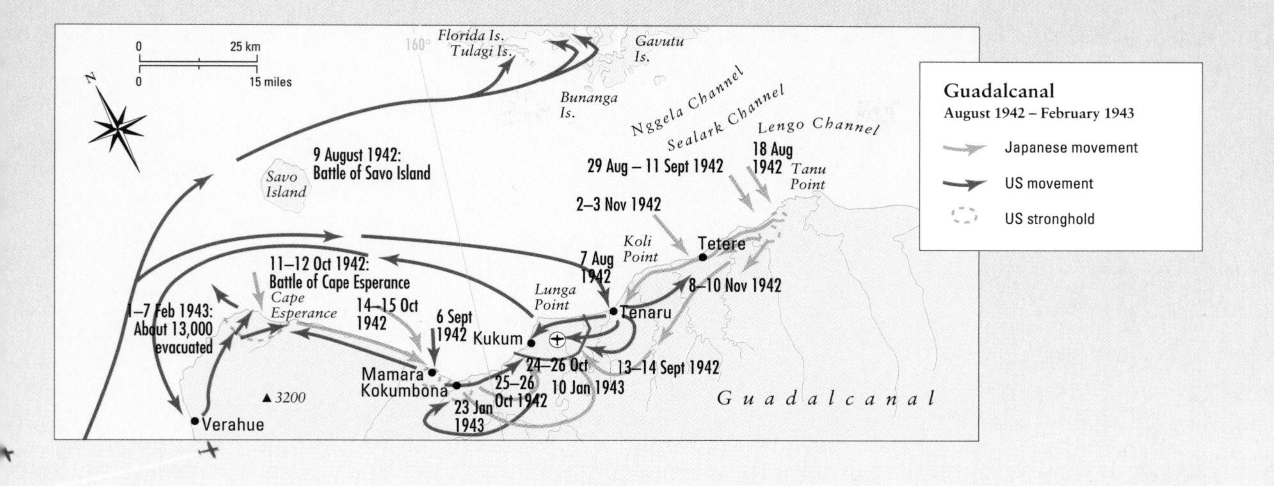

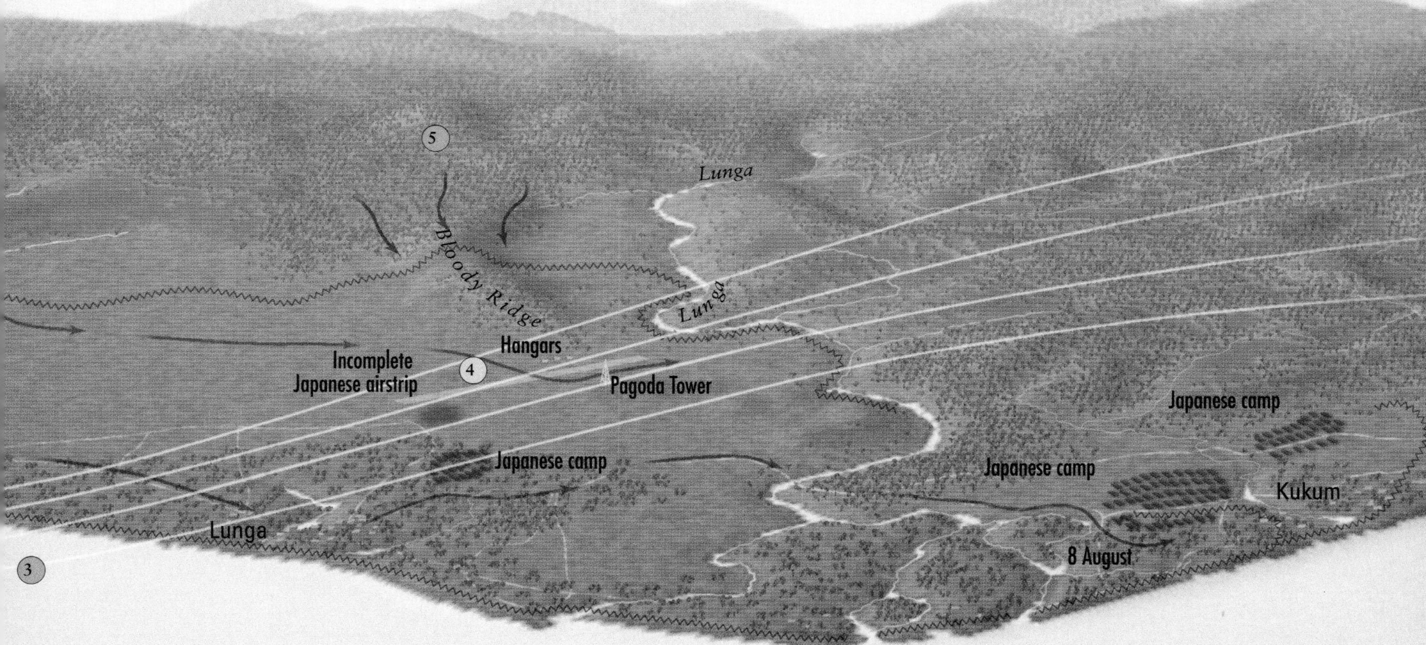

1. 7 August: US Marines land. Rapidly expanding from the bridgehead they scatter the Japanese garrison
2. 8 August: a defensive perimeter is formed around the captured airfield
3. 9 August: Japanese air strikes and intervention by naval units force US Navy to withdraw, leaving Marines isolated. They receive long-range air support and supplies brought in by destroyers during the night
4. 20 August: the airfield, now named Henderson Field, is completed and the first Marine aircraft arrive to give local air support
5. 20 Aug – 14 Sept: continuous skirmishing culminating in the Japanese attack on Bloody Ridge, which is driven off by the Marines. Despite further Japanese attacks the US build up continues and from the end of October the Marines gain the initiative

HAND GRENADES

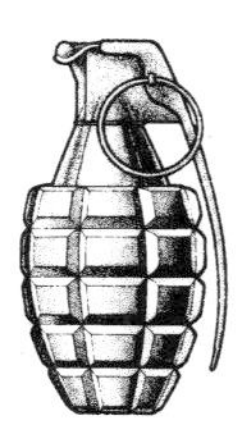

US MARK 2 'PINEAPPLE' FRAGMENTATION HAND-GRENADE

JAPANESE TYPE 97 HAND-GRENADE

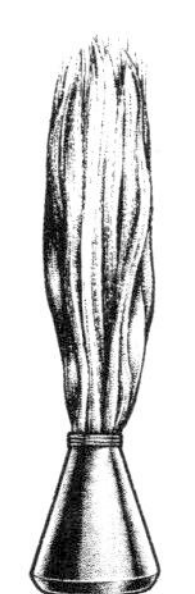

JAPANESE TYPE 3 ANTI-TANK GRENADE

On the Kakoda Trail, at Buna and at Milne Bay, Australian forces, by breaking Japanese offensives in eastern New Guinea, recorded perhaps Australia's finest achievement of the war. Australia, alone among combatant nations, had no conscription: yet one in two Australian males aged 18 to 45 enlisted voluntarily. At peak 89.4 per cent of all males aged 14 and over were in the services or employed directly in war work.

The last salvo of the US light cruiser Helena, *sunk by torpedoes fired by Japanese warships at the battle of Kula Gulf, 6 July 1943. This was the first of four closely-fought battles for the central Solomons by the end of which the Americans possessed clear advantage over the Japanese at sea.*

in a series of night bombardments and putting army formations ashore on Guadalcanal. But a major offensive against the airfield encountered withering defeat on Bloody Ridge on 12 September. Thereafter, as the seriousness of the situation in the lower Solomons slowly impressed itself upon the high command, the Japanese made a major effort to build up their forces on Guadalcanal in readiness for a renewal of the offensive: at the same time capital ships were sent into the waters that washed Guadalcanal in an attempt to neutralize Henderson Field by sustained, deliberate and heavy fire. Despite being worsted in a skirmish between cruiser forces that was dignified with the title of the battle of Cape Esperance, 11/12 October, these Japanese efforts were generally successful: equality of numbers on the island and a reduced American effectiveness in the air were achieved by the time that the Imperial Navy committed its carrier forces to a second attempt to eliminate the American outpost on Guadalcanal.

The battle of Santa Cruz, 26/27 October, with the American carrier *Hornet* and destroyer *Porter* sunk, and the carrier *Enterprise* damaged, against one Japanese fleet carrier and one light fleet carrier damaged, was perhaps one of only two carrier battles in the war when the Japanese had the better of an exchange with the Americans. But like the battle in the Coral Sea, the margin of success, plus the fact that the army's second attempt to overrun Henderson Field failed on the 23rd, was too slender to permit an effective exploitation of advantage. The losses incurred by the Japanese air groups, as well as a shortage of fuel, prevented the Japanese from pressing their advantage. In the aftermath of what was, in effect, a drawn battle, the Japanese took the decision to intensify their ferrying operations and to commit battleship and cruiser formations by night, and bomber formations by day, to the task of neutralizing Henderson Field. With the Americans also committing heavy units to its defence, the result was a three-day series of actions that broke the Japanese effort in this theatre.

In the first engagement, 12/13 November, fought at times at ranges at which torpedoes could not arm and battleship guns could not be depressed to bear upon the enemy, the Japanese lost the battleship *Hiei* and two destroyers, compared to the Americans' two light cruisers and three destroyers, with two further ships rendered *hors de combat*. In the second engagement, 14/15 November, another Japanese battleship, the *Kirishima*, was lost in one of the only two capital ship actions of the Pacific war, the Americans losing three destroyers. The loss of a battle division in these actions in many ways spelt the end of the Japanese effort, but what was no less serious in the long term was the annihilation of a troop convoy the Japanese tried to fight into Guadalcanal under the cover of its battle force. With eleven destroyers committed to the support of eleven transports, six of the transports were lost on 14 November and another four ran themselves ashore and were bombed to destruction on the following day. The loss of 70,179 tons of high-quality shipping in a single

LSTs at Guadalcanal. Though naturally it was the fighting for Guadalcanal that ultimately decided the outcome of the campaign, it was the Americans' greater ability to supply and reinforce their garrison and air formations on the island that largely determined events.

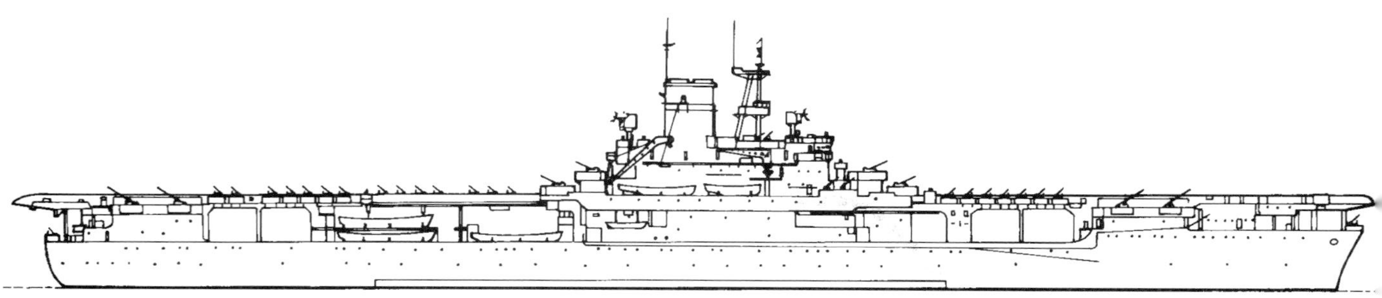

THE *WASP*

The Wasp. *18,500 tons (deep load), eighty-four aircraft, eight 5-inch, twenty 20-mm guns, 29.5 knots. Compliance with Treaty regulations was achieved primarily at the expense of anti-torpedo protection.*

24-hour period on a single mission was something that Japan could not afford. But Japan's position was even worse than these bare figures would indicate. These losses came after the destruction of 154,074 tons of service and merchant shipping in October – more than twice Japan's replacement capability – and at a time when an estimated 700,000 tons of shipping were committed to operations in the south-west Pacific. Neither the losses of 13/15 November, nor a shipping commitment of this magnitude, could be borne, certainly not indefinitely and in waters commanded by enemy land-based air power. On 31 December the Japanese high command took the decision to abandon the struggle for Guadalcanal and to evacuate its remaining forces from the island.

The surviving Japanese troops on Guadalcanal were evacuated, without loss, in the first eight days of February 1943, ending the campaign in the lower Solomons. Within a couple of weeks the Americans moved to occupy and prepare an airstrip in the Russells, foreshadowing how the campaign in the Solomons, indeed in the Pacific as a whole, was to unfold. But the campaign in the Solomons was over for the moment, and three matters are of significance in understanding its results and implications. The first of these points is the nature of land-based air power on Henderson Field that was crucially important in deciding the outcome of this campaign. In any consideration of the war at sea in the Second World War, the importance of land-based air power can hardly be understated, but the struggle for Guadalcanal is notable for the fact that the air power available on Henderson Field was primarily naval air power, and very often carrier aircraft based ashore, not conventional land-based air power. What was so important in the sinking or damaging of Japanese ships, and which so limited Japanese freedom of action, was the ability of naval aircraft to attack at low level, rather than the high- and medium-altitude attacks of heavy or medium land-based bombers.

Second, a qualitative balance began to establish

The fleet carrier Enterprise *at the battle of Santa Cruz, 26 October 1942. With her sister ship* Hornet *lost, this was one of the few carrier actions in which the balance of losses favoured the Japanese but not to the extent that they were able to seize the initiative in the lower Solomons.*

itself at sea during the campaign. At the outset, the Imperial Navy possessed clear superiority over its opponents, as the victory off Savo Island demonstrated. By the campaign's end, and even allowing for the action off Tassafaronga (30 November) when the Japanese inflicted a stinging reverse on a considerably superior American cruiser formation, a rough parity of quality prevailed. The Americans learnt from their mistakes and recast their tactics accordingly: in addition, they possessed a clear advantage in radar and communications. The qualitative improvement of American naval forces in the course of this campaign was purchased by defeats and losses, but in the event Tassafaronga, where the US Navy was very fortunate not to lose four heavy cruisers, proved to be the last clear-cut Japanese naval victory of the war. The first two of the three battles fought in mid year in the central Solomons – at Kula Gulf on 6 July and at Kolombangara on the 13th, and the action off Vella Lavella on 6 October – saw honours and losses more or less shared. But in the battles fought in Vella Gulf on 6/7 August and, in the upper Solomons in November, in Empress Augusta Bay and off Cape St George, the Americans clearly outfought the Japanese, not least because of their employment of divided

THE G4M BETTY AND B-25 MITCHELL

On paper the two aircraft were well matched though with full loads the B-25 weighed almost twice as much as the G4M. In terms of speed and ceiling there was little to chose between them. In terms of armament and payload the Mitchell carried fourteen cannon and maximum bomb load of 3,200-lbs to the five guns and 1,764-lb payload of the Betty. In range the Betty held a clear advantage, 3,748 compared to 1,500 miles, but this advantage was too dearly bought in terms of armour and self-sealing tanks. Japanese industry produced 2,446 all G4M types: American industry 9,816 all B-25 types.

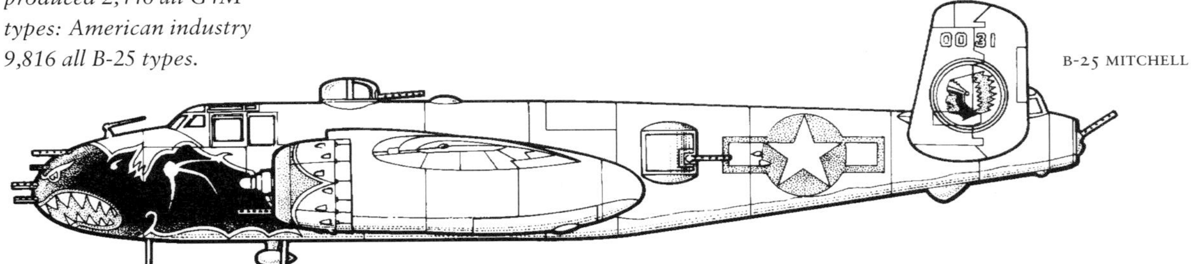

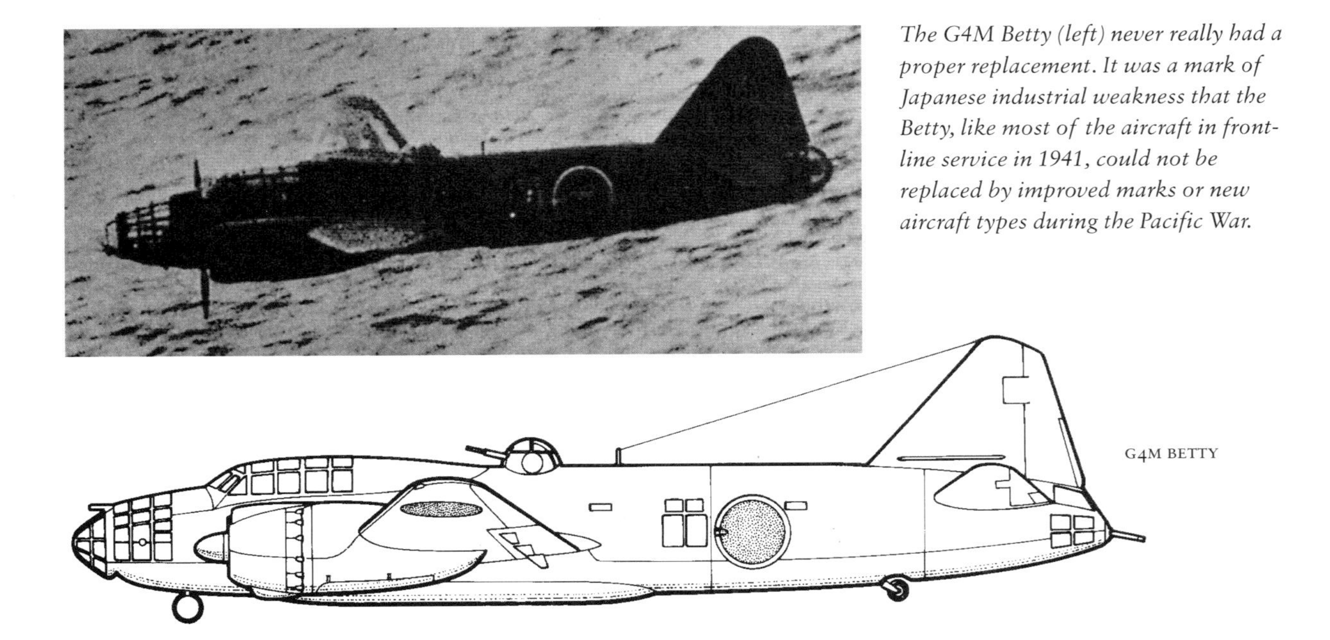

The G4M Betty (left) never really had a proper replacement. It was a mark of Japanese industrial weakness that the Betty, like most of the aircraft in front-line service in 1941, could not be replaced by improved marks or new aircraft types during the Pacific War.

forces and synchronized attacks which were hitherto the monopoly of the Imperial Navy.

The third and last point of significance about the Guadalcanal campaign is that ironically it provided vindication of the Japanese perimeter defence concept: unfortunately for the Imperial Navy, it was the US Navy that made it work. By seizing Tulagi and Henderson Field, and then committing their main formations to the defence of these bases, the Americans imposed upon the Imperial Navy the campaign that the Japanese had assumed the Americans would have to fight, and have to fight under such conditions that its defeat was assured. The reasons for such a state of affairs was varied, though four were uppermost in ensuring that the Imperial Navy fought under conditions that all but guaranteed defeat: the inadequacy of individual bases and their inability to sustain themselves in the face of a massively superior enemy; the loss of the initiative that ensured that the Imperial Navy was obliged to react to events at the cost of the balance and timing of its operations; the Japanese lack of air superiority in the immediate battle area; and the inadequacy of Japanese

The American landings on Rendova in the central Solomons were just one of five landings in the south-west Pacific on 30 June 1943: the others were near Salamaua and in Nassau Bay and on Woodlark and the Trobriands. In one two-week period, between 21 June and 4 July, the Americans conducted no fewer than ten landing operations in this area, building on successes won on Guadalcanal and New Guinea and the breaking of Japanese air power in the central and lower Solomons between April and mid June.

The keys to Allied advances in the south-west Pacific theatre were, first, the American ability to neutralize Japanese land-based air power before moving to secure objectives by amphibious assault and, second, bringing into service airfields from which the next moves could be supported and covered. Bougainville was subjected to assault on 1 November 1943. The construction of the first of three airfields began on the 9th: it was readied for operations on 9 December.

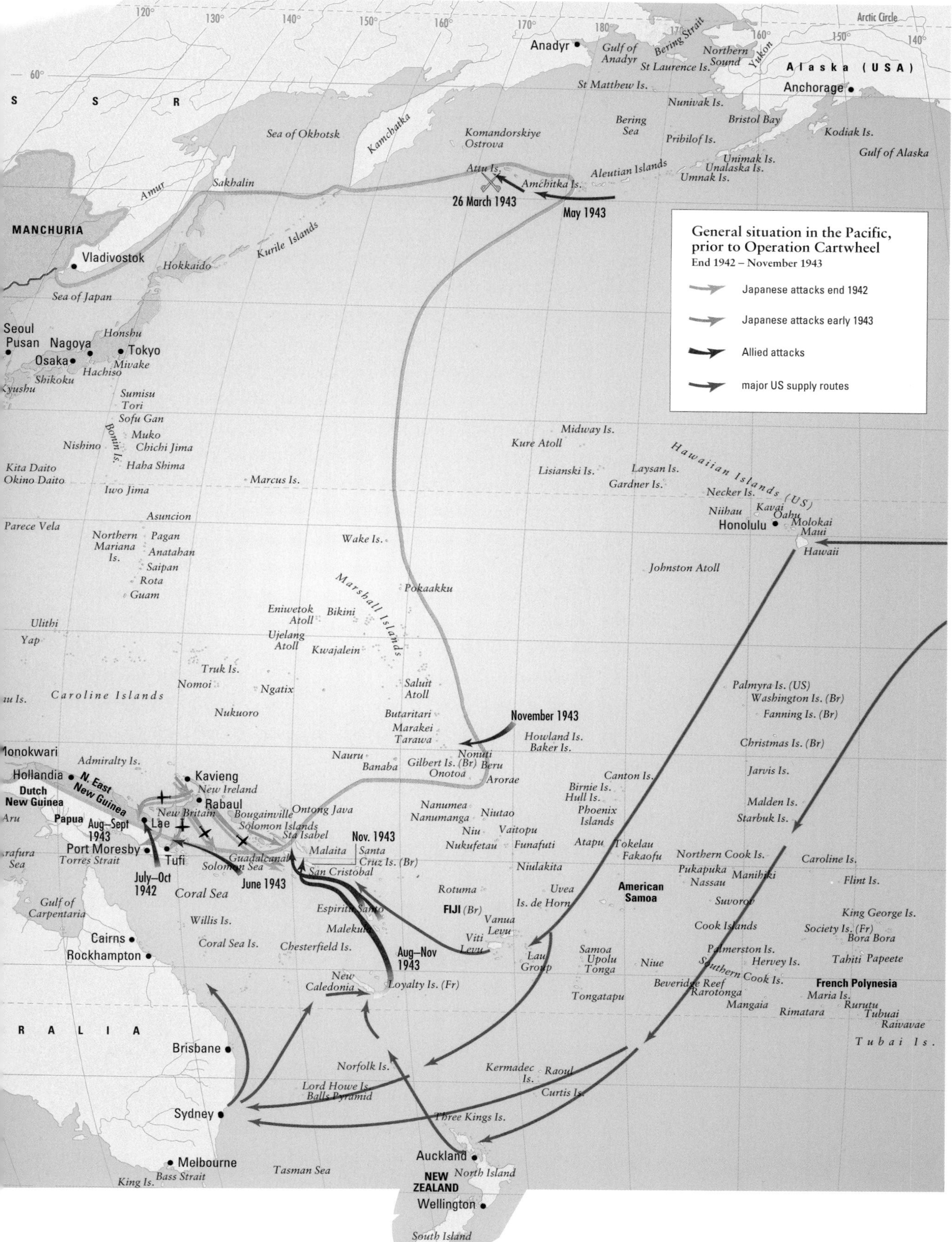

General situation in the Pacific, prior to Operation Cartwheel
End 1942 – November 1943
Japanese attacks end 1942
Japanese attacks early 1943
Allied attacks
major US supply routes
26 March 1943
May 1943
November 1943
Aug–Sept 1943
July–Oct 1942
June 1943
Aug–Nov 1943
Nov. 1943
Arctic Circle
Anadyr
Gulf of Anadyr
Bering Strait
Northern Sound
Yukon
St Laurence Is.
Alaska (USA)
Anchorage
St Matthew Is.
Nunivak Is.
Bristol Bay
Bering Sea
Pribilof Is.
Kodiak Is.
Gulf of Alaska
Unimak Is.
Unalaska Is.
Umnak Is.
Aleutian Islands
Amchitka Is.
Attu Is.
Komandorskiye Ostrova
Kamchatka
Sea of Okhotsk
Sakhalin
Amur
MANCHURIA
Vladivostok
Hokkaido
Kurile Islands
Sea of Japan
Seoul
Pusan
Nagoya
Osaka
Tokyo
Honshu
Mivake
Hachiso
Shikoku
Sumisu
Tori
Sofu Gan
Muko
Chichi Jima
Nishino
Bonin Is.
Haha Shima
Kita Daito
Okino Daito
Iwo Jima
Marcus Is.
Asuncion
Parece Vela
Northern Mariana Is.
Pagan
Anatahan
Saipan
Rota
Guam
Wake Is.
Marshall Islands
Pokaakku
Eniwetok Atoll
Bikini
Ujelang Atoll
Kwajalein
Ulithi
Yap
Truk Is.
Nomoi
Ngatix
Caroline Islands
Nukuoro
Saluit Atoll
Butaritari
Marakei
Tarawa
Nauru
Banaba
Gilbert Is. (Br)
Nonuti
Beru
Onotoa
Arorae
Howland Is.
Baker Is.
Midway Is.
Kure Atoll
Lisianski Is.
Laysan Is.
Gardner Is.
Hawaiian Islands (US)
Necker Is.
Niihau
Kavai
Oahu
Molokai
Maui
Honolulu
Hawaii
Johnston Atoll
Palmyra Is. (US)
Washington Is. (Br)
Fanning Is. (Br)
Christmas Is. (Br)
Jarvis Is.
Malden Is.
Starbuk Is.
Canton Is.
Birnie Is.
Hull Is.
Phoenix Islands
Admiralty Is.
Kavieng
New Ireland
Rabaul
New Britain
Hollandia
N. East New Guinea
Dutch New Guinea
Papua
Lae
Port Moresby
Tufi
Torres Strait
Aru
Gulf of Carpentaria
Bougainville
Solomon Islands
Ontong Java
Sta Isabel
Malaita
Guadalcanal
Solomon Sea
San Cristobal
Santa Cruz Is. (Br)
Coral Sea
Willis Is.
Coral Sea Is.
Chesterfield Is.
Espiritu Santo
Malekula
New Caledonia
Loyalty Is. (Fr)
Nanumea
Nanumanga
Niutao
Niu
Vaitopu
Nukufetau
Funafuti
Niulakita
Atapu
Tokelau
Fakaofu
Rotuma
FIJI (Br)
Vanua Levu
Viti Levu
Uvea
Is. de Horn
Lau Group
American Samoa
Samoa
Upolu
Tonga
Tongatapu
Niue
Northern Cook Is.
Pukapuka
Nassau
Manihiki
Suvorov
Cook Islands
Palmerston Is.
Hervey Is.
Southern Cook Is.
Beveridge Reef
Rarotonga
Mangaia
Caroline Is.
Flint Is.
King George Is.
Society Is. (Fr)
Bora Bora
Tahiti
Papeete
French Polynesia
Maria Is.
Rimatara
Rurutu
Tubuai
Raivavae
Tubai Is.
Cairns
Rockhampton
Brisbane
Sydney
Melbourne
Bass Strait
King Is.
Tasman Sea
Norfolk Is.
Lord Howe Is.
Balls Pyramid
Kermadec Is.
Raoul
Curtis Is.
Three Kings Is.
Auckland
North Island
NEW ZEALAND
Wellington
South Island

logistical support in terms of sustained operations. The wisdom of trying to prosecute a campaign at the most distant part of the defensive perimeter was also questionable, but merely brought to the fore the intrinsic problem of seeking to fight a defensive campaign against a superior enemy with choice in the conduct of its offensive operations. This point raises another in its turn: most of the battles that constituted the campaign were not the battles that the Imperial Navy had planned to fight. The Japanese seemed unable to adapt their battle plans to the reality of the conflict. If the Imperial Navy in the inter-war period failed to distinguish between a war, a campaign and a battle, and in this phase of the war fought the wrong campaign, the development of air power meant that the battles it fought both here in this theatre and throughout the war were not the battles for which it had prepared. In the course of this campaign the Imperial Navy lost just one cruiser, the *Furutaka*, in a surface action, and of the sixteen heavy and twenty-two light cruisers lost during the war, just four were destroyed in action with enemy surface forces, another two being shared between warships and aircraft. In contrast, land-based aircraft sank two light cruisers and shared in the destruction of one heavy cruiser and one light cruiser and carrier aircraft accounted for seven heavy and seven light cruisers and had claims on the credit for the destruction of three other units.

The period of Japanese defeat off, over and on Guadalcanal and in eastern New Guinea came at a time of British victory at El Alamein, the Anglo-American landings in north-west Africa and the Soviet counter-offensives in front of Stalingrad and Rzhev which collectively marked the Allies' wresting the strategic initiative from their European enemies. This coincidence of Axis defeats provides opportunity to consider the position of the Allied powers in the Far East at the end of 1942, and the policy decisions, mainly American, that were to shape the events of the next thirty-two months which were to end with Japan's total defeat.

Allied Strategy

The outbreak of the Pacific war forced upon the United States the obligation of leadership in the prosecution of the war against Japan and vested her with the power of decision relative to Britain in matters affecting this war and, in the longer term, the European war as well. The outbreak of war also rendered the United States the dominant western influence within China.

American strategic policy at the time of national entry into the Second World War was dominated by three considerations: the primacy of the Europe-first commitment; a confidence that the United States had the measure of Japan; and the belief that Japan's defeat had to embrace both Asian and Pacific dimensions. The latter was crucial because the belief that Japan could not be defeated without the Imperial Army on the mainland being part of that defeat was to lead the United States into a search for both an expanded Chinese and a Soviet dimension to the Japanese war. The latter proved easy to secure. At the

Tehran conference in November 1943 the Soviet high command gave an undertaking to enter the war against Japan within three months of Germany's defeat, although ironically by the time that the Soviet Union was in a position to honour this undertaking American enthusiasm for Soviet intervention was past. The China part of the American equation, however, proved much more difficult, and the American effort in this direction calls to mind the definition of the Japanese involvement in that country: the China quagmire.

The simplicity of American expectations of China's role in the defeat of Japan was to involve a host of problems that crystallized over the next three years at different levels. The twin intentions to arm and equip Chinese field armies with a view to their conducting major offensive operations, and to stage a strategic bombing campaign against the Japanese home islands from bases in southern and central China, involved a baffling array of inter-alliance, strategic, logistical and bureaucratic problems. American intentions were supposedly

The Casablanca conference, January 1943: Roosevelt, Churchill and their leading military advisers King, Marshall, Pound (First Sea Lord until October 1943), Air Chief Marshal Sir Charles Portal, Brooke, Field Marshal Sir John Dill (head of British military delegation in Washington) and Vice Admiral Lord Louis Mountbatten, chief of combined operations.

complementary, but in fact emerged as rivals to one another, and in any event they fell foul of the wishes of the Nationalist regime in Chungking that had no real interest in fulfilling the role that Washington ordained. Chungking regarded the Communists, not the Japanese, as the real enemy, and while willing to accept American aid was reluctant to undertake offensive operations that would consume military resources that were to be preserved for the post-war settling of accounts with the domestic foe.

Chungking, therefore, was quite willing to play host to an American air effort. But without any major military undertaking and the securing of the bases from which such an offensive would be mounted, a strategic bombing campaign could only miscarry. Moreover, the desire to stage an air offensive from China took no account of the implications that flowed from the basic premise that underpinned American (mis)calculations. China could only be supported and readied for her appointed tasks from India, and if the Americans were prepared to mount an airlift from bases in India that did not exist, the fact remained that, in the long term, China could only be supplied on the necessary scale by overland communications that ran through Burma. Thus the British reconquest of Burma formed a basic American requirement, and was one that Britain was not merely unable to undertake, but was determined to resist.

For the British, the reconquest of Burma represented a most hazardous undertaking, involving an advance across the mountains and through the jungles that separated India and Burma against an enemy served by good lines of communication through the Sittang and Irrawaddy valleys. But even if upper Burma was cleared sufficiently to permit the building of a road into China, the demands of the defence of that road against an intact enemy in central Burma would be equal to the capacity of the road itself, it being axiomatic that lower Burma could not be cleared of a Japanese enemy by an overland offensive staged from north-east India. Geography suggested that only an amphibious effort directed against Rangoon as the first stage of an offensive into central and upper Burma offered any realistic prospect of clearing Burma and developing an overland line of supply into China. But the demands of the European war ensured that the British could not undertake such an operation. In reality, however, the British high command had no wish to undertake such a commitment: Japanese strength in Burma, plus the existence in south-east Asia of other, more important objectives than Rangoon, were positive incentives to the British to bypass Burma in order to seek out enemy weakness, not that Washington agreed with this analysis. To add to the perversity of this situation, the American requirements for an airlift into China and an offensive into upper Burma were dependent upon a logistical infrastructure in north-east India that did not exist, and which the American high command was determined should not be developed at the expense of two undertakings that it wanted to see effected immediately. To further complicate matters, the engineer support needed for any offensive into upper Burma was not available, given the need to

Their only meeting, physical and not one of minds: Generalissimo Chiang Kai-shek, President Franklin D. Roosevelt and Prime Minister Winston Churchill at Cairo, November 1943.

develop north-east India in order to make such an offensive possible. The China–Burma combination thus threw up a series of clashes of priorities that confounded Anglo- and Sino-American deliberations, and which bred mutual exasperation and distrust.

In the Pacific, the American position was scarcely less difficult because there the US Army and Navy were involved in war with the real enemy. Bureaucratic and personnel considerations meant that after March 1942 the American effort in the Pacific was to be divided between the two services. At the heart of this inherently unsound arrangement was the Navy's refusal to put the Pacific Fleet under the command of a general, and one general in particular, and the Army's wilful refusal to allow the Navy the position of pre-eminence that the very nature of the Pacific war should have ensured. Thus were created Admiral Chester Nimitz's Pacific Ocean Areas and General Douglas MacArthur's South West Pacific Command and, like the two strands of American intention with respect to China, for most of the war these commands were as much rivals as partners. Throughout the war there was a series of attempts by South West Pacific Command to subordinate its naval counterpart and the Pacific Fleet to itself, while the army high command sought to impose a joint organization upon

Nimitz's command while ensuring that the power of decision within South West Pacific Command remained in army hands. Rather strangely, these efforts were largely successful. Even more strangely, these efforts came to success on the back of victories won by the US Navy and the Pacific Fleet: in real terms, the US Army's contribution to victory by the time that South West Pacific Command had its way in summer 1944 with the definition of the clearing of the Philippines as the American national priority was minimal.

But if inter-service rivalries were very much part of the American policy-making scene from the outset of war, the division of the Pacific into two service commands perversely proved to American advantage. National resources permitted the development of two offensives across both the central and the south-west Pacific in 1944. These cancelled out the potential advantage of Japan's central position from which to check the American efforts. However, as the Guadalcanal campaign came to an end, the American intention for the moment was limited and cautious. Originally, the Guadalcanal commitment had been adopted as the first step in an effort that was culminate with the capture of Rabaul, and in February 1943 this remained the American intent.

Fleet Admiral Chester Nimitz, Commander-in-Chief US Pacific Fleet and Pacific Ocean Area and post-war Chief of Naval Operations.

For much of 1943 relatively little change on the map occurred. While the Americans reclaimed the Aleutian Islands that had been lost in June 1942 – Attu in May and Kiska in August – the war was taken into the central Solomons by the landings in the New Georgia group in June and on Vella Lavella in August. On the same day as the landings in New Georgia the New Guinea effort began with landings on Woodlark, in the Trobriands and in Nassau Bay; Lae and Salamaua were secured in September. But by October 1943, when Finschhafen was secured, the move into the upper Solomons represented major change in two respects. By this time the American high command had settled on a bypass strategy that would avoid Japanese strength and leave Rabaul 'to wither on the vine'. The move against the Treasuries and Bougainville was one part of a double effort; the other part, the landings in the Gilbert Islands, represented the opening of the central Pacific offensive.

The central Pacific offensive was one of two massively significant developments in 1943. The first was that by November 1943, the US Pacific Fleet possessed the means to take the war to Japanese strength. By this time American shipyards had more than made good the losses that had been incurred to date. For the landings in the Gilberts the Americans were to deploy no fewer than six

The scene on Tarawa: if anything the scenes on the reef where so many amphibians came to grief was much worse. Tarawa was the one occasion when the casualty lists were more or less even, though the Japanese lists mostly consisted of dead: thereafter the balance of losses overwhelmingly favoured the amphibious assault.

fleet, five light fleet and eight escort carriers, and such numbers proved that, in real terms, the decision of the war had been reached with the opening of this offensive. Such was the disparity of numbers, and such was the widening disparity in quality of equipment, that these landings were assured of success: the Americans were able to isolate an objective from outside support and overwhelm it before the Japanese could intervene effectively. Inevitably, there was to be a cost exacted in the process, but what was to be remarkable about material and human losses was not their heaviness, but how economically victory was purchased. In any week of her war with Germany between June 1941 and May 1945, the Soviet Union lost more dead than the total American fatalities in the Pacific war. By November 1943, the Americans, in the special conditions of naval warfare, secured a numerical and qualitative superiority and stumbled across the basic 'the-more-you-use-the-less-you-lose' principle that they made their own. The subsequent advance across the central Pacific represented the application of a superiority and technique wholly absent from their conduct of operations during the Guadalcanal campaign.

The second of the two developments that took place in the course of 1943 concerned the campaign against Japanese shipping. After relatively minor losses in the opening five months of hostilities, the pace of sinkings quickened considerably between May 1942 and February 1943, and in the eight months that followed again appreciably increased. Compared to sinkings in the Battle of the Atlantic, the scale of Japanese losses was relatively modest, but, of course, this was not the relevant yardstick. By November 1943 the rate of loss bordered on the prohibitive. But no less significant was the pattern of sinkings, a pattern that has been largely obscured in post-war histories by the fact that Japanese shipping losses increased massively after October 1943 and the raising of the General Escort Command and Japanese attempts to introduce convoy for shipping. A very careful analysis of Japanese losses will reveal that increasing losses after October 1943 had very little to do with the general introduction of convoy but conformed to patterns of sinking that had been established before this time. The critical points to note in terms of sinkings were the heaviness of service shipping rather than civilian shipping losses, the relative decline of importance of the northern and south-west Pacific theatres as reflected in the decline of losses in these areas, and the simple fact that by October 1943 the central Pacific had emerged as the real graveyard of service shipping despite the fact that to date it had not played host to any significant offensive. Civilian shipping losses were not light between December 1941 and October 1943, but

JAPANESE TRANSPORT LOSSES BY COMPARATIVE PERIODS AND BY AREAS OF OPERATION

Japanese naval, military and civilian shipping losses by comparative periods (below) and by area of operation (opposite). After the cheaply won successes of the opening phase, Japanese losses quickly reached prohibitive proportions: estimated replacement capacity was 75,000 tons per month. The most serious losses were incurred by service shipping: their losses were disproportionate because of the slenderness of shipping allocated to the armed forces, and had to be replaced by shipping drawn from trade.

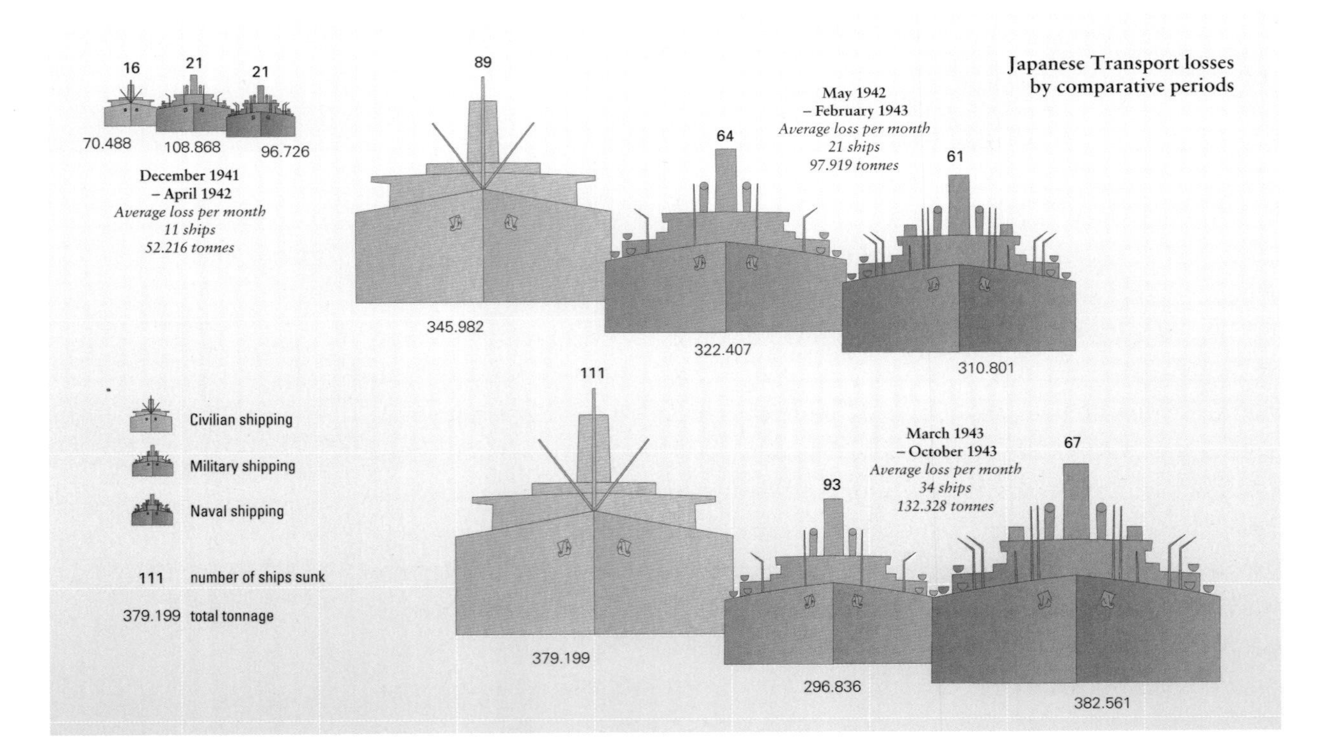

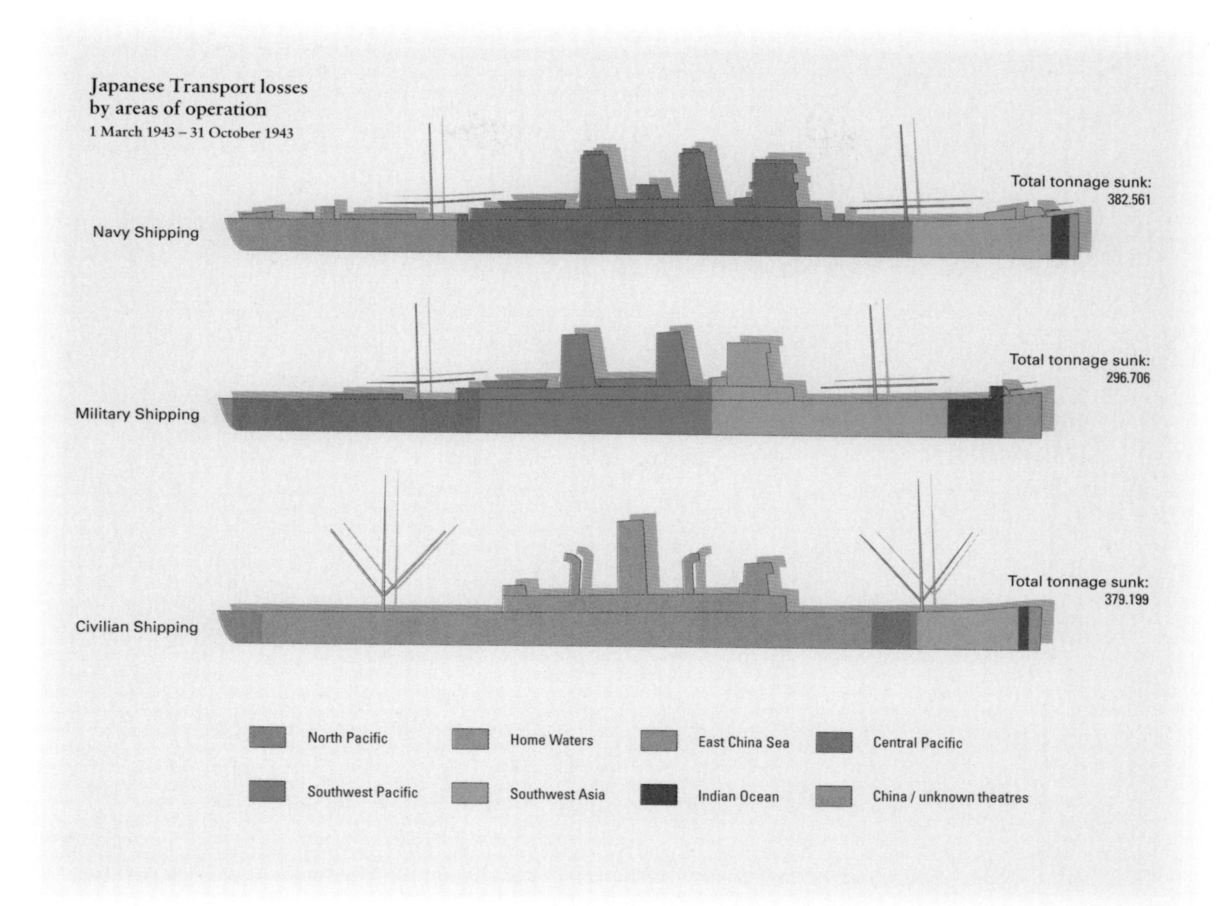

they were certainly not disastrous. The concentration of merchantmen losses in home waters and the East China Sea reflected the peculiarity of geography that forced shipping coming into Japan to use ports on the exposed east coast. What was especially serious about these losses was the evident inability of the Imperial Navy to protect shipping in an operational area that was smaller than the North Atlantic. The fact was that by October 1943 Japanese shipping had to negotiate certain narrows and was increasingly vulnerable to a submarine offensive that had assumed momentum after a very uncertain start.

What was at work by October 1943 in ensuring ever-greater American inroads into Japanese shipping strength was a combination of three matters relating to the submarine campaign. The first was American correction of various material defects, most obviously faulty torpedoes, which had hampered operations from the start of hostilities. The second was American correction of organization and doctrine that had handicapped operations in the first two years of war. For example, the priority afforded fleet operations meant that attacks upon large merchantmen, such as fleet oilers, did not figure highly in American calculations with the result that such targets were afforded a single torpedo, an insufficient investment for attacks on large, well-built merchantmen. By the third quarter of 1943 realism in such matters as torpedo allocation had

Submarines accounted for 4,446,227 tons of service and civilian shipping, some 53.48 per cent of overall Japanese losses. Of this total 1,977,198 tons was sunk in south-east Asia, 898,302 tons (of which all but 63,851 tons consisted of service shipping) in the central Pacific, 897,484 tons in Japanese home waters, and 557,696 tons in the East China Sea.

intruded upon American doctrinal deliberations. The third was the simple fact that by summer 1943 American submarine operations had assumed a scale that for the first time was significant. In June 1943 the number of sailings from Pearl Harbor exceeded twenty in a month for the first time, and in September 1943 the number of submarines at Pearl Harbor allowed monthly sailings to be sustained at that level. This fact, when combined with sailings from Australian bases, meant that from autumn 1943, the Americans were able to maintain a significant number of submarines on station, and the American ability to read Japanese shipping signals increased their effectiveness by an estimated one-third.

What all these changes – material, doctrine and growing numbers – meant was that by the third quarter of 1943 the American submarine force had readied

itself for a sustained onslaught on all but defenceless Japanese shipping, though the real points of significance are too easy to miss. By October 1943 US submarines operating from bases in the central Pacific were inflicting losses that the Japanese could barely tolerate, and this excludes losses inflicted by all other agencies of attack on Japanese shipping. What was equally significant was that between March and October 1943, when there were no major fleet operations in any part of the Pacific, American warships and carrier aircraft made virtually no contribution to Japanese losses. In October 1943 the carriers of the Pacific Fleet were poised to move for the first time in support of amphibious operations in the central Pacific. The different pieces that together spelt 'Defeat' were falling into place: Japan's strategic intent was on the point of being shredded as remorselessly as her hapless garrisons and equally hapless shipping.

At their peak in March 1944 American factories produced one aircraft every 294 seconds. The basis of such prodigious output was the production line, massive investment in new factories, pooled resources between peacetime rivals and building to settled designs with minimum in-service changes. During the war the US concentrated on eighteen aircraft specifications, only one of which post-dated 1940 in design: Japan built ninety, or, perhaps more accurately, tried to build ninety.

CHAPTER FOUR

The Third Milestone: The Road to Defeat, Failure and Collapse

November 1943 – October 1944

The front line on Wakde Island, 18 May 1944. After landings on the previous day at Arare on the New Guinea mainland, the Americans moved against Wakde in order to secure its airfield. Wakde was secured within five days but the Arare–Toem area was not cleared until September: after both had served their purpose in supporting the moves into the Philippines, they were abandoned in February 1944.

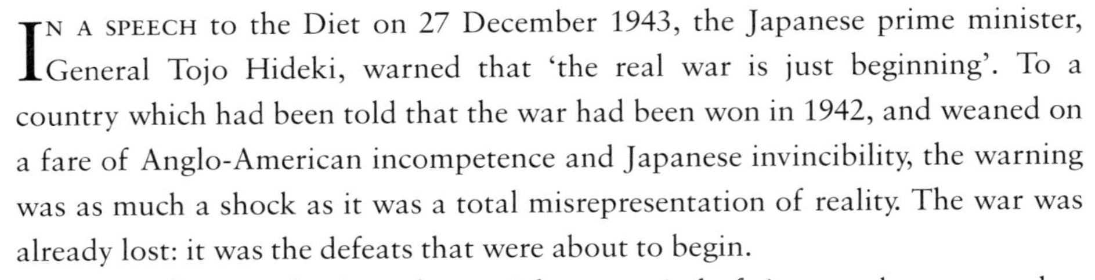

THE THIRD MILESTONE: THE ROAD TO DEFEAT, FAILURE AND COLLAPSE

IN A SPEECH to the Diet on 27 December 1943, the Japanese prime minister, General Tojo Hideki, warned that 'the real war is just beginning'. To a country which had been told that the war had been won in 1942, and weaned on a fare of Anglo-American incompetence and Japanese invincibility, the warning was as much a shock as it was a total misrepresentation of reality. The war was already lost: it was the defeats that were about to begin.

By a judicious selection of material, any period of time can be presented as being endowed with special circumstance: in a sense mendacity is the historian's trademark. But there are moments in history 'when the world turns', and, clearly, 1944 was such a moment in time. It was the year of the coming of age of the United States, when she entered into her inheritance as the greatest power in the world. It was the year that witnessed the emergence of the Soviet Union as the greatest military power in Europe. It was the year that sealed the defeat of Germany and Japan, their last faint chances of somehow avoiding ruin being destroyed, specifically in the series of defeats that overwhelmed both in the single month of June. It was a year that, by virtue of these developments, saw what had been the most powerful of the continents reduced to the status of the object of deliberations of two states, both more powerful than herself and which were historically apart from and a part of Europe.

The events of the Pacific war did not unfold in a manner that permits chronological neatness: there was no exact correlation between campaigns and battles and the structure of the calendar. There is a certain appropriateness in the fact that on 6 June 1944 American forces came ashore at Normandy and American carrier task groups sailed from Majuro in the Marshalls for the battle of the Philippine Sea, but that apart, 'the year of defeats' that sealed the fate of the remaining Axis powers, and specifically Japan, lacks 'annual exactitude'. The year in which defeat assumed reality for Japan was between 20 November 1943 and 25 October 1944, between the American descent upon Japanese bases in the Gilberts and the battle of Leyte Gulf, after which the final American victory in the Philippines (and hence astride Japan's lines of communication with the southern resources area) was only a matter of time. It was a period that witnessed two of the greatest naval battles in history, the second of which included probably the most destructive single day in naval warfare. In addition, this period saw perhaps the greatest destruction of shipping other than warships in a single day with the American raid on Truk on 17 February 1944; it saw Japanese shipping butchered to the extent that by the end of 1944, Japanese mercantile resources were inadequate to meet minimum national requirements; and it ended with the Americans in a position to take the war to Japanese home waters, with the Japanese stripped of every form of resistance but one.

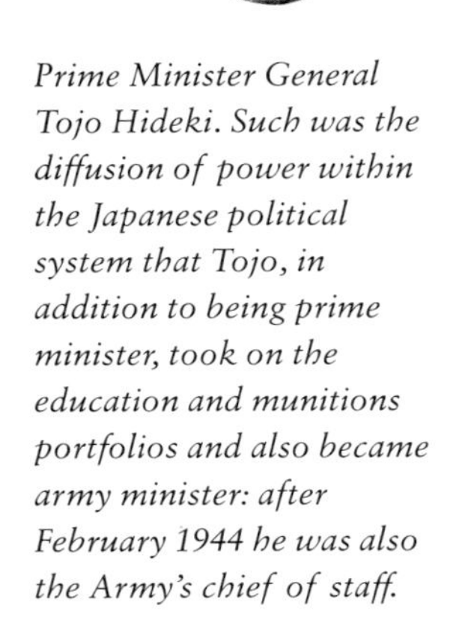

Prime Minister General Tojo Hideki. Such was the diffusion of power within the Japanese political system that Tojo, in addition to being prime minister, took on the education and munitions portfolios and also became army minister: after February 1944 he was also the Army's chief of staff.

Mementoes will tell sad tale to future generations

First published in *The Whitehaven News* on 3 August 200~~8~~6

Harry Dimond

IN 1945, when Henry Dimond was freed from a Japanese prisoner-of-war camp, he was 25 years old and weighed five-and-a-half stone.

Possessing only the leather G-string he was wearing, he was given a kit bag, by Australian soldiers, which contained clean clothes and a razor.

"My husband told me that in August 1945 the Australians were flying 400 miles to air-drop bread to the prisoners,'' said Henry's wife, 83-year-old Mary. "It was the first bread they had tasted since being captured in 1942.''

Henry, who became manager of the Rowntrees chocolate factory, in Egremont, died in 1982. Now Mary, of Thornhill, has donated her husband's kit bag to The Second World War Experience Centre in Leeds.

"I thought that the Australians, who Henry said had been so caring and good, should be remembered by future generations,'' Mary said. "I don't know why we kept the bag, but it seemed right to give it to the Centre.''

The Centre was set up to collect, document, preserve, exhibit and encourage access "to the surviving material … of the men and women who participated in the war.'' It aims to store wartime letters, diaries, artwork, maps, books, official papers and memorabilia from the era. Increasingly, it is becoming home to the memories and records of veterans' associations whose numbers are declining.

Mary is also to be interviewed about her wartime experiences, and her memories will be stored at the Centre.

Henry landed in Java in 1942 and spent the time "trying to keep ahead of the Japanese,'' Mary said. "However, he was one of 50 men in a rear party when he was captured.''

He was taken to the infamous Bicycle camp in Java, and then transported with 4,000 other prisoners, packed like sardines and lying head to toe, on a ship to Singapore. "They travelled like that for four days without ever going up on deck,'' Mary said. Henry and 2,000 of the prisoners were then sent to Kuching camp in Borneo where he remained until 1945.

"I had met Henry in 1940 when I lived in Sheffield,'' Mary said. "After he was captured I was allowed to send him 25 words a month. He received only three of my letters, but said it had made a world of difference.'' The couple married in 1948 and moved to Cumbria when Henry got a job at the creamery in Aspatria.

When the Australians entered the camp, after the Japanese had fled, they found hundreds of undelivered letters sent by desperate families to their imprisoned sons, husbands, brothers and sweet-hearts.

"My husband told me the Australians had been disgusted by the state of the prisoners they found in the camp,'' Mary said. "Henry himself weighed only five and a half stone and he said when the prisoners were being loaded onto a ship, taking them to convalesce, the Australians had lifted them like babies.''

Henry had particularly remembered how good it had felt after years of imprisonment "to stride out by the sea chatting with the Australians.''

Mary said her husband never wanted to be reminded of his time in the camp, but did talk to her about the horrific suffering.

The Australians had found instructions at Henry's camp, left by the Japanese, which stated that had the war not ended in August, the allied prisoners and civilian women and children were to be marched 25 miles to a mine, sealed in and left to die.

"In general a lot of the men didn't want to talk about their experiences,'' she said. "I wanted to donate Henry's kit-bag so that people will continue to know what happened in the war long after I'm gone.''

Between November 1943 and October 1944 Japan was defeated not in two struggles, namely in the central and south-west Pacific, but in five. The period is dominated by events in the two main theatres of operation, which rightly overshadow all other matters in terms of scale, distance and importance. But this period witnessed the continuing campaign against shipping, the defeat of the Japanese offensive into north-east India that exposed upper Burma to invasion, and the start of the land-based bombing of the Japanese home islands. In addition, the Japanese launched an offensive throughout southern China directed against the airfields from which this bombing effort was staged. All these efforts command attention in their own right, and somewhat oddly, perhaps the most important of these in the sense of long-term consequence was the one effort in which the Japanese commanded a measure of success.

The campaign in southern China proved of crucial importance, if not in the outcome of the Second World War then in weakening the

BELOW: *Vice Admiral Marc A. Mitscher.*
LOWER: *Japanese naval yard at Dublon Island under attack during the carrier raid on Truk. In Operation Hailstone 35 transports and merchantmen were sunk. In one 24-hour period, 17 February 1942, the Japanese lost three months' shipyard production.*

Yunnan, 1943. Chinese nationalist formations marching to the Salween front. Despite the good order shown in this photograph, Chinese route marches were notorious both for natural wastage and casual executions carried out by Chinese nationalist officers, and by the state of troops on arrival.

Chungking regime. The Imperial Army's offensive, code named Ichi-Go, was the largest Japanese land operation of the war, involving 620,000 Japanese troops, and served to undermine the credibility of Kuomintang authority even as the end of the Japanese war became discernible. Elsewhere, the defeat of the Japanese 'March on Delhi' in front of Imphal and Kohima, the first stage in what amounted to a clearing of Burma by June 1945, rehabilitated British prestige on the sub-continent and throughout south-east Asia; it provided an Indian Army that was soon to be ripped apart by the partition of the Raj with a very real, final victory that paid in full for past defeats and humiliation. At the same time, the campaign against Japanese shipping, as noted earlier, assumed critical proportions. In stating matters thus, one acknowledges the nature of

victory in total war: while certain efforts clearly are more important than others, every little counts in the product of the whole, and very little is to be gained in any attempt to assess relative contributions beyond recognition of different worth.

Across the western Pacific

This period of the war was to open with two related efforts over three months: the destruction of the more important Japanese garrisons in the Gilberts and Marshalls, and a series of operations in New Guinea and the Bismarcks that resulted in the bypassing and isolation of Rabaul. Then, after a two-month respite from landing operations, while American carrier forces rampaged throughout the central Pacific as far west as the Palaus, the Americans conducted landings at Aitape and Hollandia on the northern coast of New Guinea on 22 April 1944. From these positions the Americans moved against Japanese holdings in western New Guinea in May, before the main effort in the central Pacific unfolded in mid June with landings in the Mariana Islands. With the Japanese having abandoned the policy of forward defence and dignified the Vogelkop–Truk–Marianas line with *ne plus ultra* status, the landings in the Marianas forced the Imperial Navy to give battle. Its subsequent defeat at the battle of the Philippine Sea bared the whole of the western Pacific to an

Indian soldiers in the fighting conditions of north-east India and northern Burma. Such vegetation, limiting an advance to a single soldier at arm's length, partly explains British and Japanese reluctance to consider offensive operations in this theatre.

Island, flight deck and two F6F Hellcats of the US fleet carrier Essex. *In the course of the strategic advance across the Pacific, the carrier air group became increasingly defensive with more fighters and fewer strike aircraft.*

American advance. With the Marianas and bases for a strategic bombing offensive against the Japanese home islands secured, the revelation of Japanese weakness throughout the Philippines as a result of the carrier raids of 9/10 and 12/14 September prompted the American decision to abandon the proposed landings on Mindanao in favour of an accelerated move into the Visayans. With the landings in the Palaus too far advanced to be cancelled, the result was that American forces landed on Leyte on 20 October. This landing marked the end of an advance of some 2,200 miles in thirteen months since Huon Gulf had been secured, and it provoked one last despairing effort by the Imperial Navy to fight

The landings on Makin by troops from the 27th Infantry Division, 20 November 1943: the landings were supported with fire support from four battleships and four cruisers, with three escort carriers operating in support. Makin was secured within four days but the fight for the island was overshadowed by the battle for neighbouring Tarawa.

'the decisive battle' in which it continued to believe until it ceased to exist. The battle of Leyte Gulf was, in fact, a three-part affair, the actions off Cape Engano and in the Surigao Strait complementing the action in Leyte Gulf itself. In reality, this battle was really only one part of an effort that had begun with the American carrier raids on Formosa and the Philippines two weeks before, and which continued for a full month after the main-force engagements and immediate follow-up operations between 23 and 28 October. The American victory at Leyte Gulf ensured ultimate victory throughout the Philippines and exposed the approaches and the home islands to direct Allied attack.

With the moves by Allied forces into the Treasuries and northern Choiseul in the Solomon

THE SOUTH-WEST PACIFIC 1943–4

In 1943 relatively few islands or towns changed hands as both sides reorganized in the aftermath of the campaigns on Guadalcanal and in eastern New Guinea. None the less the Americans conducted a series of operations that ensured control of the central Solomons and eastern New Guinea, before beginning a series of operations in November 1943 aimed at neutralizing and bypassing Rabaul: this was achieved by February–March 1944 with the acquisition of Manus and Emirau. Thereafter, with US carrier forces operating in the central Pacific, the Americans were free to develop their offensive operations along the north coast of New Guinea.

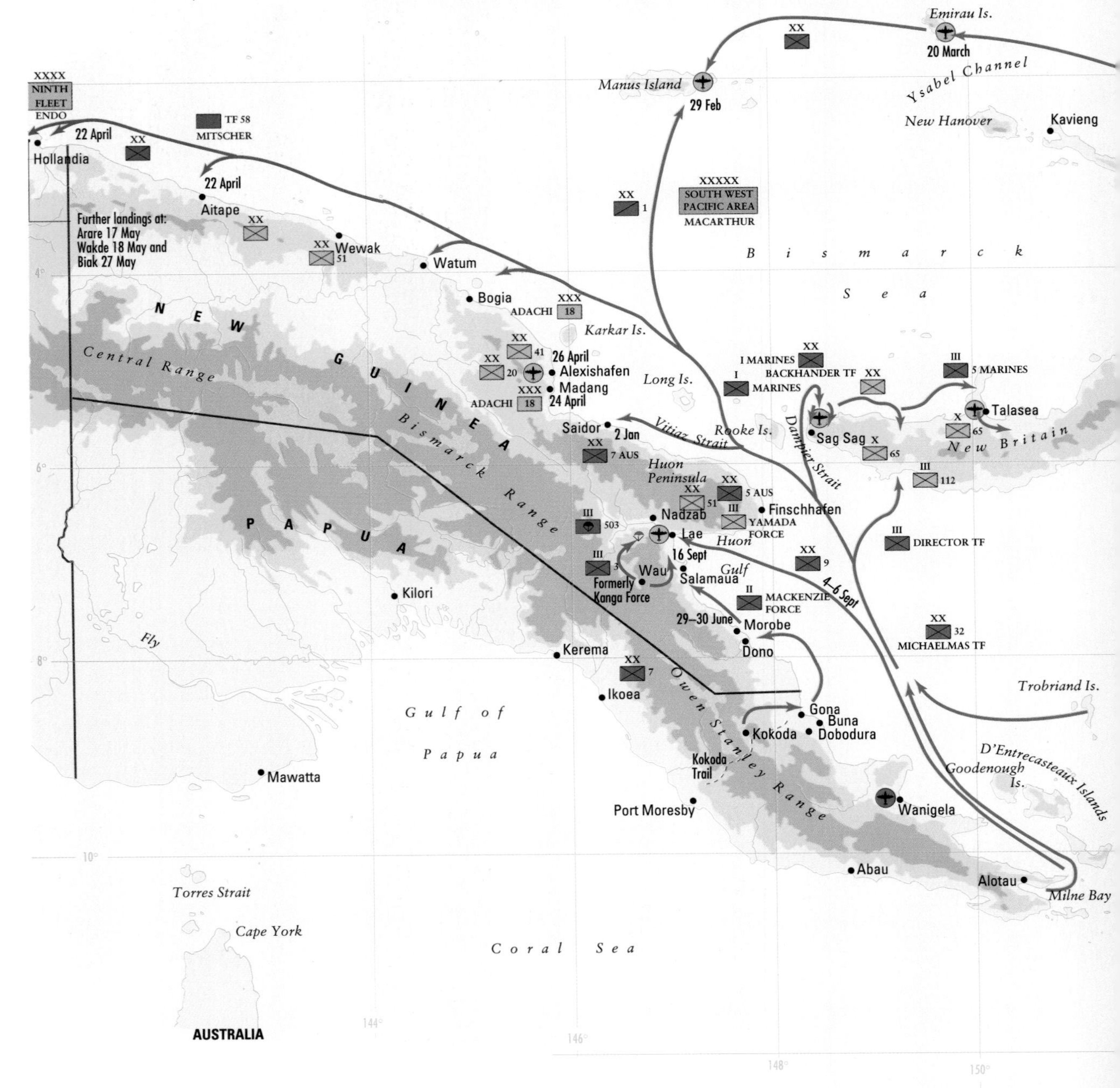

Major Generals Holland Smith and Charles Corlett in the attack transport Cambria. *Corlett was army divisional commander at Kwajalein, Holland Smith a somewhat tempestuous Marine Corps commander of exceptional ability but little patience and tact. His dismissal of an army general of the same name on Saipan led to bitter inter-service recriminations.*

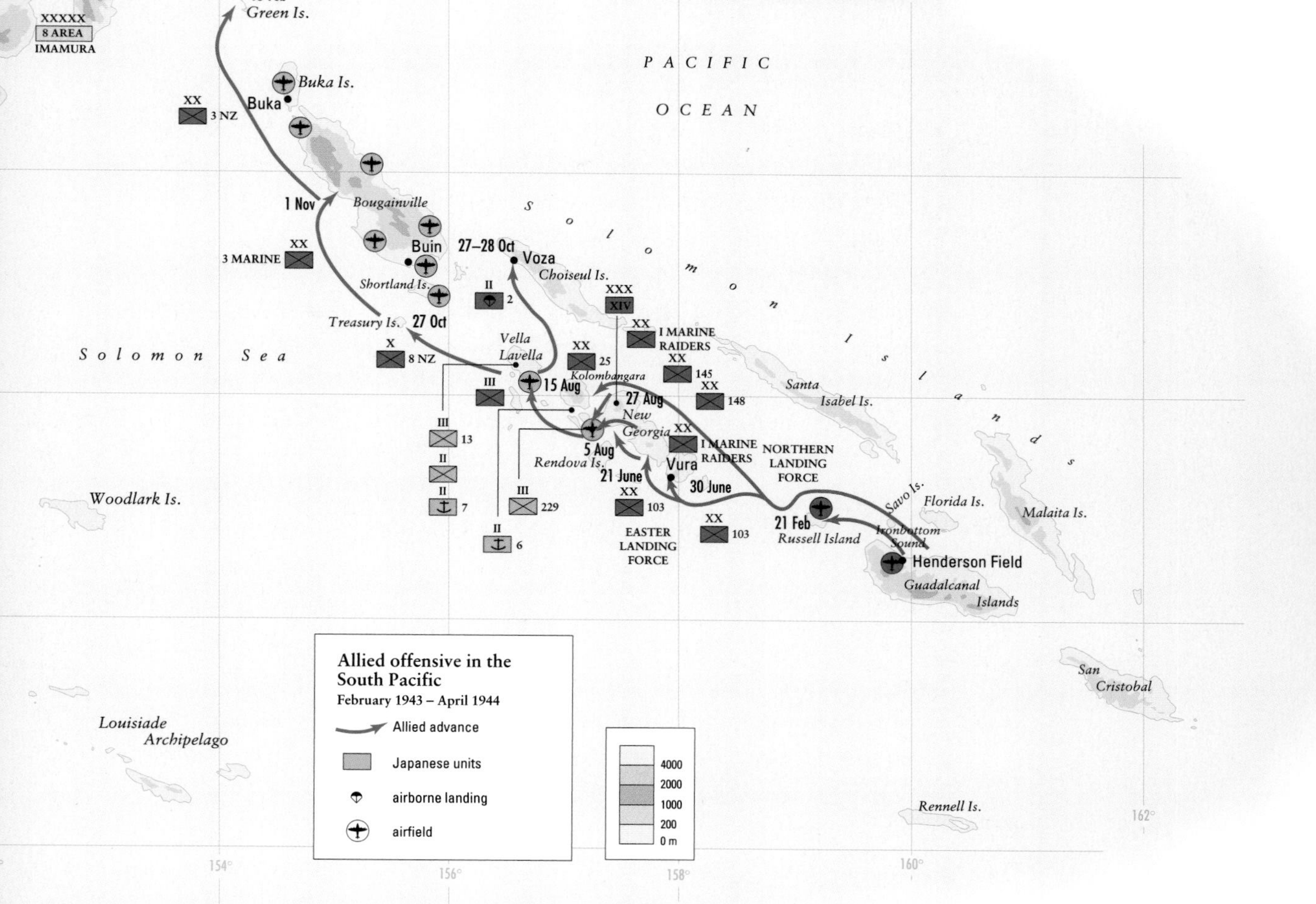

The landings on Cape Gloucester, western New Britain, by the 1st Marine Division on 26 December 1943. Conducted without carrier and battleship support, Operation Dexterity was one of the last Allied operations that completed the ring around Rabaul. By the war's end Japanese forces on New Britain were confined to no more than a close perimeter around Rabaul.

Islands as the prelude to landings in Empress Augusta Bay on 1 November 1943, the Allied victory began to assume substance. The Japanese, who had put carrier air groups ashore at Rabaul intending to contest any enemy move into the upper Solomons, sent a cruiser force into the Bay and initiated a closely fought night action which was narrowly won by the Americans. The Imperial Navy then committed another cruiser force to Rabaul, but the American carrier raid of 5 November mauled the formation two hours after it arrived at the base. In addition, this strike, plus the raid of 11 November, accounted for the greater part of the air groups at Rabaul. These reverses, plus the clear American victory in the destroyer battle off Cape St George on 25 November, forestalled the possibility of sustained Japanese resistance in the upper Solomons. On Bougainville the 3rd Marine and 37th Infantry Divisions side-stepped the main concentrations of Japanese forces and secured fighter and bomber strips around Cape Torokina from which to cover operations into the Bismarcks; the Japanese 6th Infantry Division's attempt to overrun American positions was broken during March 1944. With Allied forces in New Guinea moving to secure Cape Gloucester on 26 December and Saidor on 2 January 1944, the 3rd New Zealand Division's landings in the Green Islands on 15 February and the American landings in the Admiralties two weeks later isolated Rabaul. Forces from South West Pacific Command occupied Manus in the Admiralties in February 1944, and the occupation of Emirau by the 4th Marine Division on 20 March completed the encirclement and neutralization of Rabaul. Largely intact Japanese forces on New Britain withdrew into the base, where they were to remain mostly unmolested and helpless until the end of the war.

The ease with which these various efforts unfolded prompted two demands on the part of South West Pacific Command, first that the next moves in this theatre should be directed to Aitape and Hollandia, some 400 miles beyond present positions, and second that these offensives, and South West Pacific Command itself, should be afforded priority in the conduct of the Pacific war. With the Japanese holding the equivalent of a corps around and in front of Wewak, the Aitape–Hollandia initiative was to be afforded a planning code name – Reckless – that would have been sufficient comment upon it, but for two facts of life: the ability to read Japanese signals had alerted the Americans to the weakness of Japanese forces in the Aitape and Hollandia areas, and by this time the Allies possessed sufficient land-based air power to neutralize Japanese air formations in these areas without undue difficulty. Despite appearances to the contrary, the Aitape–Hollandia proposal was both reasoned and reasonable, a somewhat unusual state of affairs with reference to MacArthur and South West Pacific Command headquarters.

The second demand, however, was somewhat different. The product of planning future operations, it grew from the inter-service rivalries within the American high command that had resulted in the establishment of two commands in the Pacific, but its immediate origin lay in the reaction, both

public and military, to the Gilberts campaign. Very simply, between 21 and 29 November American forces drawn from Nimitz's Pacific Ocean Areas command secured six atolls in this group, and in so doing opened the way to further offensives into the Marshalls and Carolines. In breaking open one key part of Japan's outer perimeter defences the Americans registered a very real strategic success, but it was a success overshadowed by the alleged heaviness of losses, specifically those incurred by the 2nd Marine Division on Tarawa. In truth, a total of 3,301 casualties on Tarawa was light in terms of the overall numbers employed in this operation: the public outcry on this score reflected both an unreasonable expectation and the fact that to date in the Pacific war American casualties had been unconscionably light. In very large measure, the problems that attached themselves to the Tarawa endeavour stemmed from a number of planning errors and the fact that this was the first set-piece amphibious assault undertaken by American forces in the war: the subsequent campaign in the Marshalls, 31 January – 4 February 1944, was to demonstrate vastly improved technique, most obviously in terms of close air and fire support. Such was the ease with which Kwajalein was secured that uncommitted forces were moved forward to secure Eniwetok on 17 February.

Tarawa, November 1943. The first major assault landing conducted by American forces, the offensive in the Gilberts was noted for errors of planning without due allowance for water depths and exits from beaches and by inadequate fire support. None the less by the time of the offensive in the Marshalls, and with more escort carriers becoming available for the close support role, most of the deficiencies that marred Operation Galvanic had been remedied.

This second demand was resisted by a navy high command that argued that no offensive into the western Pacific could be developed without clearing the island groups of the central Pacific, and that there could be no offensive from the south-west Pacific inside the line of the Carolines and Marianas that left the Japanese in possession of these islands. The logic of this argument was unanswerable, and the wonder of South West Pacific Command's demand was that it was ever seriously considered. But, inevitably, even in success the central Pacific priority had to make certain concessions: whether the Philippines were to be cleared or bypassed was not resolved; the Marianas argument was underpinned by the decision to stage a future strategic bombing offensive in the islands; and the Pacific Fleet's carriers would support the Aitape–Hollandia operation on New Guinea. But what was more immediately relevant, confirmation of the central Pacific priority was attended by the decision to bypass rather than attempt to take Truk. The carrier force was thus freed for offensive operations throughout the central Pacific. The occupation of Eniwetok took place on the same day that the carrier force struck Truk in a raid anticipated by the Imperial Navy and which it knew, given the losses of its carrier air groups and cruiser force at Rabaul, it could not resist. The main Japanese fleet units had been withdrawn to the Palaus and thence to Singapore or the home islands, ruining Japanese strategic intention in the process. With no fleet at Truk to provide support, Japanese formations at Aitape and Hollandia were overwhelmed by the American forces which landed on 22 April after six major Allied bombing raids between 30 March and 16 April had destroyed 351 Japanese aircraft in these areas. Such was the extent of success that American forces were able to move against Arare on 17 May and Wakde the next day.

OPPOSITE: *A Liberator of the VII Air Force over Kwajalein in October 1944. Compare the US installations with those of the Japanese on 31 January 1944 and after bombardment, 3 February.*

VOUGHT F4U-2 CORSAIR

First flown in May 1940, the Corsair was superior to most land-based fighters. Various problems delayed deliveries until mid 1942 and ensured that first deployment was to shore-based squadrons. Ultimately deployed to carriers, the Corsair saw service as a fighter, night-fighter and fighter-bomber.

ABOVE TOP: *Kwajalein, 31 January 1944.*
ABOVE BOTTOM: *Kwajalein, 3 February 1944.*

These efforts compromised Japanese strategic intentions and plans that were being recast even as American preparations for the Arare/Wakde landings were put in hand. The loss of Hollandia exposed Japanese holdings around Sarmi when it was the Japanese intention to hold this area as part of their main line of resistance in the south-west and central Pacific. Accordingly, the Japanese revised their plans to ensure that their main defensive effort was made on the Vogelkop, Sarmi being held as a forward base. However, the equivalent of one of two divisions dispatched to New Guinea was lost at sea off north-east Celebes on 6 May. As a result, the Japanese high command on the 9th designated Halmahera in the Indies and Sorong as the new centres of resistance in this theatre. In effect, the Japanese ceded a thousand miles of coastline in seventeen days, but to no real purpose or effect. No individual or group of positions, whether in western New Guinea or the Indies, could be sustained in the face of assault. Moreover, because the Imperial Navy recognized that its carrier force could not hope to meet its American counterpart on an equal basis, the conferring of a *ne plus ultra* status on the Guinea–Truk–Marianas line went hand-in-hand with the intention to use shore-based air power to balance accounts. By holding certain bases and using shore- and carrier-based air formations to complement one another, the Japanese high command anticipated that it would be able to give battle on the basis of equality when the Americans moved against the Palaus. In reality, the only real chance the Japanese had of meeting the Americans on an equal footing was if the US attacked the Palaus without striking Japanese air bases on either or both flanks. There was no good reason for the Americans to move against the Palaus without first eliminating these air bases, most obviously those in the Marianas. American operations in

The American move against Japanese islands was notable for modest but cumulatively important losses inflicted on Japanese air strength and shipping. Kwajalein was a major Japanese air and submarine base: the raid of 5 December 1943 by groups numbering three fleet and two light fleet carriers resulted in the destruction of five naval transports of 24,190 tons and fifty-five Japanese aircraft.

LEFT: *Admiral Richmond Kelly Turner, amphibious task force commander in operations in the central Pacific.*
RIGHT: *Vice Admiral Ozawa Jisaburo. Generally regarded as one of the Imperial Navy's best junior admirals in the early stages of the war, Ozawa's misfortune was to be dealt a losing hand by the time he reached command. His carrier force was out-fought at the Philippine Sea and played the sacrificial role at Leyte: he was one of the very few admirals of any navy to have preserved his reputation despite having had two flagships sunk under him.*

February and March, and then against Hollandia, underlined their ability to isolate and overcome any garrison and base before Japanese naval and land-based air forces could intervene in their defence.

The battle of the Philippine Sea

With the Marianas the main American objective, the next phase of operations opened with the 41st US Infantry Division's landings on Biak Island, New Guinea, on 27 May. At the same time heavy fighting was taking place on the mainland around Arare and Toem in the aftermath of the Wakde landing. Despite having chosen Halmahera as its main centre of resistance and thereby tacitly having written off Biak, the Imperial Navy somehow convinced itself that it could fight its 'decisive battle' in defence of Biak. Its attempts to do so were both halting and, in light of the seriousness of its intention, somewhat bizarre. By the time the Japanese were able to gather adequate forces for even a minor effort at Biak, the Americans showed their hand with the start of carrier operations that neutralized Japanese air power in the Marianas and isolated these islands from any possibility of effective support from the Bonins. On 15 June American forces came ashore on Saipan. By dusk on the 22nd the whole of the southern part of the island, with the exception of one headland, had been cleared. With the capture of Garapan on 2 July generally regarded as marking the final phase of operations on Saipan, the island was declared secure on the

OPPOSITE: *Landings on Cape Sansapor on 31 July 1944 completed the American advance along the northern coast of New Guinea from Huon Gulf in just eleven months and carried the war to the eastern Indies and southern Philippines.*

9th. Guam was assaulted on 21 July, Tinian on the 24th and both islands were secured within a month. Their being cleared, and the whole of the southern Marianas being secured, was the product of a supremacy established when the Japanese attempt to contest the landings on Saipan was broken in the battle of the Philippine Sea on 19/20 June.

The battle of the Philippine Sea was one of two major battles between June and October 1944 marred by controversies which obscured the fact that in both actions the Americans secured overwhelming victories. In the case of the battle of June 1944, the American carrier force won a three-fold victory. By fighting defensively and *en masse*, American carrier air groups annihilated their opposite numbers to the extent that the Japanese carrier air groups were never reconstituted before the end of the war. No less importantly, off Saipan the American carrier task forces secured overwhelming advantage in terms of position and timing relative to the campaign on the Marianas. In addition, the Americans won a forward base for operations into the western Pacific from which a bombing campaign against the home islands could be staged.

Against these realities of numbers, position and time, the escape of the bulk

A dead Japanese soldier and a destroyed tank in northern Saipan in late June 1944. The Americans declared Saipan secure on 9 July after a defence by a 32,000-strong garrison that died almost to the last man. Some 22,000 Japanese civilians on the island killed themselves rather than be taken captive.

AIR RAID OVER SAIPAN

The landings on Saipan, 15 June, were the largest undertaken by the US Navy thus far in the war: the 551 ships of TF42 put ashore 67,451 men on the island. Fire support was provided by 7 battleships, 11 cruisers, 8 escort carriers and 38 destroyers. The covering force, which was to fight and win the battle in the Philippine Sea, mustered 7 fleet and 8 light carriers, 7 fast battleships, 21 cruisers and 97 destroyers.

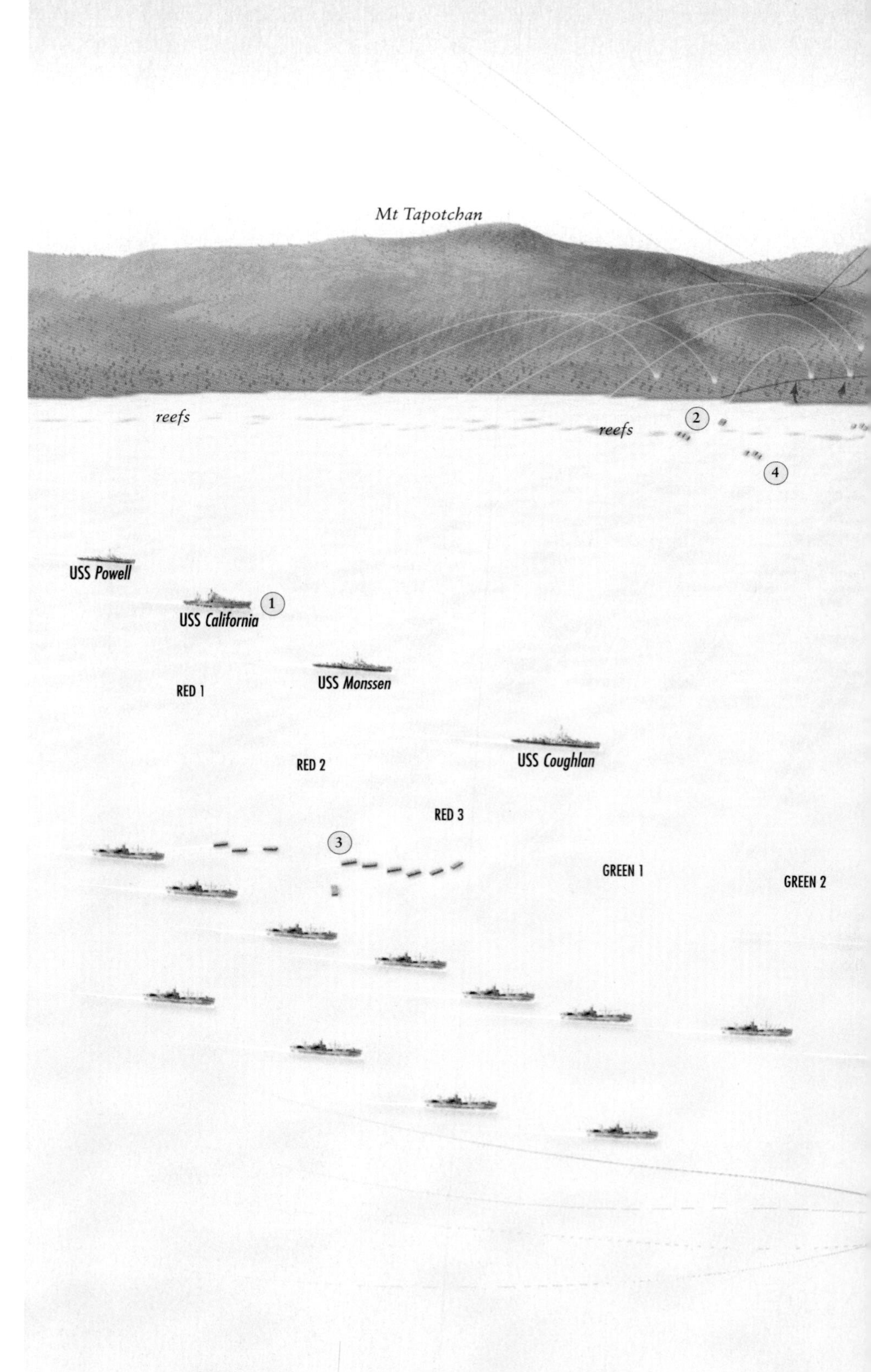

(1) 15 June, 4 am: Warships bombard Japanese positions and roads leading to Kanoa beach

(2) 5.42 am: landings begin

(3) Amphibious support vehicles disembark from landing ships

(4) Four support gunboats approach the beach followed by further landing ships and craft at approximately 8 minute intervals. By just after 9.00 am 8,000 marines are on shore

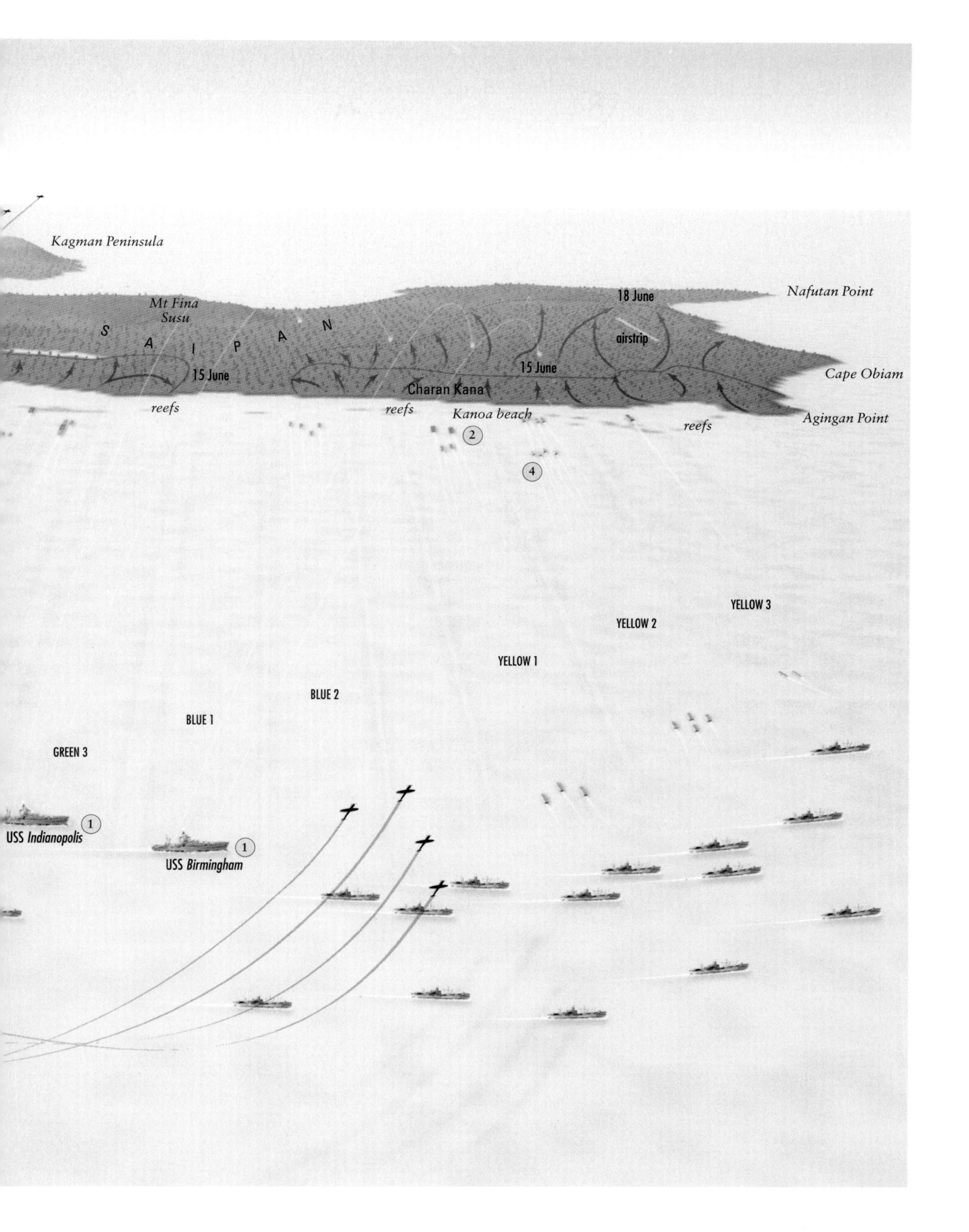
Kagman Peninsula
Mt Fina Susu
SAIPAN
15 June
reefs
Charan Kana
reefs
Kanoa beach
2
4
15 June
18 June
airstrip
Nafutan Point
Cape Obiam
reefs
Agingan Point
YELLOW 3
YELLOW 2
YELLOW 1
BLUE 2
BLUE 1
GREEN 3
1
USS Indianapolis
1
USS Birmingham

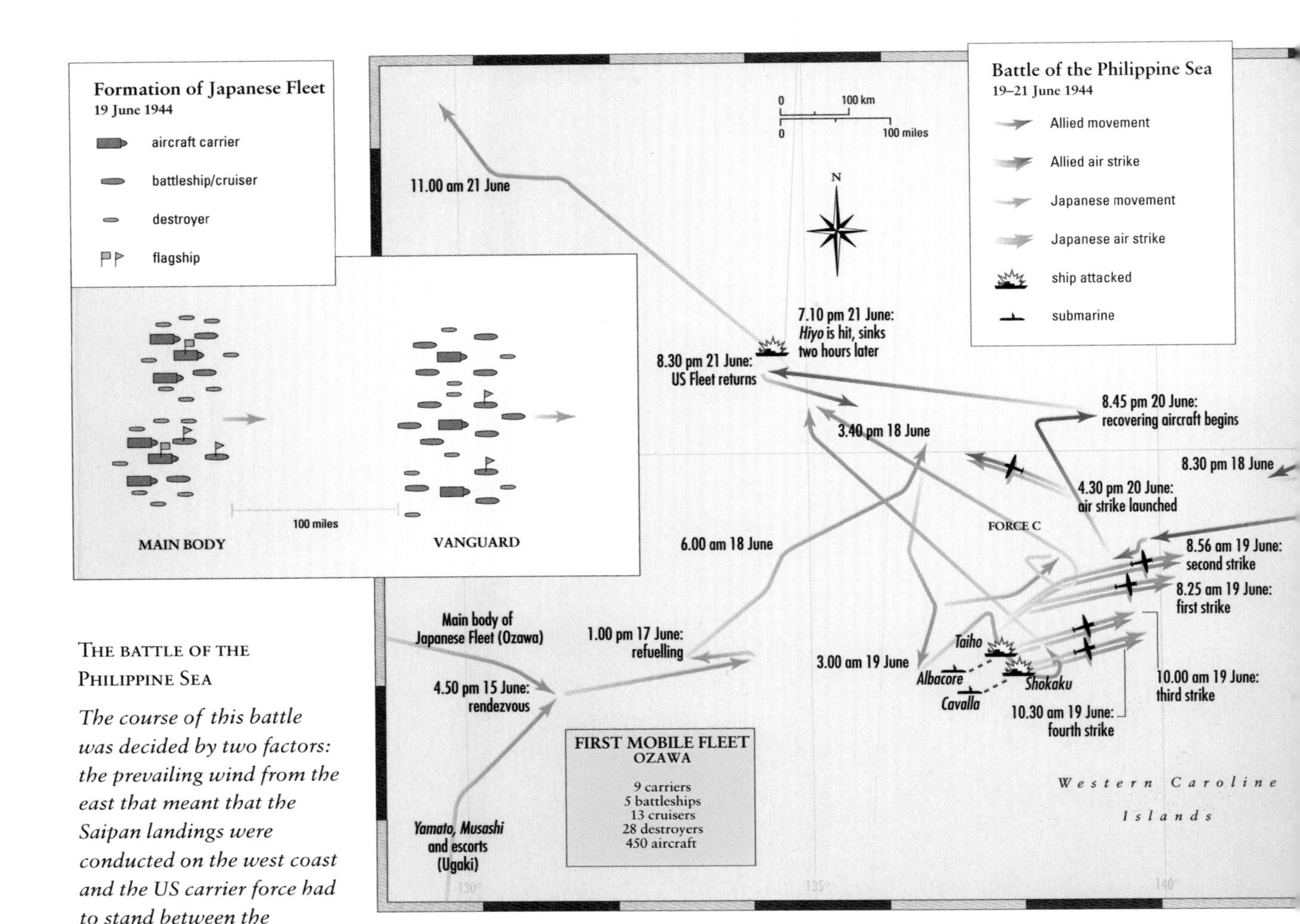

THE BATTLE OF THE PHILIPPINE SEA

The course of this battle was decided by two factors: the prevailing wind from the east that meant that the Saipan landings were conducted on the west coast and the US carrier force had to stand between the amphibious forces and the approaching Japanese. With reconnaissance aircraft of superior range, the Japanese carrier groups were able to strike at the Americans while their own carriers were invulnerable to air attack: none the less the Japanese lost two carriers to submarine attack during the course of their offensive operations. By standing on the defensive and concentrating their fighters to meet incoming Japanese attacks, the Americans fought and won a defensive victory that was overwhelming: Japanese carrier air groups were never reconstituted in the remainder of the war.

of the Japanese carrier force was of no very great consequence, and in any event much of the criticism of the American conduct of operations that allegedly allowed the Japanese task forces to escape was misconceived on two counts. The extent of Japanese carrier losses was not known at the time and, with three fleet carriers – the *Shokaku*, the *Taiho* and the *Hiyo* – sunk, was much more serious than was anticipated. In addition, given that in this battle the Japanese held the advantage of position because American forces could not close unless allowed to do so, the success recorded on 19/20 June was probably as much as could be reasonably expected.

The day when American forces came ashore on Saipan (15 June 1944) was also the day of the first strategic bombing raid on the Japanese home islands conducted by American land-based heavy bombers, previous raids on the outlying Kuriles excepted. The attack on the steel works at Yawata on Kyushu was staged from bases within China. Given the fact that the first American bomber operations within China were in March 1943 and by November had reached as far as Indo-China, Hainan and Formosa, the various developments that ran parallel to the twin drives across the Pacific demand proper

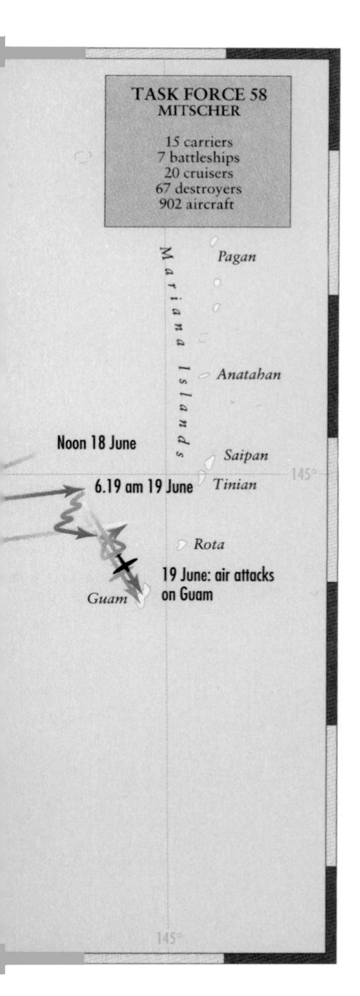

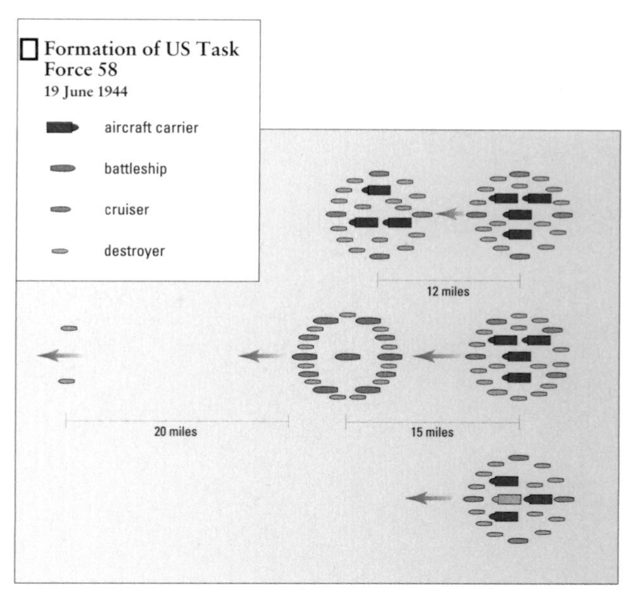

The very symbol of victory. Astern of the fleet carrier Essex *are the light carrier* Langley, *the fleet carrier* Ticonderoga *and the battleships* Washington, North Carolina *and* South Dakota. *In company were four cruisers and eighteen destroyers. TG 38.3 was about to enter Ulithi, 23 November 1944.*

In order to take the war to Japanese home waters the US Navy had to keep its fleets at sea for periods unknown since the passing of sail: the Okinawa campaign, for example, involved the carrier force being at sea continuously between 14 March and 13 June. This was only possible by a vast logistical tail across the whole of the Pacific in order to ensure the supply, effectiveness and morale of main forces. Here, an LST, built in Chicago, is photographed passing bombs to the fleet carrier Hancock.

consideration at this point. The American endeavour in China set in train a series of events that were to result in the American diplomatic débâcle that coincided with the devastating victory in the battle of Leyte Gulf. As it was, on 15 June 1944 on the continental mainland, it was Japan that stood on the brink of both a victory and a defeat: a victory throughout southern China, the last Japanese victory of the war and one, like all the others since 1937, which availed Japan nothing; and a defeat in north-east India and Burma that was all but total and overwhelming.

The Burma Campaign

The defeat on the Indian sub-continent had its origins in the events of 1942–3, specifically the shared British and Japanese view that offensive operations across the mountains that formed the border between Burma and India had little to recommend them. Without any means to undertake a major offensive, in the November 1942 – May 1943 campaigning season, the British undertook what was to become known as the First Arakan offensive, in which the equivalent of two divisions were totally outfought and suffered humiliating defeat at the hands of two Japanese regiments. At the same time, however, the

British infiltrated raiding columns into the Myitkyina–Mandalay area in an operation that achieved in newspaper inches infinitely more than it ever recorded on the ground. In real terms this operation achieved nothing of any significance other than pushing the local Japanese command into consideration of a spoiling offensive into India: given the certainty of eventual British superiority in this theatre, a Japanese defensive policy could only postpone defeat. Thus with the 1943–4 dry season, the Japanese Burma Area Army opened a two-part offensive effort, a diversionary attack in the Arakan by one division drawn from the 28th Army, and the main effort, by three divisions from the 15th Army, on the Kalewa–Homalin sector that was to reach Imphal and Kohima by late March and early April 1944 respectively. But despite being able to surround both places the Japanese found their offensive stalled for two reasons: this time, there was no general British withdrawal when outflanked as there had been in 1942 and 1943, and air transport allowed isolated British forces to be reinforced and supported so that the Japanese formations

Cutting Japanese lines of supply in Burma: a detachment preparing to blow up a rail bridge during the first Chindit operation in the Myitkyina–Mandalay area, February–March 1943. This operation registered only temporary inconvenience but was a factor in the process that led to the Japanese army undertaking its ill-considered 'March on Delhi' in 1944.

THE RECONQUEST OF BURMA

Facing three Allied offensives, the Japanese planned to fight the main defensive battle around Mandalay. The British response was to conduct a series of landings in the Arakan and to make the main offensive effort below Mandalay. The Japanese attempt to respond to the latter resulted in their being forced into two major actions at Mandalay and Myitkyina: their defeat at both exposed the whole of Burma to reconquest in the 1944–5 season.

surrounding them paradoxically found themselves besieged. Japanese success depended on the capture of supplies, and their refusal to admit failure resulted in the destruction of Japanese formations in front of Imphal and Kohima over the next three months. While Kohima was relieved as early as 18 April, the Japanese siege of Imphal was not broken until 22 June, by which time they had lost two-thirds of the force of 85,000 men with which they had entered India.

What made the Japanese defeat in north-east India worse was the fact that the campaign unfolded at the same time as two other offensives within this theatre, a Sino-American thrust into upper Burma, specifically directed through the Hukawng, Mogaung and Irrawaddy valleys against Myitkyina and the 18th Infantry Division, and a Chinese offensive on the upper Salween River. The first effort was closely fought, and resulted in the capture of the airfield at Myitkyina on 17 May and of Kamaing one month later, although the town of Myitkyina was not taken until 3 August. On the Salween the understrength 56th Infantry

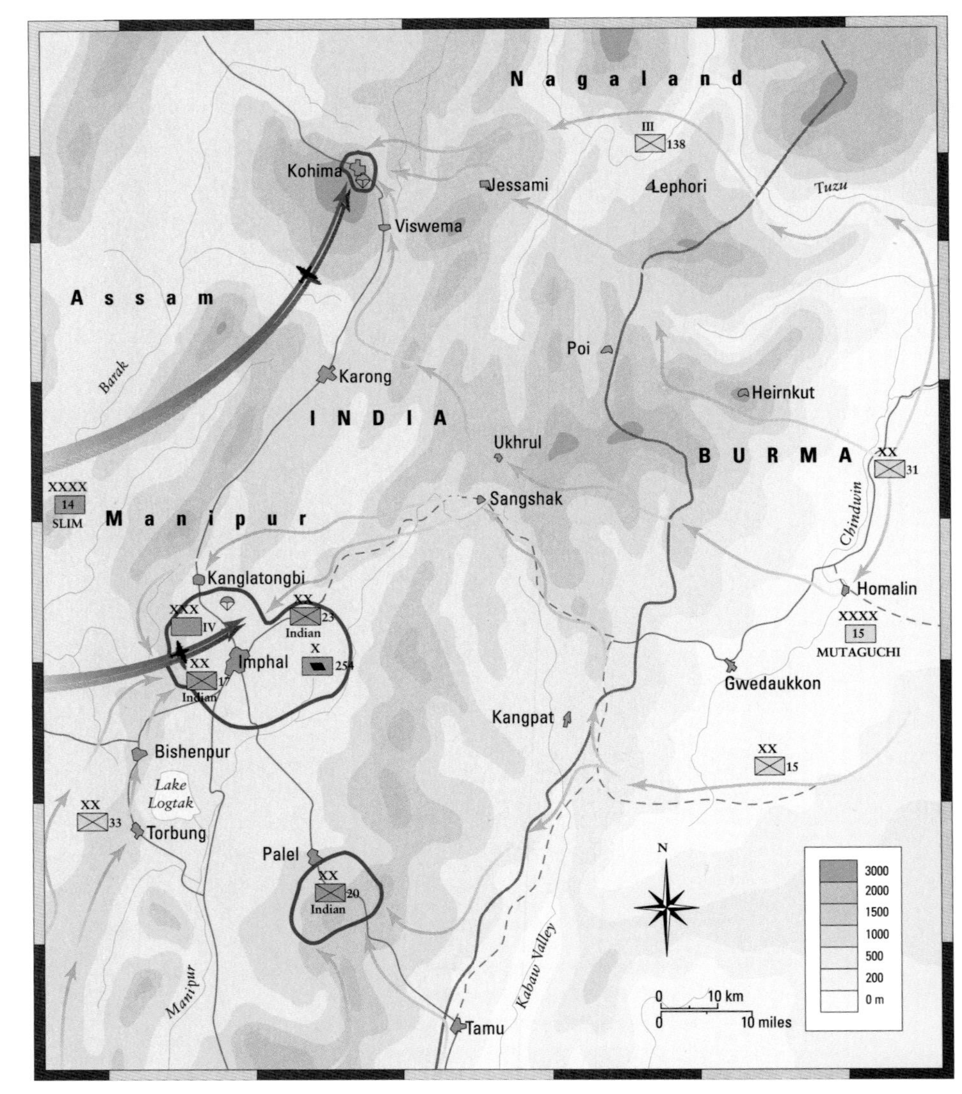

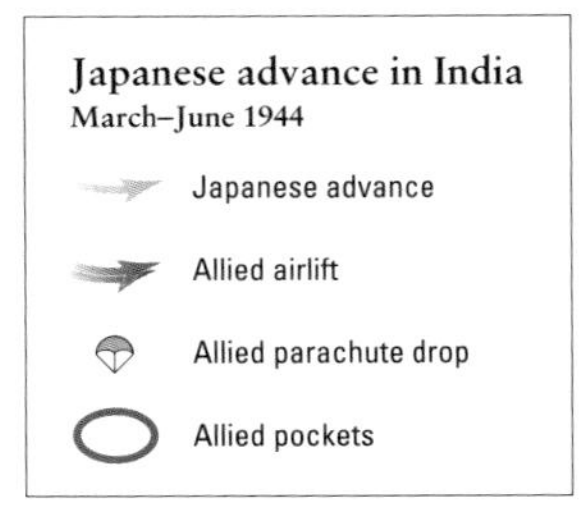

THE MARCH ON DELHI

After a successful though costly holding operation in the Arakan, the main Japanese offensive in 1944 narrowly missed trapping major British forces south of Imphal before reaching forward to Kohima and Imphal. The Japanese effort at Kohima was broken inside a couple of weeks but at Imphal a four-month siege was conducted with British forces sustained by air supply: the Japanese refusal to admit defeat in front of Imphal compromised their ability to offer a serious and sustained defence of Burma in 1945.

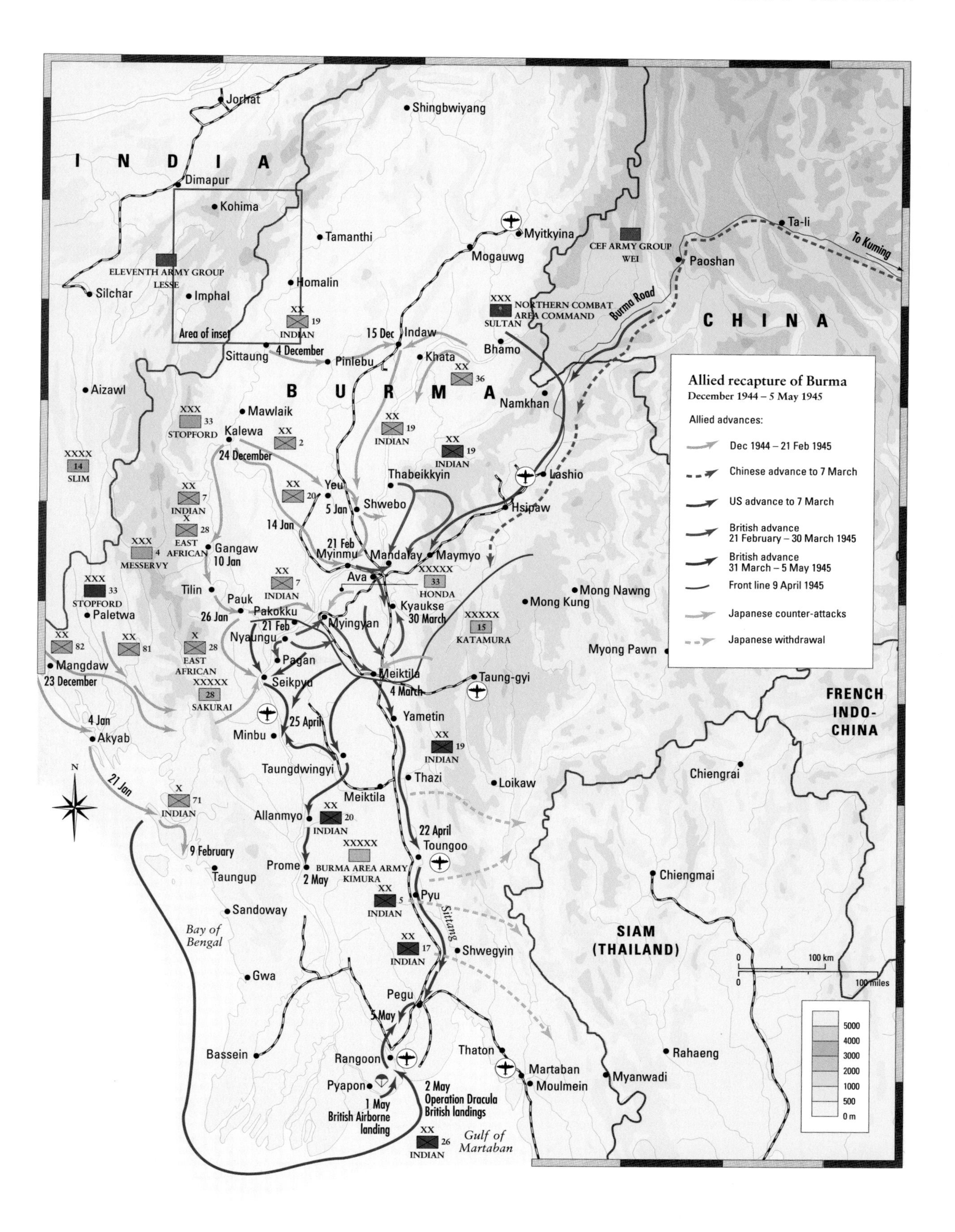

Allied recapture of Burma
December 1944 – 5 May 1945
Allied advances:
Dec 1944 – 21 Feb 1945
Chinese advance to 7 March
US advance to 7 March
British advance 21 February – 30 March 1945
British advance 31 March – 5 May 1945
Front line 9 April 1945
Japanese counter-attacks
Japanese withdrawal
I N D I A
B U R M A
C H I N A
SIAM (THAILAND)
FRENCH INDO-CHINA
Jorhat
Shingbwiyang
Dimapur
Kohima
Tamanthi
Myitkyina
Mogauwg
CEF ARMY GROUP WEI
Ta-li
To Kuming
Paoshan
ELEVENTH ARMY GROUP LESSE
Silchar
Imphal
Homalin
NORTHERN COMBAT AREA COMMAND SULTAN
Burma Road
Area of inset
19 INDIAN
15 Dec
Indaw
Bhamo
Sittaung
4 December
Pinlebu
Khata
36
Namkhan
Aizawl
Mawlaik
33 STOPFORD
Kalewa
2
19 INDIAN
14 SLIM
24 December
Thabeikkyin
Lashio
Yeu
5 Jan
Shwebo
Hsipaw
7 INDIAN
20
28 EAST AFRICAN
14 Jan
4 MESSERVY
Gangaw
10 Jan
21 Feb
Myinmu
Mandalay
Maymyo
Ava
33 HONDA
Mong Nawng
Tilin
7 INDIAN
Mong Kung
33 STOPFORD
Paletwa
Pauk
26 Jan
Pakokku
21 Feb
Kyaukse
30 March
15 KATAMURA
Myingyan
Nyaungu
82
81
28 EAST AFRICAN
Myong Pawn
Mangdaw
23 December
Pagan
Meiktila
Taung-gyi
Seikpyu
28 SAKURAI
4 March
4 Jan
Akyab
25 April
Yametin
Minbu
19 INDIAN
Chiengrai
Taungdwingyi
Thazi
Loikaw
21 Jan
71 INDIAN
Meiktila
Allanmyo
20 INDIAN
22 April
Toungoo
9 February
BURMA AREA ARMY KIMURA
Prome
2 May
Taungup
Chiengmai
5 INDIAN
Pyu
Sandoway
Sittang
Bay of Bengal
17 INDIAN
Shwegyin
Gwa
Pegu
5 May
Bassein
Rangoon
Thaton
Martaban
Moulmein
Myanwadi
Rahaeng
Pyapon
1 May British Airborne landing
2 May Operation Dracula British landings
26 INDIAN
Gulf of Martaban
0 100 km
0 100 miles
5000
4000
3000
2000
1000
500
0 m
N

Division, part of the Japanese 33rd Army, was able to fight a series of very successful rearguard actions that denied a force of some 72,000 Chinese troops control of Ku-feng and Chiang-chu until 19/20 June, and it was not until September that the Chinese were able to secure Tengchung. By that time the Japanese had survived the immediate crisis in Burma, albeit at a very heavy price. The Imphal–Kohima attack cost the Japanese the means and opportunity to meet the Myitkyina and Salween offensives: defeat at Imphal–Kohima denied the Japanese the means to defend Burma in 1945 because the losses incurred in 1944 could not be replaced. In seeking to insure themselves against defeat by an offensive in 1944, the Japanese ensured their own defeat in a defensive battle in 1945.

As the tide of war turned against them Japanese military formations found themselves committed to the defensive with no real addition to their strength compared to the period 1941–2 when various matériel *weaknesses were disguised by possession of the initiative and local superiority of force.*

But what added a special significance to these events was the Chinese dimension. In the Myitkyina offensive Chinese divisions performed very respectably, but on the Salween the Chinese performance was at best indifferent. Moreover, the Salween offensive was undertaken by the Chungking authorities only after intense American pressure, Washington for the first time tiring of Nationalist procrastination and evasion. The American threat to suspend aid forced Chungking's hand and the Japanese invasion of Honan province in April exacerbated the situation still further. In a little more than a month the Japanese were able to secure the Chengchow–Hankow line and thereby open a direct supply line between Peking and Yoyang, by which stage the main Japanese effort, staged from the Ichang–Yoyang area against Changsha and

Aerial resupply was the key to Chindit survival, but this was small change compared to the efforts made to insure British forces against defeat in the Arakan, Imphal and Kohima when supply aircraft were diverted to Burma from the Mediterranean. The advance from the Chindwin almost to Rangoon was made possible only by supply aircraft.

ABOVE: *General Sir William Slim, commander of the British 14th Army, with Air Vice Marshal S. F. Vincent, Air Commanding-in-Chief No. 224 Group in Burma, in 1945. The air forces in India and Burma tended to be 'the forgotten air forces', but their operations were critical to Allied success.*

RIGHT: *Seemingly at a loss for something vitriolic to say, Lieutenant General Joseph Stilwell on the banks of the Tanai in northern Burma. Clearing the Japanese from this area was the first step in the move into the Hukawng valley, completed by late January 1944.*

Hengyang with formations from the 1st and 12th Armies, was about to begin.

This offensive began on 27 May (the same day Biak Island was invaded) and from the outset seemed to have a hypnotic, paralysing effect upon Chungking's armies. Changsha fell on 16 June after token resistance, and Hengyang was assaulted on the 28th, but here the Japanese were frustrated by Chinese commanders of ability and independence of thought that rendered them anathema to Chungking. Hengyang finally fell on 8 August without the Nationalist regime making any effort to relieve it. Thereafter, the Japanese offensive was resumed, though much of its pace had been lost, and it was not until November that Kweilin and Liuchow were taken. With Japanese forces from coastal enclaves and in northern Indo-China joining the offensive, Tokyo was able to announce gains that had resulted in the establishment of uninterrupted overland communications between Manchoutikuo and Singapore on 28 November, though in effect this counted for nothing. Without the means to establish secure rail communications, the whole of the Japanese effort throughout central and southern China after April 1944 was effort wasted. These gains, plus other minor acquisitions that were made after December 1944 with the Japanese occupation of Tushan and Tuyun, were relinquished in spring and summer 1945 as Japanese forces in China were thinned in order to provide for the defence of Manchoutikuo. The Soviet Union's declaration in April 1945 that it would not renew the 1941 non-aggression treaty when it expired was taken to mean Soviet intervention in the autumn, hence the transience of whatever success Operation Ichi-Go commanded.

The events on the Salween river and throughout central and southern China provoked a double crisis for the Chungking regime, both with the United States and domestically. The defeats of 1944 could not be dismissed lightly since the situation was very different from the one that had prevailed in the previous period of defeat, 1937–8. In 1944 China was not without allies. She had armies that had been well supplied, and possessed in Chiang Kai-shek a leader who claimed and was afforded international stature and whose legitimacy in large measure rested upon national resistance to the invader. Such resistance was conspicuously lacking in 1944, and the collapse in certain parts of central and southern China was

Inseparable from the nickname 'The Peanut' given him by Stilwell, Chiang Kai-shek is seen here seeking to inspire the Chinese people.

marked by the massacre of fleeing Nationalist troops by enraged local populations who for years had been subjected to Nationalist corruption and incompetence. Nationalist passivity and evasion of military responsibility had reaped its inevitable result by 1944, with a government and military that was largely incapable of offering either effective, honest administration, or any form of serious resistance to the Japanese. It was in such circumstances that Washington wholly misjudged the situation. In July the Roosevelt administration demanded that Chiang Kai-shek's American chief of staff be vested with command of all Nationalist forces. The Americans, however, refused

The Pacific Situation 1944

By 1944 the US Navy had such carrier and amphibious strength that it could sustain a dual offensive across the Pacific. The Japanese were forced to give battle for the Marianas and then the Philippines. Until mid 1944 American policy favoured bypassing Luzon, but in the event the landings in Leyte were the prelude to a major campaign in the islands.

'I shall return.' The return of General MacArthur to the Philippines at Leyte, October 1944. On MacArthur's left is his chief of staff, Lieutenant General Richard Sutherland: eighth from the left is Colonel Carlos Romula, who made his name in 1942 as a broadcaster from the Philippines. Precedence and etiquette should have decreed that the person leading the party was Sergio Osmena, president of the commonwealth of the Philippines, seen here on the left.

to consider ending aid to Chungking or to seek Chiang's removal from the scene. In such circumstances Chiang's refusal to accede to the American demand and his insistence on the recall of Washington's would-be commander in China could have only one result: American acquiescence at the end of October 1944, in the last days before the presidential election in the United States and at the same time as the Americans fought and won the battle of Leyte Gulf. In effect, Washington was rendered the prisoner of Chungking for the remainder of the war.

American strategy and Japanese shipping

It has already been noted that the American victory in the Philippine Sea exposed the whole of the Japanese position in the western Pacific to further American advances, and this, plus the fact that

Tokyo was brought within range of American heavy bombers based in the Marianas, marked the end of the Pacific war in positional terms: the fall in July of the Tojo administration that had taken Japan to war in 1941 was tantamount to recognition of this fact. But victory off, over and in the Marianas brought to Washington the problems of choice in the future prosecution of the war, and three factors were critically important here. First, the basic idea of an advance across the Pacific in order to effect a landing in China to join with Chinese Nationalist forces died with the events of spring and summer 1944 in China, and with it wavered the priority afforded the capture of Formosa. Second, in summer 1944 the American high command moved from the premise that an invasion of the Japanese home islands *might* be necessary to the conclusion that the invasion of the home islands would have to be undertaken. It therefore became clear that the possession of bases in the western Pacific from which to stage landings would be essential. Third, the South West Pacific Command's insistence upon the reconquest/liberation of the Philippines, rather than bypassing the islands, had a singleness and simplicity of purpose that alternatives lacked. In the immediate aftermath of the battle of the Philippine Sea, the US Navy considered the suggestion of an immediate move against Okinawa which was all but undefended at that time. It may be that in securing Guam and Tinian the US Navy passed up the very real opportunity of taking Iwo Jima without undue difficulty, but the lack of any clear priority for the navy meant that the army-backed Philippines option was endorsed and accelerated in September once the extent of Japanese weakness in these islands was realized.

Thus were resolved American priorities and timetable, and the irony of the

JAPANESE SHIPPING LOSSES BETWEEN MARCH 1943 AND NOVEMBER 1944

The quickening pace of the war against shipping is shown by losses that all but tripled between the period March–October 1943 and July–November 1944. What is also significant about the figures is the impact of service shipping losses in the period November 1943 – June 1944 and the massive inroads made into Japanese resources by carrier aircraft after November 1943.

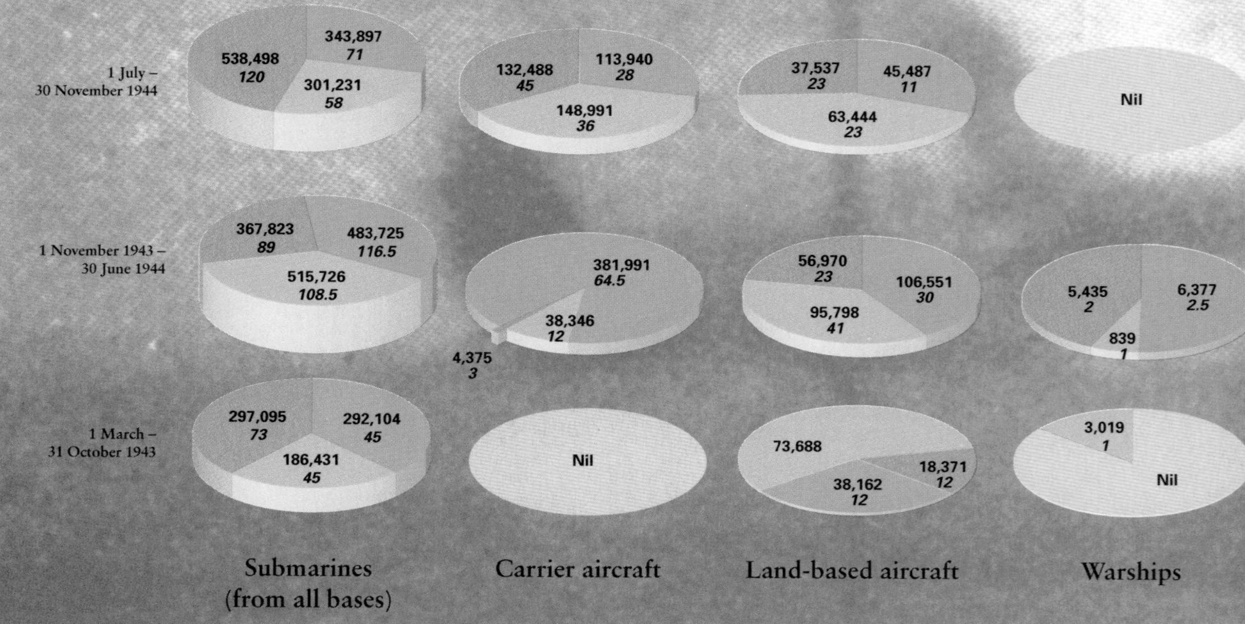

process has been noted elsewhere: the endorsement of a US Army agenda came on the back of operations on the part of the US Navy, the scale and scope of which represented something that was new in the conduct of war at sea: not since the age of sail had a fleet been able to conduct sustained operations continuously into waters nominally controlled by its enemy, though this aspect of operations was only one part of the significance of this foray. The other part has been but seldom acknowledged, and it relates directly to the campaign against Japanese shipping.

In setting out the story of the destruction of Japanese shipping, the creation of an escort command by the Imperial Navy in November 1943 – with the princely total of eleven ageing destroyers, sixteen escort destroyers and four gunboats under command – holds a special place, albeit for a somewhat perverse reason. The Japanese implementation of convoy without any understanding of the principles of convoy and without adequate numbers to provide proper escorts has been generally regarded as critical in ensuring increased, not reduced, losses. There is no disputing the general point, at least not in the long term: with many Japanese convoys being afforded only one or two escorts of very uncertain quality, the introduction of convoy concentrated targets without making any provision for a commensurate increase for their defence. But a very careful analysis of Japanese shipping losses in the months after the formation of the General Escort Command, in the period between November 1943 and June 1944, reveals that the real increase in losses was incurred not among merchantmen but by the shipping allocated to the two armed services.

Moreover, and specifically in this period between Tarawa and Saipan, even

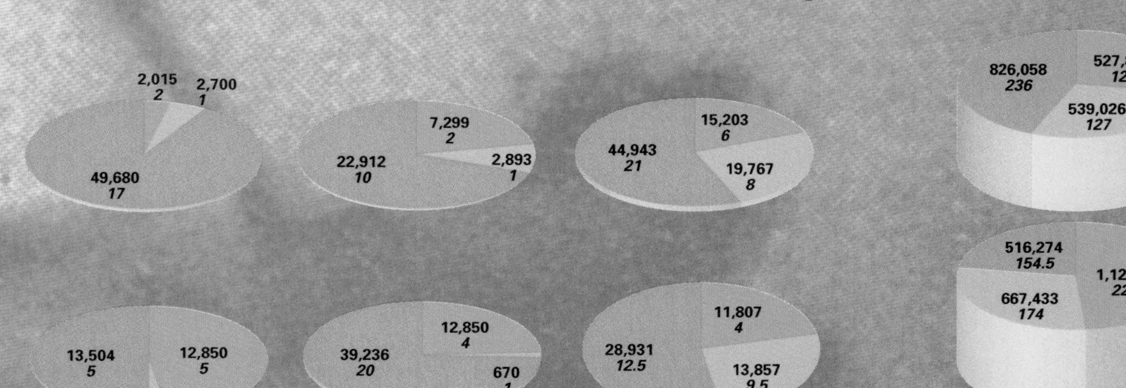

As US escort carriers withdrew from Leyte on 25 October no fewer than seven of their number were struck by kamikaze aircraft, with the result that one, the St Lo, *was sunk and four extensively damaged: the* St Lo *was hit even as a F6F Hellcat tried to land on her.*

allowing for the increase of losses incurred by the merchant marine and the very significant increase of losses in south-east Asia, the real increase of losses was not registered on routes to and from the southern resources area but in the central Pacific by service shipping. What was equally significant was that, while sinkings by submarines and land-based aircraft doubled, the real increase in Japanese losses was caused primarily by carrier aircraft in the course of main-force operations, and by submarines deployed in support of those operations rather than committed to the *guerre de course* against shipping. The same point applied to Japanese losses to carrier aircraft after June 1944, but in this period the increased toll on shipping exacted by submarines reflected their increased numbers, their operating from forward bases in the Marianas and their increasingly aggressive tactics that were in large measure the product of an awareness of American superiority in all aspects of *matériel* and training.

The story of the campaign against Japanese shipping in this phase of the

Between 25 October and 13 January 1945 144 ships were hit by kamikazes with 19 sunk and 70 damaged extensively: 3 fleet carriers were forced to withdraw from the battle. Off Okinawa, of 525 US warships in action 22 were sunk and 254 incurred some form of damage with another 14 landing craft and auxiliaries sunk and another 117 damaged.

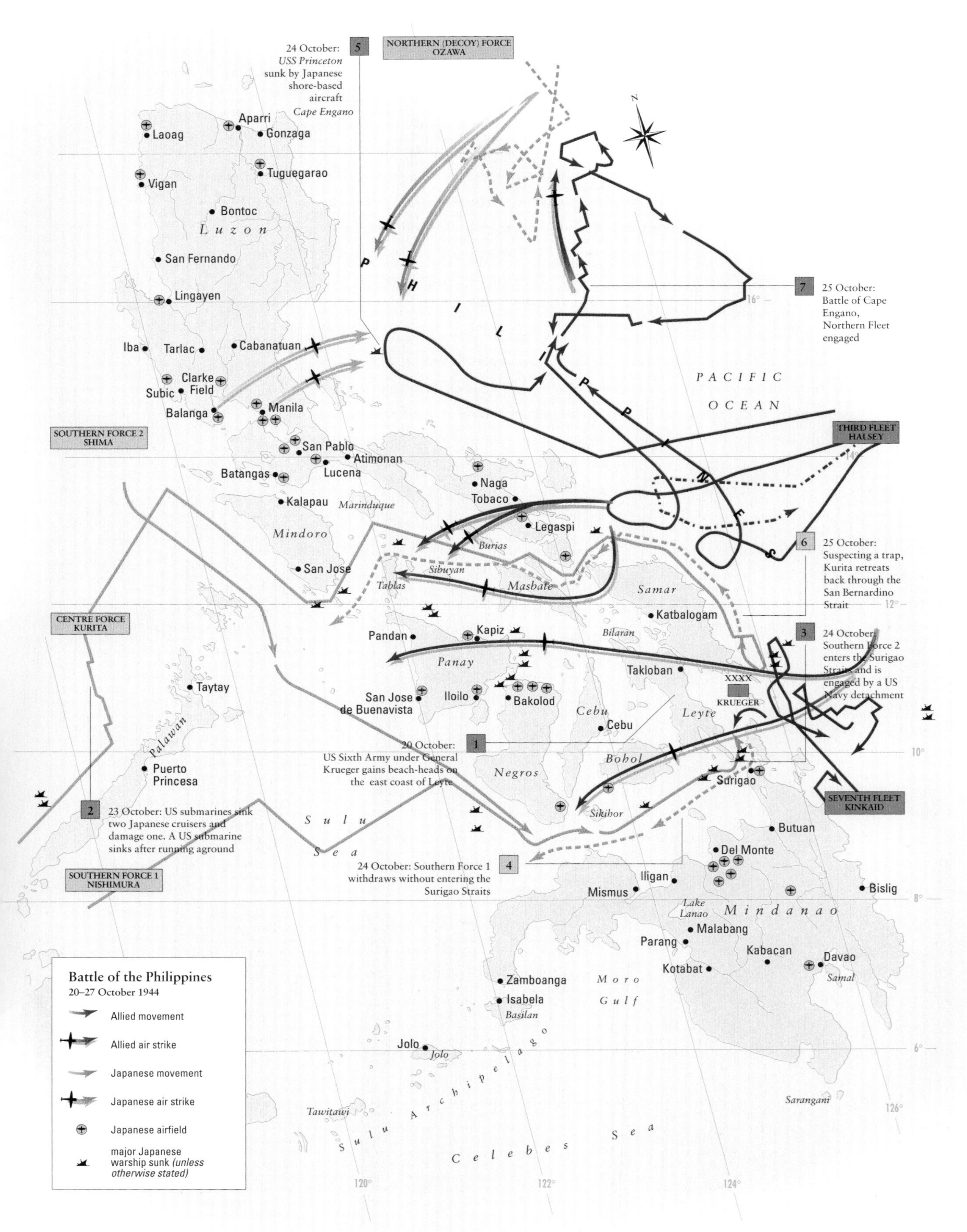
24 October: USS Princeton sunk by Japanese shore-based aircraft Cape Engano
5
NORTHERN (DECOY) FORCE OZAWA
7
25 October: Battle of Cape Engano, Northern Fleet engaged
SOUTHERN FORCE 2 SHIMA
THIRD FLEET HALSEY
6
25 October: Suspecting a trap, Kurita retreats back through the San Bernardino Strait
CENTRE FORCE KURITA
3
24 October: Southern Force 2 enters the Surigao Straits and is engaged by a US Navy detachment
XXXX
KRUEGER
1
20 October: US Sixth Army under General Krueger gains beach-heads on the east coast of Leyte
SEVENTH FLEET KINKAID
2
23 October: US submarines sink two Japanese cruisers and damage one. A US submarine sinks after running aground
SOUTHERN FORCE 1 NISHIMURA
4
24 October: Southern Force 1 withdraws without entering the Surigao Straits
PHILIPPINES
PACIFIC OCEAN
Laoag
Aparri
Gonzaga
Vigan
Tuguegarao
Bontoc
Luzon
San Fernando
Lingayen
Iba
Tarlac
Cabanatuan
Subic
Clarke Field
Balanga
Manila
San Pablo
Atimonan
Batangas
Lucena
Naga
Tobaco
Kalapau
Marinduque
Mindoro
Legaspi
Burias
San Jose
Sibuyan
Tablas
Masbate
Samar
Katbalogam
Bilaran
Pandan
Kapiz
Panay
Takloban
Taytay
San Jose de Buenavista
Iloilo
Bakolod
Cebu
Leyte
Palawan
Cebu
Puerto Princesa
Bohol
Negros
Surigao
Sikihor
Sulu Sea
Butuan
Del Monte
Iligan
Mismus
Bislig
Lake Lanao
Mindanao
Malabang
Parang
Kabacan
Kotabat
Davao
Samal
Zamboanga
Isabela
Basilan
Moro Gulf
Jolo
Jolo
Sulu Archipelago
Tawitawi
Sarangani
Celebes Sea
16°
14°
12°
10°
8°
6°
120°
122°
124°
126°
N
Battle of the Philippines
20–27 October 1944
Allied movement
Allied air strike
Japanese movement
Japanese air strike
Japanese airfield
major Japanese warship sunk (unless otherwise stated)

war may be best related by reference to the progressive collapse of convoy routes primarily under the impact of American operations. In the space of eight months, from December 1943 until August 1944, thirteen routes were all abandoned because of the immediate military situation, but scarcely less significant were the other routes that were closed for different reasons. The direct route between the home islands and the Palaus was abandoned as early as March 1944 because of shortage of escorts, shipping instead being directed from the home islands to Formosa and thence to the Palaus in a newly initiated convoy system. The delays inherent in such an arrangement were accepted, at least until July when this route in turn had to be abandoned with shipping redirected through Manila. The direct route between Balikpapan and Manila was abandoned in June 1944 as a result of the predatory activities of American submarines in the Sulu and Celebes Seas, while October 1944 saw the Imperial Navy close the Singapore–Medan route in part because of British submarine operations in the Malacca Strait. But evidence of the increasingly desperate Japanese position was provided in August 1944 with the closing of the Takao–Hainan and Hong Kong–Hainan routes because of shipping shortages and, in the case of the former, by the need to divert what shipping was available from the iron ore trade to bauxite. With the Manila–Saigon route abandoned in September as a result of lack of escorts, the American advance into the western Pacific in summer 1944 in effect resulted in the collapse of the Japanese 'centre'. The Japanese lines of communication in the Sea of Japan and Yellow Sea and within south-east Asia remained more or less intact, and, indeed, nine such routes remained at least nominally operational until the end of the war. The problem for the Imperial Navy was the routes between the two, between the home islands and the area which supplied the natural resources vital to the Japanese war effort.

The part that American carriers played in this process can be understood by reference to four of their operations in this period. First, the raid on Truk, the main Japanese base in the central Pacific, accounted for 3 light cruisers, 3 destroyers and 5 other warships of 34,267 tons, and 33 auxiliaries and merchantmen of 199,525 tons. Second, the raid on Koror, in the Palaus, on 30 March accounted for 12 minor warships of 5,634 tons and 22 ships, all but one drawn from the services, of 126,817 tons. Third, in the operations that formed the softening-up phase prior to the battle of the Philippine Sea, carrier aircraft accounted for 5 warships of 4,741 tons and 13 transports of 45,358 tons: to these totals, moreover, have to be added 5 destroyers of 9,077 tons and 8 naval and 3 military ships of 64,920 tons that were sunk by American submarines in this same phase of operations, plus 4 submarines and a minelayer sunk by warships of the screens. Fourth, the carrier raids on the Philippines in September 1944 that prompted the decision to advance the timetable for the landing at Leyte accounted for 19 warships, 53 service ships and merchantmen of 199,854 tons, and an estimated 1,000 Japanese aircraft. In terms of destruction of

OVERLEAF: *An interesting photograph in two respects. First, airborne landings were somewhat rare during the Pacific war, but Kamiri airstrip, seized by the landing on Noemfoor on 2 July 1944, witnessed two: both jumps resulted in high casualties amid airfield equipment on the 3rd and on an already compacted runway on the 4th. The airfield received its first aircraft on 21 July. Second, the photograph is a fake, though why it should be so is unclear: there are authentic photographs of these jumps. This consists of two, probably three, obviously put together for press release.*

THE BATTLE OF LEYTE GULF

After a series of strikes in September by carrier air groups that compromised Japanese defensive capability in the islands, the US landed on Leyte. With a deployment area equivalent in size to western Europe, the Japanese committed three forces to the defence of Leyte: one was offered as bait while two forces were to move through the Visayans to attack American shipping on Leyte. The defensive battle was not well conducted, with American forces watching the Visayans withdraw even as the Japanese forces negotiated the islands: the one force that did reach Leyte Gulf was subjected to major losses as it tried to escape, after having achieved very little in the way of sinking US warships.

Once, a photograph of a carrier and the guns of a battleship would have carried clear implications of defender and defended: by 1944, however, roles had been reversed. Here the Iowa *is having a quiet word with an Essex-class newcomer fresh from the yard.*

OPPOSITE: *The Japanese Kagero-class fleet destroyer* Amatsukazi *under attack, and about to be sunk, by a B-24J Mitchell from the 345 Bombardment Group, 14th Air Force, off Amoy, southern China, 6 April 1945.*

shipping the impact and importance of carrier force operations cannot be understated, especially as the Japanese services were obliged to replace their losses by requisitioning from an already inadequate merchant marine. The only occasion when the American carriers deliberately sought out merchantmen and were not directly tied to the requirements of an assault landing was in January 1945. In the course of a ten-day rampage through the South China Sea and off the Ryukyus, carrier aircraft accounted for 58.5 service ships and merchantmen of 222,653 tons, two dozen warships being sunk *en passant*. When the sinkings of supporting submarines and warships are added to such results, the importance of main force operations as a complement to the *guerre de course* cannot be doubted. And to this point can be added another, and one which equally leaves little to doubt. In 1944 Japanese shipyards produced 1,699,000 tons of new shipping, an amount almost double the 900,000 tons assumed by Japanese pre-war planning to represent maximum output in any year. By any standard, the 1944 production represented a remarkable effort, but it was still not enough to safeguard national interest, not least because by March 1944 the amount of shipping laid up was equivalent to the 1941 projected annual

production total, or 18.96 per cent of national shipping resources. This apart, Japanese shipping production was simply set aside by the overwhelming extent of losses: in 1944 Japanese losses totalled 983 service and merchant ships of 3,937,541 tons, or nearly fourth-fifths of the shipping with which Japan began that year.

Leyte Gulf

The operations of the American carrier force outside battle is essential to an understanding of the battle of Leyte Gulf, the greatest single battle in naval history and one fought over 115,000 square miles between fleets that deployed across an area three times as large. The conventional account of the battle would exlain it in terms of two decisions, the first of which was to accelerate operations in the Philippines with the substitution of landings on Leyte in the place of those that had been planned for Mindanao: the landings at Noemfoor and Sansapor in July, on Morotai and Peleliu on 15 September, and the occupation of Ulithi on 23 September may be added to the account for good measure. The second decision, and the one on which attention had invariably concentrated in terms of the action itself, was that taken by Halsey. His decision led to the American carrier support formations in Leyte Gulf being left uncovered and subjected to attack by Japanese surface forces on 25 October when the carrier and battle forces of Halsey's 3rd Fleet were withdrawn. This attention, both in the immediate aftermath of the battle and for decades afterward, was largely muddled. The issue of divided command was paraded as explanation of the unfortunate sequence of events whereby the San Bernardino Strait was left unguarded, but this was essentially irrelevant: the issue was not command but role and responsibilities.

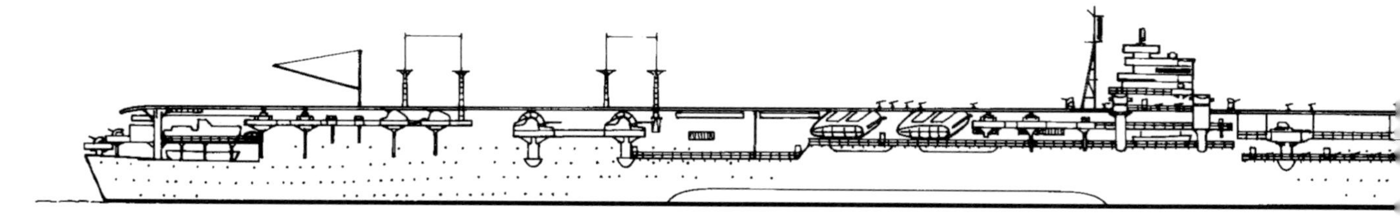

THE *ZUIKAKU*

On a full load displacement of 32,105 tons, in October 1944 the Japanese fleet carrier Zuikaku *could carry a maximum of eighty-four aircraft, a defensive armament of ninety-six 25-mm guns and six 28-barrelled rocket launchers. With a top speed of 34.25 knots, she and her sister ship* Shokaku *were the best Japanese carriers to be built. The* Shokaku *was sunk by a submarine in the Philippine Sea, the* Zuikaku *by carrier aircraft off Cape Engano during the Leyte action.*

The battle itself is generally considered in terms of 24–25 October, yet the real significance of Leyte is not simply what happened in the four days of the overall battle between the 23rd and 26th – when the fleet carrier *Zuikaku*, the light fleet carriers *Chitose*, *Chiyoda* and *Zuiho*, the battleships *Musashi*, *Fuso* and *Ymashiro*, 6 heavy and 4 light cruisers, 9 destroyers, 1 submarine and 2 amphibious ships were sunk – but in the desparity of forced deployed for battle and Japanese losses not just in this battle but in the subsequent follow-up phase, On the first score, opposed to the 4 carriers, 9 battleships, 20 cruisers and 35 destroyers of the Japanese 1st Mobile Fleet were 46 carriers, 12 battleships, 25 destroyers, 162 destroyers, 56 escorts, 29 submarines and almost as many American oilers with the 3rd and 7th Fleet as Japan as a nation had possessed in 1941. Expressed another way, at Leyte the Americans had more destroyers than the Japanese had carrier aircraft. The relationship between numbers and the outcome of battle was never more obviously demonstrated. On the second score, the sheer scale of destruction in this battle, and specifically in the course of the various actions fought on 25 October, has served to obscure the extent of the Japanese defeat and American victory both before and after the main force action when American carrier aircraft ranged over the Philippines against Japanese warships and shipping stripped of support.

Between 29 October and 30 November 1944 the Imperial Navy lost 50 warships of 129,511 tons – including the battleship *Kongo* – in Philippine and immediately adjacent waters during American follow-up operations. In addition a total of 48 service ships and merchantmen of 201,216 tons were lost in these same waters and in these same operations. The context of these losses can be gauged by the fact that total Japanese losses in all theatres and to all causes in this same period numbered 65 warships of 224,547 tons and 105 service and merchant ships of 440,171 tons. Lest the point be forgotten, before the outbreak of hostilities the Imperial Navy calculated shipping losses would be in the order of 900,000 tons in any year.

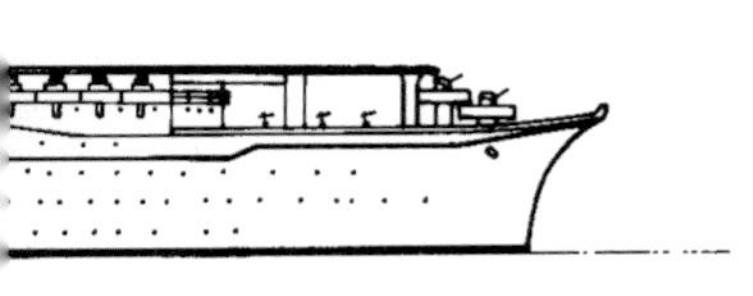

In other works this author has used the analogy of history being like a piece of string in that it consists of strands woven together to produce the whole, but unlike a piece of string the strands of history are neither equal nor regular in the weave. Japan's defeat, and the reasons for that defeat, conform to this analogy, and the battle of Leyte Gulf marks the point where the various strands of Japan's defeat recognizably began to be woven together. Defeat in battle was clearly the most important of the strands, and after Leyte Gulf the Imperial Navy was never again able to offer battle with a balanced force: after November 1944 the Imperial Navy was reduced to coastguard status and was barely able to perform even that role.

But the real point of Leyte lay in the coming together of all of the elements that contributed to victory and defeat in total war: military defeat at sea, on land and in the air; the dimensions of time and position in the conduct of war; the failure of Japan's strategic intent in Burma and China, and more generally throughout the conquered territories in being unable to win the endorsement of fellow Asians for her war effort; the faltering Japanese industrial, financial and trading effort; the Japanese inability to protect shipping. It is impossible to state with any finality when Japan's defeat became assured, perhaps 7 December 1941, perhaps November 1943. But October 1944 saw the various elements of defeat come together and into place.

CHAPTER FIVE

The Last Milestone: Supremacy and Victory

November 1944 – August 1945

The decisive factor in war: *the will of infantry to move forward.*

THE LAST MILESTONE: SUPREMACY AND VICTORY

THREE VERY separate matters contribute to a full understanding of the final phase of the Pacific war. The first is the sortie of the battleship *Yamato* in support of the garrison on Okinawa and her sinking in attacks by 179 strike aircraft from the carriers of Task Force 38 in the East China Sea on 7 April 1945.

The sortie of the *Yamato* was ordered in full awareness that she would not survive the mission, and the fact that she carried enough fuel for only a one-way voyage is well known. Less well known is the fact that she was ordered to sail because the Imperial Navy considered it dishonourable for the ship that bore the ancient name of Japan to survive the surrender of the country. Equally obscure is the fact that the foray was mounted after the Imperial Navy relieved the merchant fleet of one month's supply of fuel. This was at a time when every ton of oil was needed for the merchant marine if Japan was to have any chance of avoiding mass starvation and when 200,000 barrels of oil – compared to the 20 million with which Japan had gone to war – remained in stock. At the Tokyo War Crimes Tribunal it was the Imperial Army that bore the brunt of national guilt and failure but, other than the demise of the *Yamato*, few if any episodes better illustrate the conceit and irresponsibility of an Imperial Navy that was infinitely more culpable than the Imperial Army for the war that began in December 1941. The Imperial Navy wrecked limitations treaties that afforded Japan security and in 1941 insisted on war with the United States. When that war was lost and its own failure apparent, it contemptuously subordinated nation and society to its own concept of service honour rather than seek, however unavailingly, to discharge its duty to the state it was supposed to serve.

The second concerns exceptionally heavy Japanese shipping losses in the last months of the war, between 1 April and 15 August 1945, when Japan lost 210 warships of 440,293 tons, 77 service auxiliaries and transports of 224,532 tons and 400 merchantmen of 741,574 tons. Although these losses were not much greater than those incurred by the Allies in the single month of November 1942, allowing for ships laid up or damaged beyond economical repair, they amounted to three-fifths of the real total of tonnage available to Japan on 31 March 1945.

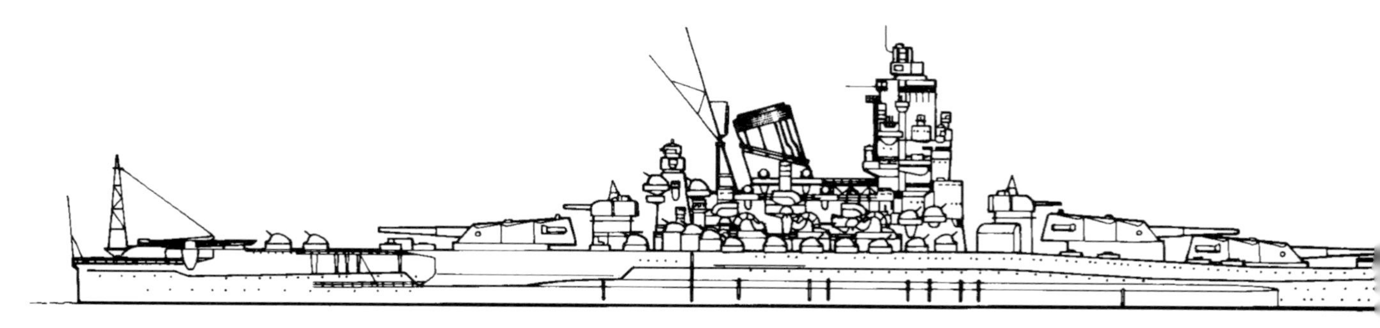

THE YAMATO

The fleet flagship and bearer of the ancient name of Japan, the Yamato *was endowed with a 16.1-inch belt, a triple bottom and elaborate sub-division which resulted in 1,147 watertight compartments. In 1943 she lost two secondary turrets in order to accommodate more tertiary AA weapons, and in April 1945 carried 146 25-mm guns.*

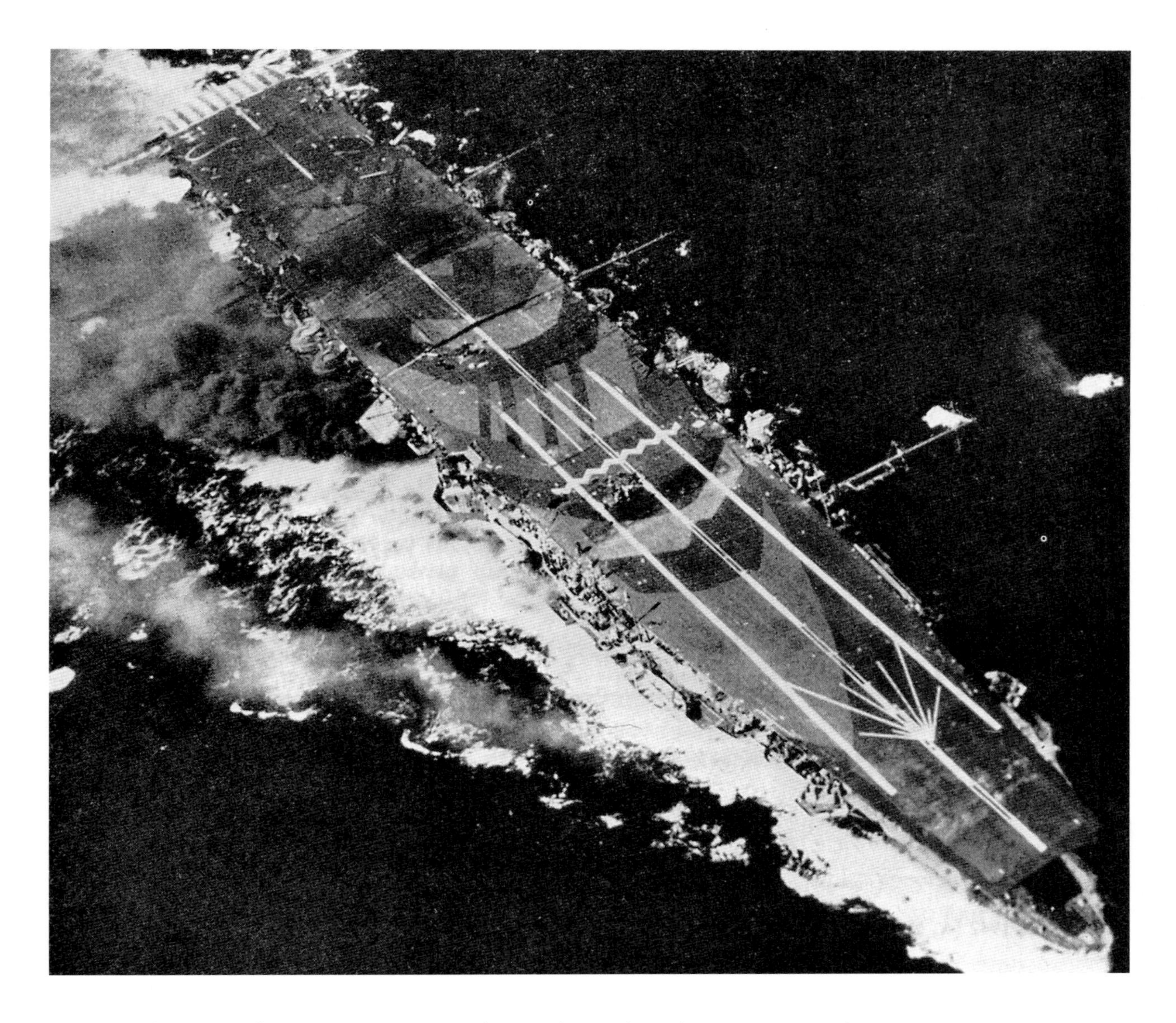

The light carrier Zuiho *under attack, 25 October 1944. The Japanese Navy's policy of converting a number of fast oilers and liners to serve as carriers resulted in some of the worst carriers of the Second World War, mainly because of practically non-existent damage control systems. The* Zuiho *was one of the better of these and was in the Philippines and at Midway, Santa Cruz and the Philippine Sea before being sunk at Leyte.*

But what is perhaps even more significant about these losses concerned cause and location. Leyte Gulf represented the swansong of the American submarine campaign against Japanese shipping. The American return to the western Pacific meant that the campaign against Japanese shipping in 1945 was to be spearheaded by land- and carrier-based aircraft that could carry this effort into waters denied submarines, and could conduct their operations more quickly and directly than could the latter. The submarine campaign in 1945 therefore slowed as these other forms of taking the war to the Japanese merchant fleet moved to centre stage.

Moreover, as submarines fell from their position of pre-eminence, mines accounted for a minimum of 25 warships of 31,840 tons and 170

The destruction of the Yamato. *In the company of one light cruiser and eight destroyers, she was committed to a one-way mission in support of forces on Okinawa. Caught 130 miles from Kagoshima with no air cover, she was overwhelmed by aircraft from nine carriers, being hit by perhaps as many as eleven torpedoes and seven bombs. Her light cruiser and four destroyers were also sunk, 7 April 1945.*

service and merchant ships of 302,172 tons as Japan's defences were very literally engulfed. With the Americans using five different influence systems and a total of 200 different types, the scale and diversity of their mining ensured that Japanese defensive measures were all but overwhelmed. But what is even more telling about the losses in the last months of the war is that in July 1945 a total of 123 merchantmen of 254,549 tons were sunk, and, as testimony of the totality of Japan's defeat and the extent to which she had lost any real element of strategic mobility, 120 merchantmen were lost in Japanese home waters: just three merchantmen of 2,820 tons were lost in all other theatres other than the seas that washed Japan. Put at its most simple and with scarcely any exaggeration: in July 1945 nothing moved outside Japanese home waters, and between a third and a half of what did move in home waters was sunk.

The third matter concerns the circumstances that surrounded the meeting of the Supreme War Council scheduled for the evening of 8 August 1945 to discuss whether or not to accept the terms of the Potsdam Declaration of the United Nations demanding Japan's immediate and unconditional surrender. This meeting was called two days after the American attack on Hiroshima with an atomic bomb. With Soviet entry into the war and the attack on Nagasaki only a matter of hours away, the meeting had to be cancelled because 'one of Council's members had more important business elsewhere'. It is difficult to discern any matter that could have represented 'more important business' than consideration of the question of the nation's immediate and unconditional surrender. The episode was final comment on the Japanese system and organization in the Second World War that very literally defies belief.

The final phase of the Japanese war is perhaps best examined under six headings: the series of defeats that separately and together overwhelmed the Imperial Army; the annihilation of the Imperial Navy; the campaign against Japanese shipping; Japan's industrial and economic prostration by war's end; the strategic bombing campaign against the home islands; and the Soviet intervention. There is an obvious interconnection between these subjects. But while it is somewhat difficult to disentangle the various strands of defeat, immediate attention must be directed to the most obvious and direct: the defeat of the Imperial Army in the field.

The fleet carrier Amagi *was rendered* hors de combat *on 24 July 1945 when, in addition to routine operations involving 570 Superfortresses, no fewer than 1,747 carrier aircraft attacked the Kure naval base and ships in the Inland Sea on that day, accounting for 1 battleship, 1 fleet and 2 escort carriers, 1 heavy cruiser, 1 chaser, 3 naval transports and 9 merchantmen.*

A British patrol from the 14th Army in the battle of the Sittang Bend in the final stages of the campaign in Burma: at war's end some 110,000 Japanese troops remained in Burma east of the Sittang but their effectiveness had been destroyed by defeat and lack of supplies.

Leaving aside events in Manchuria in August 1945, the Imperial Army was defeated in the course of five separate campaigns: in the Pacific on the islands of Iwo Jima and Okinawa; in Burma, the Philippines and the Indies. Of these, the individual defeats in south-east Asia demand little consideration because at this stage of proceedings anything that happened beyond the inner zone of Japan's defences was of no real account, at least in terms of the outcome of the war. The most obvious proof of this was in the Indies where Australia, which with New Zealand had been casually and ungraciously denied a central Pacific role by the United States as the war moved away from their shores, found employment for her forces with the landings at Tarakan on 1 May, in Brunei Bay on 10 June and at Balikpapan on 1 July. More substantially, in Burma in December 1944 a British advance from Sittaung and Kalewa resulted in the establishment of three bridgeheads over the Irrawaddy River during January and February. Signals intelligence enabled the British 14th Army to fight with an exact knowledge of the Japanese order of battle and intentions and, accordingly, it was able to drive through Nyaungu against Meiktila while the main Japanese strength was pinned around and in Mandalay. In two separate battles, both

lasting about one month, Japanese forces in upper Burma and those directed against Meiktila were destroyed. By the end of March 1945 the collapse of Japanese resistance throughout upper and central Burma, plus the availability of transport aircraft, enabled the British offensive to extend into lower Burma. In the course of April what had been considered impossible over the previous two years, the reconquest of Burma by means of an overland offensive from north-east India, was achieved, though in fact the Arakan was cleared by a series of landing operations and Rangoon was taken (1/3 May) by amphibious assault ahead of both the monsoon and the columns advancing from the north. Even after the loss of Rangoon some 115,000 Japanese troops remained in Burma, but these were mostly in Tenasserim or east of the Salween River and were powerless to have any influence on proceedings. The war was to end with the British in effect having cleared Burma and preparing for landings in Malaya. What this effort achieved with respect to original terms of reference is interesting. The first overland convoys reached Chungking via Tengchung on 20 January and via Bhamo on 4 February, but the overland

If air resupply was crucial to the British advance in Burma in 1945, scarcely less important were rivers that formed the natural lines of communication and supply. Supplies brought overland from the Imphal area to the Chindwin were vitally important in sustaining the initial advance of British forces to Mandalay. The photograph shows a supply convoy of American-supplied DWCKS on the lower Chindwin, with orders being given in semaphore.

supply route on which the Americans lavished so much money and emotional investment handled just 7.19 per cent of all material supplied to China between February and October 1945.

RETURN TO THE PHILIPPINES

The Philippines campaign ran parallel to these efforts. The US 6th Army undertook six major landing operations in the Visayans and on Luzon. These were the initial landings on Leyte in October 1944 and the subsequent landings in Ormoc Bay on 7 December 1944 which had the effect of breaking Japanese resistance on Leyte. The landings on Mindoro on 15 December 1944 served as a stepping stone to the main endeavour in the Philippines campaign, namely the liberation of Luzon, which opened with the landings in Lingayen Gulf on 9 January; and the landings on Samar and Palawan in February 1945, which complemented the main efforts directed towards Luzon, and marked the start of the clearing of the

Chinese forces in the final stages of the battle for Bhamo in northern Burma, November–December 1944. Bhamo was cleared after a month-long siege on 15 December 1944: with the Burma Road thus cleared of Japanese forces the first overland convoy to Kunming since 1942 arrived in February 1945.

central passage through the islands. Thereafter the American offensive in the group divided into two parts. Less importantly, after 19 February 1945 no fewer than twelve major assaults and some thirty other landings were conducted in the central and southern Philippines with the aim of freeing both the people and the sea routes through the islands. For the most part these operations were on a modest scale and directed against an enemy defensively dispersed, which had committed and lost its best formations in the defence of Leyte. Despite having some 110,000 troops in these islands at the end of the war, the Japanese were unable to offer effective resistance anywhere in the Visayans and by August 1945 retained organized formations only in central Mindanao.

The Burma and China theatres necessitated the building of a modern communications system, in what had previously been a peaceful backwater of north-east India. Probably everything shown in this photograph – road, huts, telephone lines and vehicles – was American made and supplied.

The campaign in the northern Visayans and on Luzon was the more important of the two efforts in the Philippines, and in effect its outcome was assured with the Japanese defeat on Leyte, acknowledged on 19 December with the decision to abandon the struggle for control of an island where 202,000 US combat troops found employment. With this victory the Americans were left free to strike at will throughout the Philippines with all the advantages bestowed by a central position. In fact, their main effort was directed, like the Japanese effort of 1941, to Lingayen Gulf and across the central plain to Manila. Again like the Americans in 1941, the defence did not seek to deny the capital but to concentrate in the field with a view to drawing as many enemy formations as possible into a protracted campaign. In 1945 the Japanese chose to make their main defensive effort not on the Bataan Peninsula, but in the mountains of north-east Luzon. The fragmentation of Japanese forces meant that Manila was defended in the course of a month-long campaign that reduced the city to the dubious status of the most heavily damaged Allied capital in the world after Warsaw by the time it was finally liberated on 3 March. Thereafter the Americans were able to clear central and southern Luzon without difficulty and take possession of everything of real political and military value on the island. The campaign on Luzon was to continue until July 1945 when US formations were withdrawn from major operations, though at the end of the war, 15 August 1945, the equivalent of five American divisions still remained in the field in the Philippines. With sixteen American divisions committed at some stage or another to the overall campaign in the Philippines, the campaign in the islands was the first large-scale campaign undertaken by the US Army in the Pacific war and cost the Japanese about 400,000 lives. Whether the final result confirmed the claims that had been made by South West Pacific Command in justification for a policy of clearing the Philippines is questionable. What is undeniable, however, is that the defeat of the Japanese in battle in the Philippines facilitated the rehabilitation of American power both in the archipelago and more generally in south-east Asia after the war in a way which a bypassing of the islands probably could never have achieved. In the short term securing Leyte Gulf and Manila Bay provided Allied naval forces with bases from which to carry the war into the Ryukyus and Japanese home waters.

Iwo Jima and Okinawa

The other two campaigns that contributed to Japanese military defeat were somewhat different. The story of the final phase of the war in the Pacific has invariably been told in terms of the American landings on and clearing of Iwo Jima and Okinawa, and rightly so: singly and together they possessed critical importance. These two campaigns represent the final closing of the ring around Japan. The campaign on Iwo Jima began on 19 February 1945, that on Okinawa on 1 April: the islands were declared secured on 26 March and 30 June respectively. On the eight square miles of Iwo Jima, where the Japanese had deployed the reinforced 109th Infantry Division with about 25,000 troops as garrison, some 2,400 Japanese personnel were killed or captured after the island was declared secure, and resistance continued into June. The value of the island was nevertheless revealed as early as 4 March when the first of 2,251 B-29 emergency landings took place, and one week later US fighters began operations from airfield complexes that ultimately covered half the island. The first fighter escorts for B-29 bombers were flown from Iwo Jima on 7 April, and, less well known, the first raids by fighters, escorted by B-29s from the Marianas, were flown on 16 April. Okinawa, however, was somewhat different from Iwo Jima. It was to provide the US with airfields from which the campaign against the home islands was supplemented, but its real value lay in the forward anchorages it afforded. More importantly, its position astride Japan's lines of communication with south-east Asia meant that no oil tanker reached Japanese waters from the southern resources area after March 1945.

Okinawa, like Saipan, housed a substantial Japanese civilian population indoctrinated with tales of American brutality, and the offensive was very different from other island campaigns. The Japanese 32nd Army, with some 131,000 troops under command, in effect ceded the central and northern part of the island in order to concentrate forces for a defensive campaign on the Shuri Line, and here lay the major significance of this campaign. Japanese policy was to force the Americans to fight a protracted campaign within range of aircraft concentrated in the home islands. The air campaign was the most important single part of a final despairing Japanese attempt to influence events to their advantage by an equalization of resources 'by other means'. War, as von Clausewitz has taught us, is a contest of moral and physical resources by means of the latter, and is a political phenomenon: thus it follows that the determinants of war are political rather than physical. A careful reader would have noticed that elsewhere it was noted that the Japanese defeat in the Second World War was comprehensive but for one dimension, which was left undefined. This was a willingness to accept death as the means and end of resistance. The Japanese ethic saw and accepted death as a means of resistance in the sense that after 25 October, off Leyte Gulf, Japanese forces, in the form of kamikaze units, died in order to fight. On this single day, suicide attacks sank one and damaged seven escort carriers, three extensively. Throughout the first four months of the campaign in the Philippines, suicide aircraft struck at American warships, but if the greatest single day's achievement of this form of attack was on 25 November when the fleet carriers *Essex* and *Intrepid* and the light fleet carrier *Cabot* were forced from the battle with serious damage, it was in the campaign for Okinawa that the greatest kamikaze effort was mounted, and to no avail. Sailors who fought to live defeated airmen who died to fight, and in so doing pointed to the limitations of political and moral factors in the conduct of war, and to the fact that there was no effective substitute for conventional air power. Moreover, with the loss of some 3,000 aircraft in the Philippines and another 7,000 in the

With Mount Suribachi in the background, D-Day, H-Hour: the 5th Marine Division at Iwo Jima, 19 February 1945. Iwo Jima was subjected to the longest preliminary bombardment of the Pacific war. The island was first bombed on 10 August 1944 and subjected to forty-eight raids by the end of October: the first bombardment by warships was on 8 December 1944.

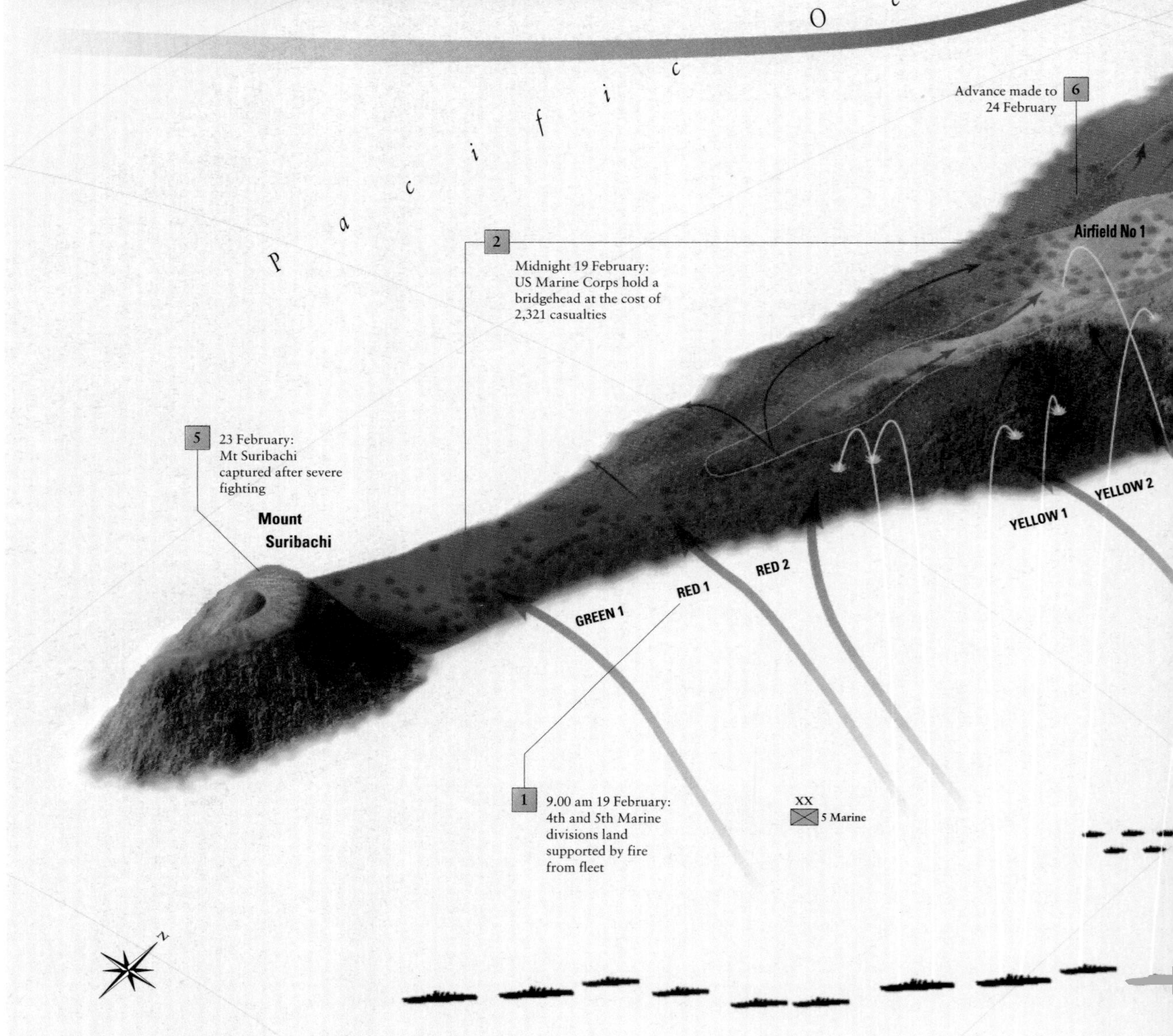

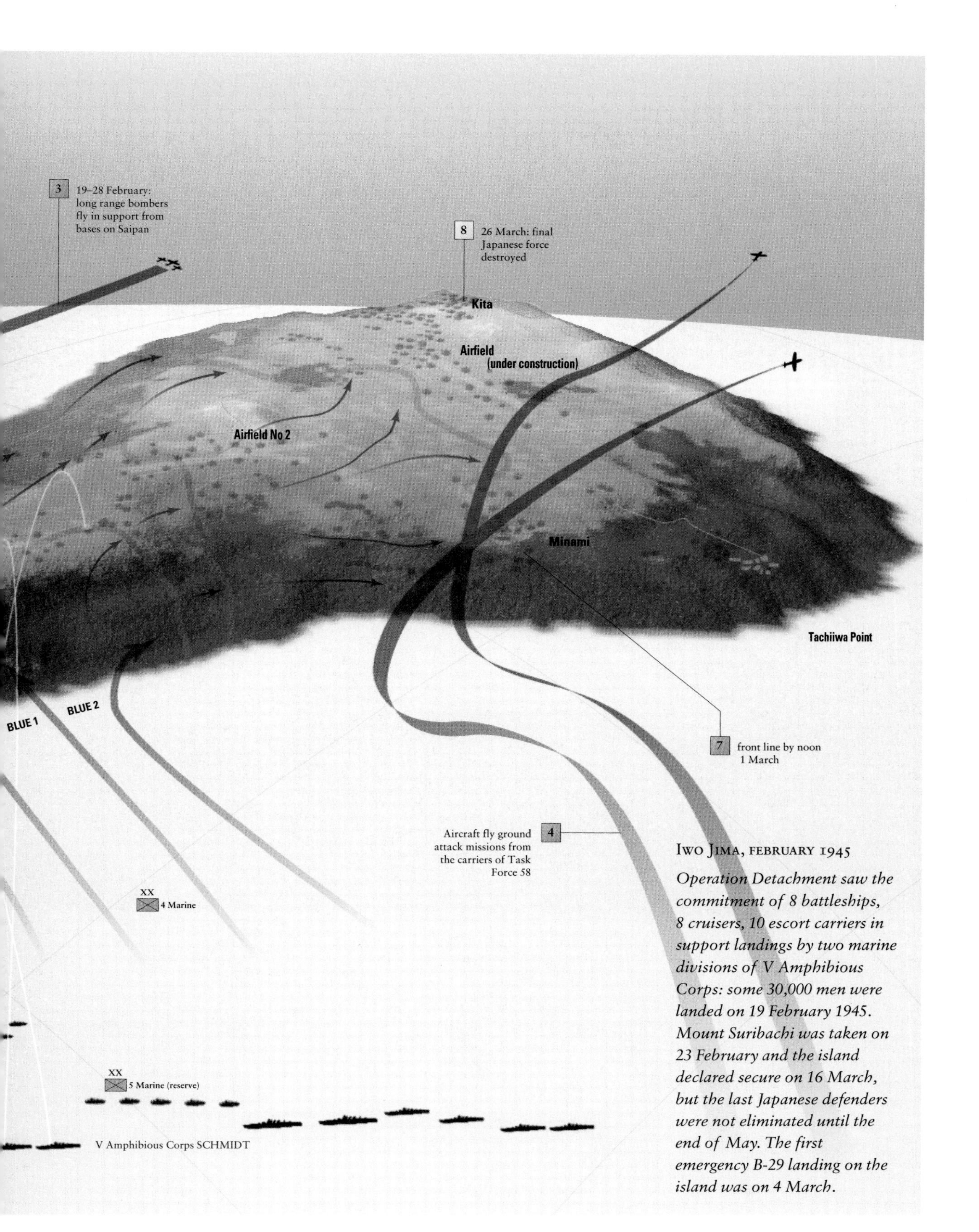

IWO JIMA, FEBRUARY 1945

Operation Detachment saw the commitment of 8 battleships, 8 cruisers, 10 escort carriers in support landings by two marine divisions of V Amphibious Corps: some 30,000 men were landed on 19 February 1945. Mount Suribachi was taken on 23 February and the island declared secure on 16 March, but the last Japanese defenders were not eliminated until the end of May. The first emergency B-29 landing on the island was on 4 March.

THE *RANDOLPH*

The Essex-class fleet carrier Randolph*: 34,880 tons (deep load), ninety-one aircraft, twelve 5-inch, thirty-two 40-mm, forty-six 20-mm guns, 32.7 knots. She first saw action in February 1945 in the raid on the home islands but an unwanted claim to fame lies in the fact that she was the only carrier to be hit by a kamikaze while in base, at Ulithi on 11 March 1945.*

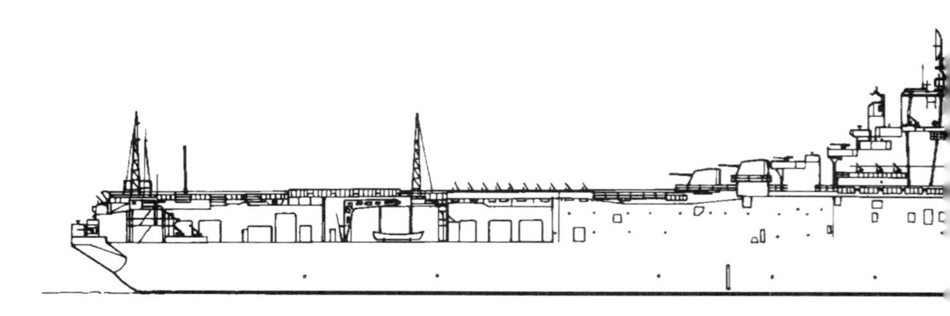

Self-defence for an Essex-class carrier in three forms: the quadrupled 40-mm, single 20-mm and single 5-inch guns. By summer 1945 the US Navy had decided upon a standard 3-inch tertiary weapon as the best compromise between rate of fire and weight of shell as counter to the kamikaze.

struggle for Okinawa, recourse to kamikaze tactics meant that the Japanese could not simultaneously prepare for a conventional air battle in defence of the home islands and undertake kamikaze offensives off Okinawa: even the most successful kamikaze effort over the Philippines and Okinawa could only have one outcome, namely the exhaustion of Japanese air strength and the certainty of its self-immolation by the end of 1945.

Moreover, while the shock wrought by the employment of suicide forces was very real, it was one that lessened with time, and certainly by the end of the Okinawan campaign the Americans, by a recasting of tactics and deployment, could beat the kamikazes. In terms of readiness for the invasion of the home islands, the Americans had moved into a position of strength that ensured that the air battle would be won, though very little attention is ever paid to what such a simple statement of the situation involved. The number of carriers gathered off Okinawa is sometimes cited as evidence of this strength – and sixty fleet, light and escort carriers saw employment off the Ryukyus – but perhaps the more pertinent measure of strength was the 90,662 missions flown by American carriers in the course of the Okinawa campaign: of this total 53,077 were flown by the fleet and light fleet carriers between 14 March and 8 June, while the remaining 37,585 were flown by escort carriers prior to the end of June. With such numbers in hand, and with British carriers arriving on station, the Americans planned that

The final phase of the campaign on Okinawa: marines clearing the caves in southern Okinawa, 14 June 1945. The eighty-two-day campaign for the island left 110,000 Japanese dead. Some 7,400 chose captivity, the first appreciable prisoner haul of the war.

OPPOSITE: *The New Mexico-class battleship* Idaho *in action off Okinawa in late March 1945. The pre-invasion bombardment forces assembled off Okinawa after 26 March 1945 included ten old battleships, the total in second-line service, more than the number then in British service.*

the landings on Kyushu would be directly supported by a carrier force of ten fleet and light fleet carriers while another force, with twenty fleet and light fleet carriers, was assigned the covering role. In short, if war is a contest of physical and moral forces, the latter cannot offset too severe a material deficit, and this was the reality that unfolded in the Philippines and the Ryukyus between October 1944 and June 1945. Tacit acknowledgement of this was provided by the fact that 7,400 prisoners were taken on Okinawa, the first occasion when Japanese soldiers surrendered in any appreciable numbers.

In the course of the Okinawan campaign the American carrier task force was continuously at sea for ninety-two days; even the short-haul British carrier force was at sea in two separate periods of thirty-two and thirty days. Such capability was unprecedented since the age of sail, and the logistical effort needed to sustain such undertakings was immense. No less serious, and in a sense more relevant for what was to come, was the effort needed to conduct assault landings. With the preliminary bombardment lasting seventy-two days, certain of the ships bound for Iwo Jima began loading in the previous November, and one of the divisions committed to this battle went ashore with food sufficient to supply the city of Colombus, Ohio, for thirty days and with,

Though most of the landings in the Philippines other than on Leyte and Luzon were relatively small, the operations in Moro Gulf on 17 April 1945, while not involving carriers and capital ships, none the less saw the commitment of two infantry divisions. Rocket-firing landing craft, converted from standard LCT (2) or (3), were notorious for their eccentricities of handling, but when aligned correctly could saturate a beach area over a frontage of 750 yards.

perhaps somewhat excessively, enough cigarettes to supply every single man with twenty a day, every day for eight months. With hospitals prepared on Saipan and Guam to receive casualties, the scale of support needed for the two armies, 14,000 combat aircraft and naval forces (including 100 carriers) that were to be involved in landings in Honshu begins to come into perspective, as does one other matter, an historical fact that could be regarded as trivia but for its obvious significance in terms of illustrating the extent of national disparity of strength and resources both in the war as a whole but specifically at this stage of proceedings. In the campaign off Okinawa, between March and June 1945,

On 19 March Japanese land-based aircraft bombed the fleet carriers Wasp *and* Franklin. *Though the* Wasp *was able to extinguish her fires quickly and was fully operational within fifty minutes of being hit, the* Franklin *was crippled by five hours of explosions that at one stage left her dead in the water. Under tow her fires were extinguished and power ultimately regained, and by noon on the 20th the carrier was able to make 14 knots and she reached Ulithi under her own power on 24 March. With 832 dead and 270 wounded, the* Franklin *was the most heavily damaged carrier to survive the war, though she never returned to service other than in a ferrying capacity. Not the least remarkable aspect of her survival was that she was crippled while 55 miles from the coast of Japan but none the less was able, with the help of her companions in TG 58.2, to survive and clear the danger area.*

American naval forces were supplied with a greater amount of petrol, oil and lubricants than Japan as a nation imported in the whole of 1944.

Attacking the home islands

The securing of the Marianas, the Philippines and Okinawa provided the Americans with the bases from which to stage the invasion of the home islands, and it was the American intention to move initially against Kyushu in November 1945 and then against Honshu, specifically across the Kondo Plain to Tokyo, in March 1946. The prospect of landings in the home islands did not command enthusiasm on two counts. First, in the course of 1945 the Japanese deployment of forces within the home islands was closely monitored by American intelligence, and with the Imperial Army anticipating where enemy forces would be obliged to land the American high command drew the obvious conclusions. The second was self-evident: the example of Japanese resistance on such places as Saipan, Iwo Jima and Okinawa was regarded as a

Okinawa Campaign

Realizing the impossibility of offering resistance on beaches, the Japanese intention was to cede most of Okinawa while standing on prepared lines in the south of the island. The Japanese hoped to conduct a protracted defence that would result in the Americans having to commit the carrier force to prolonged operations within range of conventional air and kamikaze strikes mounted from the home islands. The margin of superiority available to the Americans at this stage of proceedings confounded Japanese intentions.

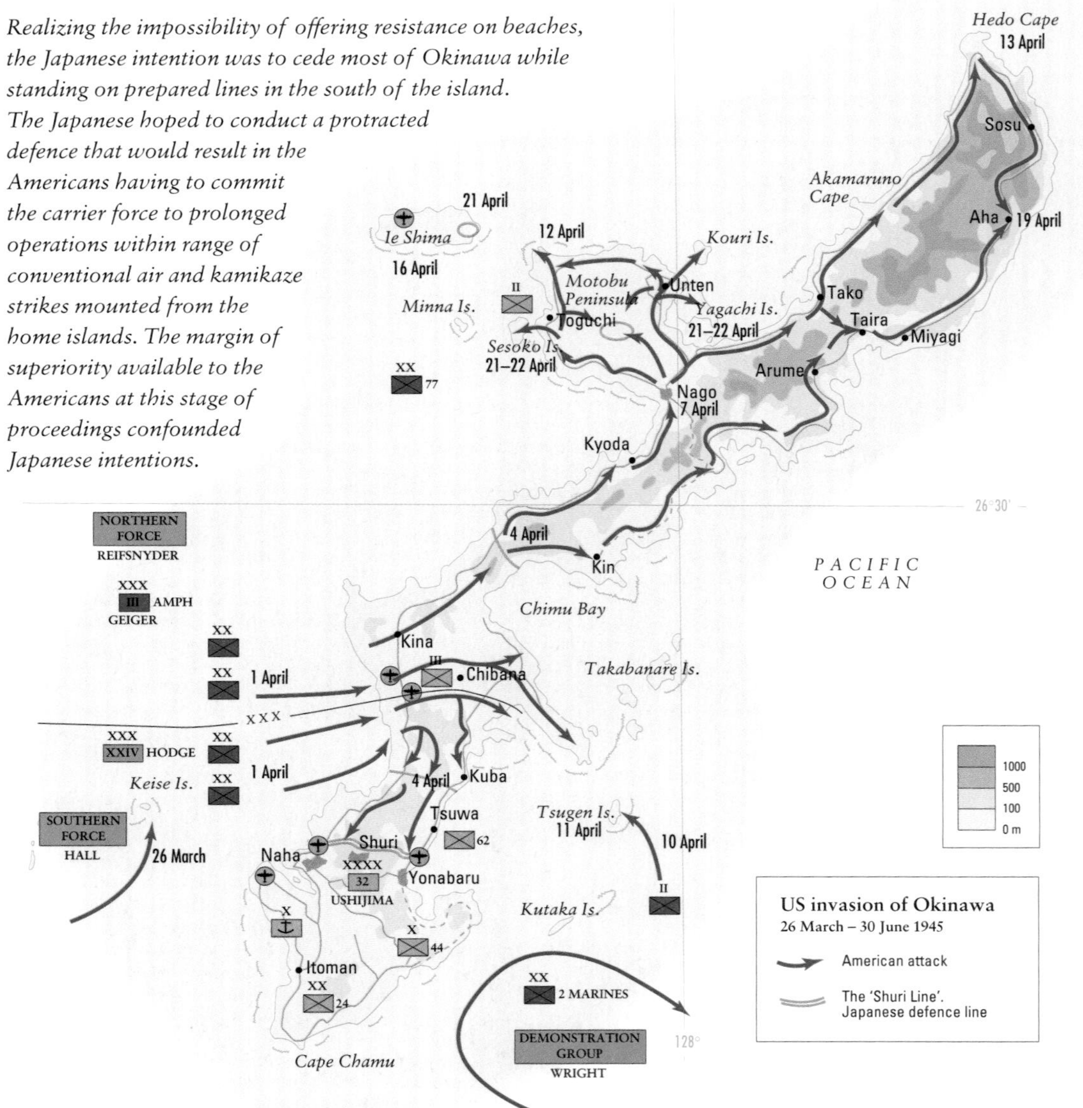

The scene off Haguishi beach, Okinawa, where troops from XXIV Corps landed on 1 April 1945. The concentration of shipping so close to the shore so early in proceedings indicates that the Japanese made little attempt to oppose the landings at the water's edge: by the end of the first day the Americans had secured a beachhead 3 miles deep and 10 miles in frontage.

foretaste of what could be expected in the event of the invasion of the home islands. In this respect, the Japanese aim in the conduct of last-ditch defence in the islands proved both successful and self-defeating. The Japanese hoped and intended to wear down American resolve, to force the Americans to the conclusion that a negotiated end to the war was preferable to a campaign on the main islands. In reality, there was little basis for such hopes. The quality of Imperial Army formations in the home islands was somewhat uneven: the classes of 1944 and 1945 were all but untrained, and even the good divisions lacked the transport, communications and armour synonymous with effectiveness. Moreover, in planning for the defence of the home islands the Imperial Army, which rejected the idea of arming the civil population for a war

Beach scene on Okinawa, 13 April 1945. With a minimum of forty-four landing ships and craft in sight, the scale and complexity of logistic support begins to come into perspective: in fact, by mid April American logistical problems were mounting as demand outstripped earlier logistical estimates.

to the death, was simply unable to force civilian evacuation of landing areas, and in any event it faced an impossible dilemma in planning the conduct of the defence against amphibious landings. If it attempted to defend the home islands at the water's edge, then its formations would be subjected to the full force of American *matériel* advantage; on the other hand, formations held inland were highly unlikely to be able to get into battle in time to affect its outcome other than in swelling the total of Japanese casualties. In this respect the example of the Okinawa campaign was salutary. Such was the disruption of Japanese

In five major raids between 10 March and 25 May 56.3 of Tokyo's 110.8 square miles were destroyed. Two-fifths of Japan's 'big six' cities – Tokyo, Osaka, Yokohama, Nagoya, Kobe and Kawasaki – were destroyed in the course of eighteen firestorm raids prior to 15 June 1945.

airfields and command facilities in the home islands as a result of American carrier operations that it took the Japanese a week after the American landings on Okinawa to organize air strikes in direct support of the 32nd Army: there is no reason to suppose that the Japanese could have done any better in the event of landings in the home islands. In reality, and despite the hesitations of the American high command, there was never any real prospect of the Imperial Army's securing the success that had eluded the German armed forces in Normandy.

Iwo Jima and Okinawa caused the Americans to hesitate but not to flinch, in part because they had other means of taking the war to the home islands. These were the combination of bombing

and, after 14 July 1945, bombardment by warships, primarily American. The warships were a bonus, their symbolism being both obvious and ironic: in a war that for the British began with the loss of two capital ships in the South China Sea on 10 December 1941, the bombardment of Hamamatsu on the night of 29/30 July was the last occasion when a British battleship fired her guns in anger.

The bombing campaign, however, was of a different order in terms of scale, impact and results, even if it began very uncertainly and was attended initially

Japanese Type D Koryu submarines in a wrecked dock at Kure naval yard, September 1945. The Japanese planned to have 570 Koryus in September for the defence of the home islands: in the event only 115 had been completed.

Harry S. Truman became president of the United States on 12 April 1945 on the death of Franklin D. Roosevelt. He attended the Potsdam Conference in July and authorized the use of atomic weapons after the Allied declaration of the 26th was rejected by the Japanese.

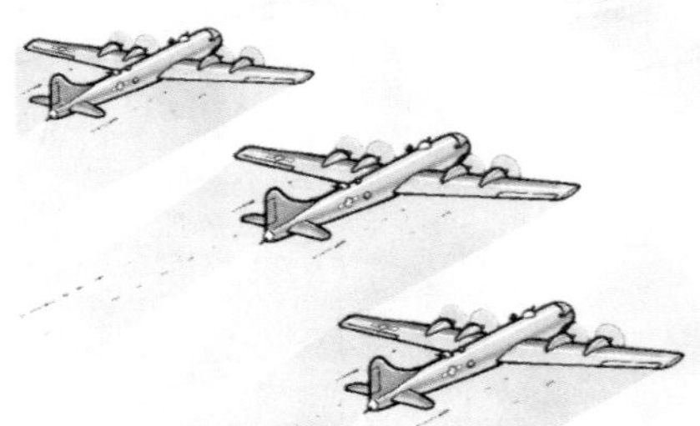

TOKYO FIRE RAID, 29 MAY 1945

Japanese cities, with their narrow streets, closely packed and lightly constructed buildings with few parks, were peculiarly vulnerable to firestorm raids. Tokyo was subjected to five raids that devastated 56.3 of its 110 square miles. One-third of neighbouring Kawasaki was razed in a single attack: 44 per cent of Yokohama was levelled in the course of two raids.

1. First wave of bombers (B-29s) drop high explosive bombs to cause structural damage
2. Following waves drop incendiary bombs, to set alight damaged areas
3. Japanese anti-aircraft fire attempts to disrupt the bombing run and destroy attacking aircraft
4. Japanese fighters intercept bombers, bombers respond with defensive fire. Later in the bombing campaign only tail guns would equip the B-29, allowing a greater bomb load to be carried

Superfortresses over Japan: seven of the 454 B-29s committed against Yokahama on 29 May when some 6.9 square miles or slightly more than one-third of the city was destroyed in a firestorm attack. 517 bombers were initially committed but only 454 found their target: this attack was the first to be afforded protection by P-51 Mustangs of VII Fighter Command.

by failure. Between November 1944 and February 1945 the attacks on the home islands from bases in the Marianas were conducted on too small a scale – only one wing was available for operations – and at altitudes too high to be effective. Furthermore, air defence inflicted a debilitating 5 per cent loss rate on the B-29 Superfortresses. After March, and in spite of the distractions of the mining commitment and operations against airfields on Kyushu and Shikoku in support of the Okinawa enterprise, the American bombing offensive became increasingly effective to the extent that by the end of the war 43.46 per cent of sixty-three major Japanese cities had been laid waste, 42 per cent of Japan's industrial capacity had been destroyed and some 22 million people had been killed, injured or rendered homeless.

Such devastation, inflicted in just five months, was primarily the result of three factors, namely the increase in the number of aircraft committed to the bombing campaign, the deployment of area bombardment tactics and the peculiar nature of Japanese cities. After March 1945 the Americans abandoned precision bombardment in favour of low-altitude attacks, notable for the employment of incendiaries. Lack of road space and parks, heavy population density and the relative flimsiness of Japanese construction meant that Japanese cities were peculiarly vulnerable to fire storms, as the extent of destruction indicated only too well. The high, or low, point of this effort – the Tokyo raid

OPPOSITE: *A Japanese military transport under attack in Ormoc Bay in the course of the Leyte campaign, November 1944.*

JAPANESE MERCHANT SHIPPING LOSSES

The changing pattern of Japanese shipping losses can be ascertained by reference to the location of sinkings over different periods of the war. Suffice to note one matter: by war's end Japanese shipping was at a standstill outside home waters despite the vast areas that remained under Japanese control. By July 1945 Japan's strategic mobility was no more, and she could not have sustained herself in terms of basic food requirements beyond November.

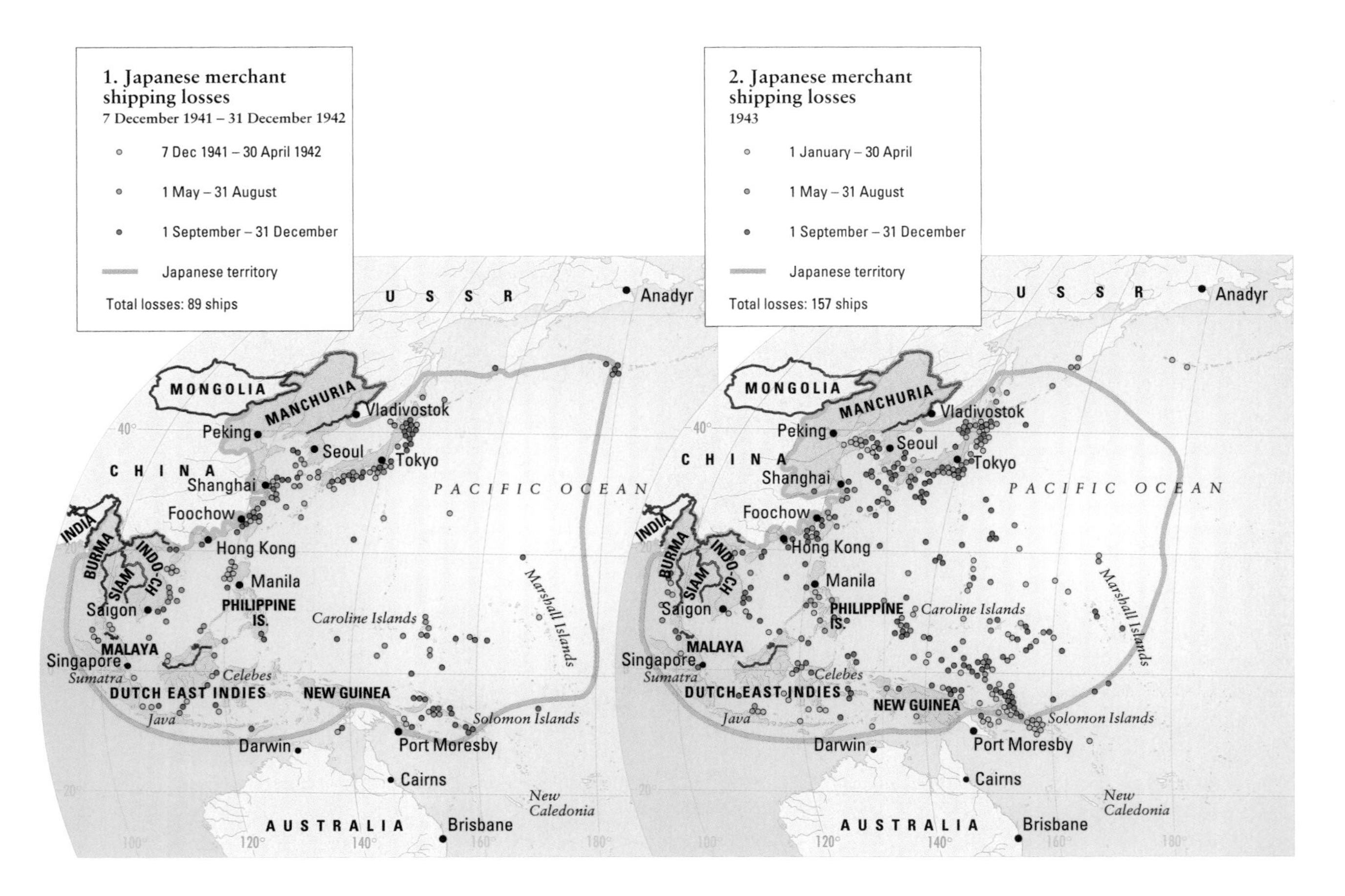

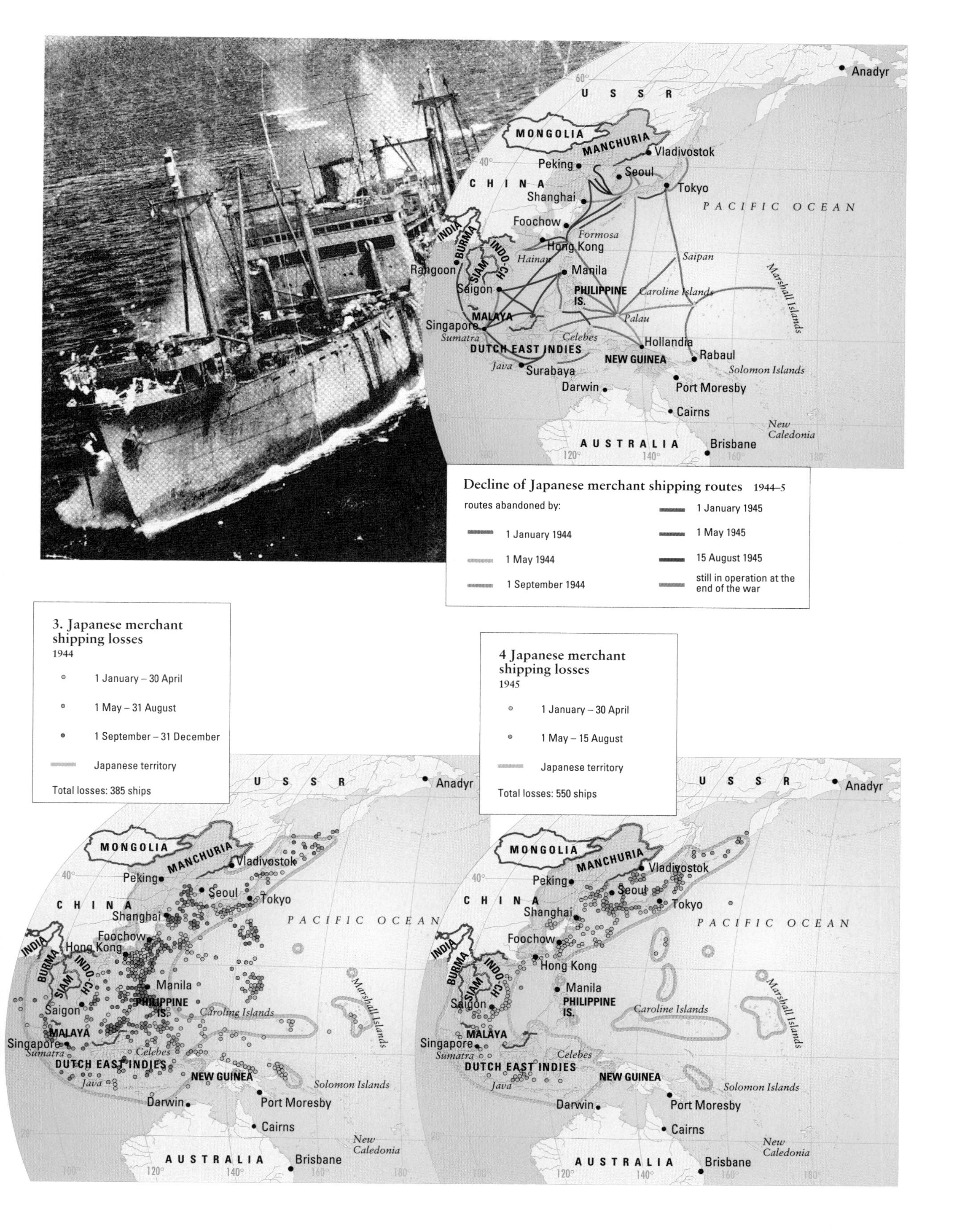

Decline of Japanese merchant shipping routes 1944–5
routes abandoned by:
1 January 1944
1 May 1944
1 September 1944
1 January 1945
1 May 1945
15 August 1945
still in operation at the end of the war
U S S R
Anadyr
MONGOLIA
MANCHURIA
Vladivostok
Peking
Seoul
C H I N A
Tokyo
Shanghai
PACIFIC OCEAN
Foochow
Formosa
INDIA
BURMA
Hong Kong
INDO-CH
SIAM
Hainan
Saipan
Rangoon
Manila
Saigon
PHILIPPINE IS.
Caroline Islands
Marshall Islands
MALAYA
Singapore
Palau
Sumatra
Celebes
Hollandia
DUTCH EAST INDIES
NEW GUINEA
Rabaul
Java
Surabaya
Solomon Islands
Darwin
Port Moresby
Cairns
New Caledonia
AUSTRALIA
Brisbane
3. Japanese merchant shipping losses 1944
1 January – 30 April
1 May – 31 August
1 September – 31 December
Japanese territory
Total losses: 385 ships
4 Japanese merchant shipping losses 1945
1 January – 30 April
1 May – 15 August
Japanese territory
Total losses: 550 ships

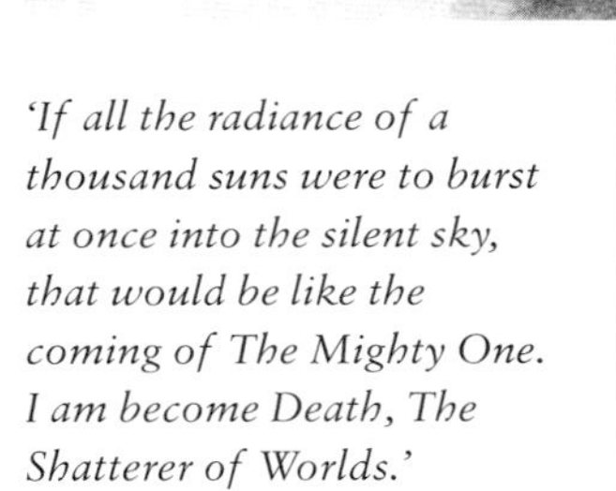

'If all the radiance of a thousand suns were to burst at once into the silent sky, that would be like the coming of The Mighty One. I am become Death, The Shatterer of Worlds.'

The Bhagavad Gita, *xi, 12, 32.*

The attack on Nagasaki (top) and the aftermath at Hiroshima (right).

of 9/10 March 1945 which left 124,711 killed or injured and 1,008,005 homeless – is well known, and the critical importance of the B-29 Superfortress is acknowledged, specifically the growth of XX Bomber Command to a strength of five wings by the end of hostilities. But the B-29 offensive was only one part of the final air assault on the home islands, and was complementary to the efforts of heavy, medium and fighter-bombers from Iwo Jima and Okinawa, as well as naval aircraft. With fighters from carriers operating combat air patrols over Japanese airfields, and air groups providing ECM and harassing night attacks, the Americans overwhelmed Japan's air defences to the extent that they were able to announce targets in advance, with obvious effect on Japanese morale. The revelation of Japan's defencelessness, a patent inability to resist declared American intention, was a major factor in the progressive demoralization of Japanese society in the course of 1945. In the words of one commentator, it 'continued to fight throughout 1945 from habit', but the debilitating effect of the air offensive can be gauged by absenteeism rates that touched 80 per cent in major industrial enterprises and even 40 per cent in Kyoto, which was never bombed. That only 68 per cent of the Japanese population in July 1945 believed that the war was lost may seem highly implausible, but the fact was that only 2 per cent of the population was of such an opinion one year earlier: the greater realism induced by taking the war to the Japanese home islands was clearly the product of the strategic bombing offensive.

Moreover, there was another matter intimately associated with this campaign: the air offensive most certainly affected both Japanese will and ability to resist, and it also completed the process of blockade. Strategic air forces had mined the Shimonoseki Strait through which most shipping entered the Inland Sea by spring 1945. This was part of a process that fulfilled its operational code name – Starvation. By spring 1945 Japanese industry was in or about to enter 'end-run production', and the

JAPANESE MERCHANT SHIPPING LOSSES

The introduction of convoy of shipping in November 1943 did nothing to curb Japanese losses: the system itself collapsed as the Americans reached into the western Pacific. At war's end the only convoy routes remaining to the Japanese were short-haul from the Asian mainland. Of Japanese merchant shipping losses almost four-fifths, both by numbers and tonnage, were lost in home waters and the southern resources area: by numbers almost half of merchant shipping losses were in home waters.

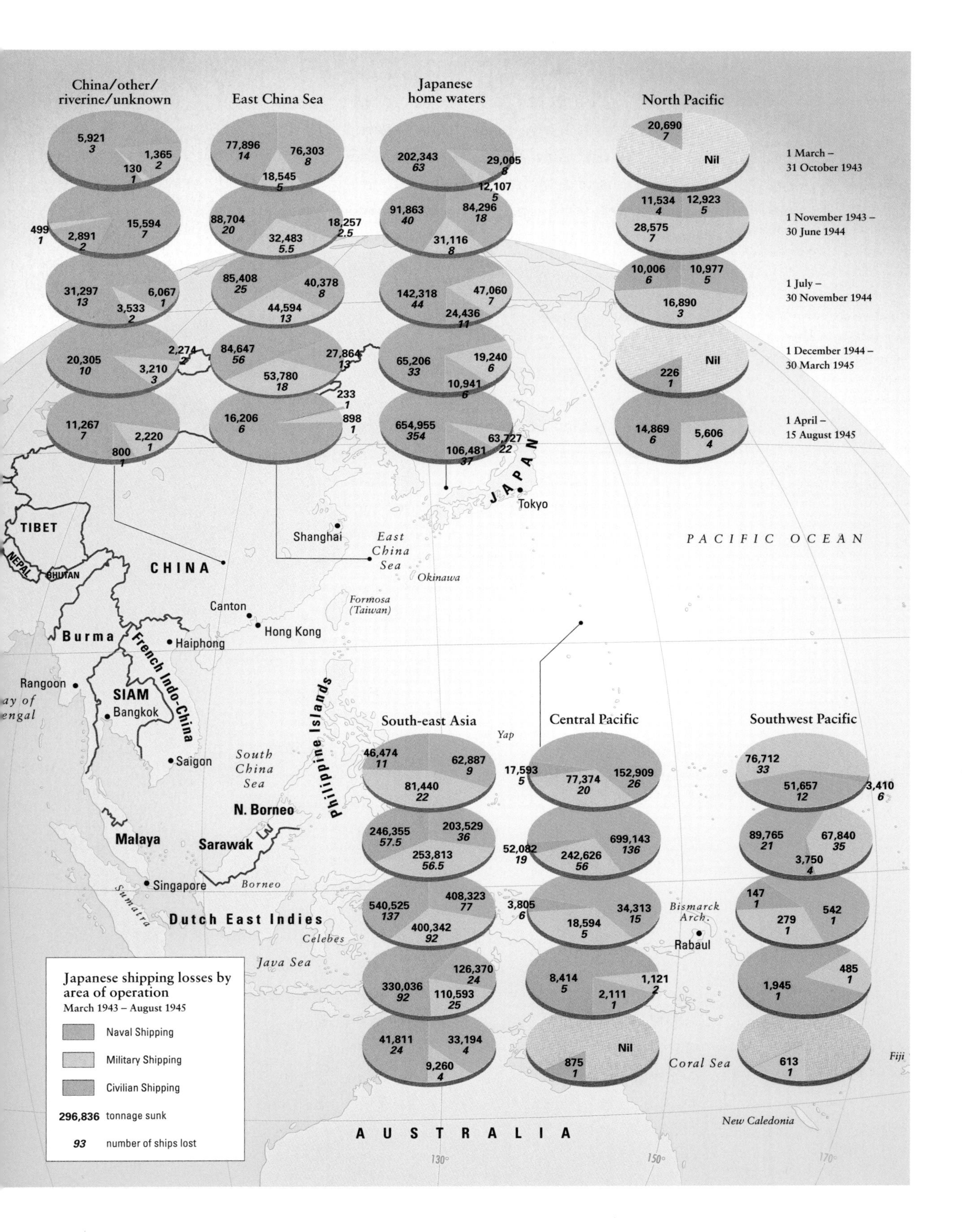

China/other/riverine/unknown
East China Sea
Japanese home waters
North Pacific
1 March – 31 October 1943
1 November 1943 – 30 June 1944
1 July – 30 November 1944
1 December 1944 – 30 March 1945
1 April – 15 August 1945
South-east Asia
Central Pacific
Southwest Pacific
TIBET
NEPAL
BHUTAN
CHINA
Burma
French Indo-China
SIAM
Malaya
Sarawak
N. Borneo
Borneo
Philippine Islands
Dutch East Indies
JAPAN
Tokyo
Shanghai
East China Sea
Okinawa
Formosa (Taiwan)
Canton
Hong Kong
Haiphong
Rangoon
Bangkok
Saigon
South China Sea
Singapore
Sumatra
Celebes
Java Sea
Yap
Bismarck Arch.
Rabaul
Coral Sea
New Caledonia
Fiji
PACIFIC OCEAN
AUSTRALIA
130°
150°
170°
Japanese shipping losses by area of operation
March 1943 – August 1945
Naval Shipping
Military Shipping
Civilian Shipping
296,836 tonnage sunk
93 number of ships lost

bombing offensive was increasingly directed against unused capacity rather than production. By war's end the Japanese power industry was able to produce double requirements, such was the extent of idleness in Japanese manufacturing industry for want of raw materials. Indeed, such was the Japanese double failure in terms of the protection of shipping and cities that after the end of the war the US strategic bombing survey suggested that, all other considerations being discounted, Japan could not have sustained herself beyond November 1945. Certainly in terms of the conduct of the strategic air offensive, in summer 1945 the US Army Air Force was warning of its rapid exhaustion of suitable targets to attack. As it was, the Japanese high command admitted its helplessness with the acknowledgement that 'the most troublesome possible course' that the Allies could follow would be to suspend all operations other than air bombardment. Japan faced the certainty of mass starvation in winter 1945–6 had the war continued into the new year, such was the utter inadequacy of the administrative margins on which she was obliged to work by summer 1945.

The potentially disastrous consequences of defeat dawned on the Japanese high command in the course of 1945. Its real concern was not so much defeat as social revolution in its aftermath, and increasingly in 1945 there was recognition of the threat presented by Soviet intervention. In the spring and summer of 1945, therefore, the Japanese high command made increasingly desperate attempts both to deflect the Soviet Union from intervention in Manchuria and to

JAPANESE SHIPPING LOSSES

Between December 1944 and March 1945, Japanese shipping losses remained at crippling levels mainly because carrier and land-based aircraft maintained their rate of sinkings. In the war's final phase losses increased primarily because of mining while the returns of carrier aircraft, increasingly committed to the air battle over the home islands, declined.

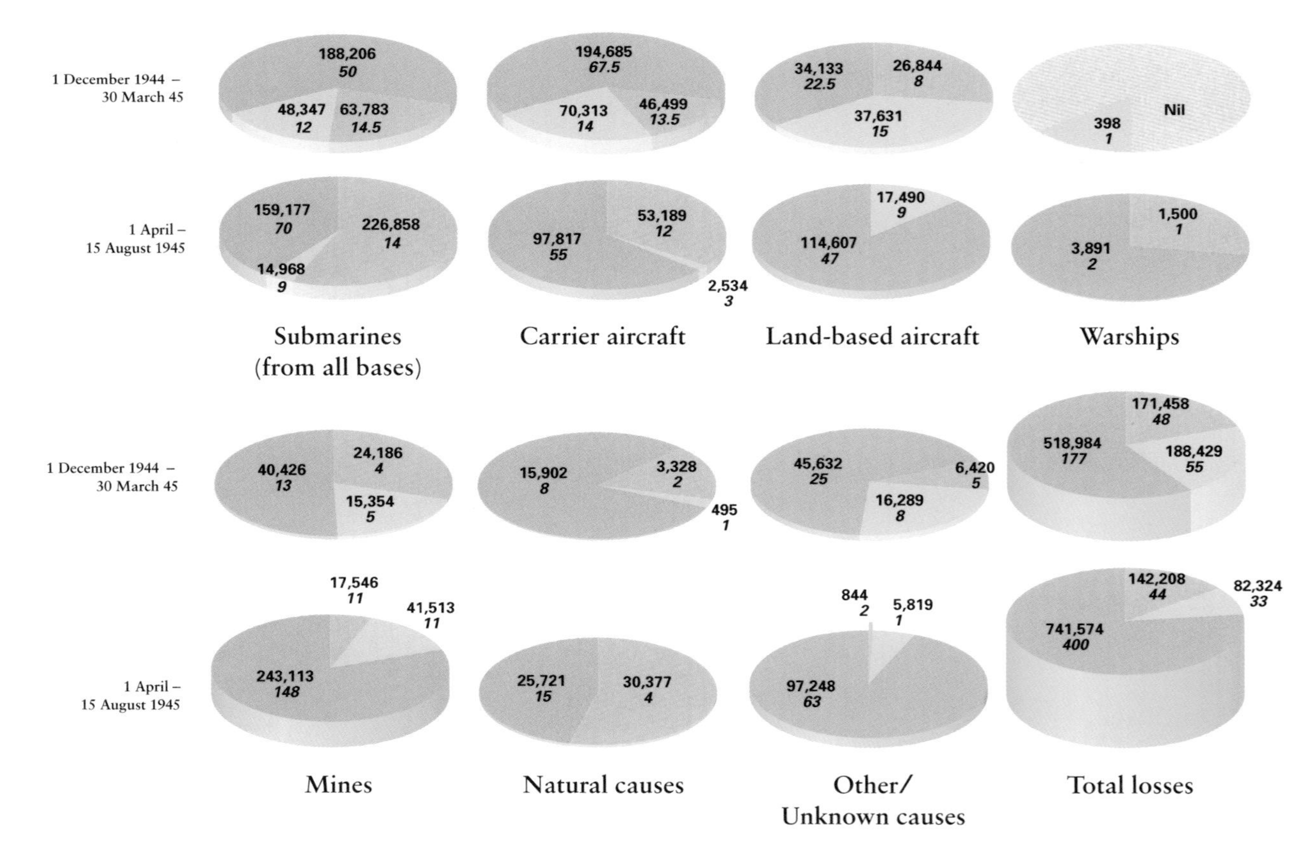

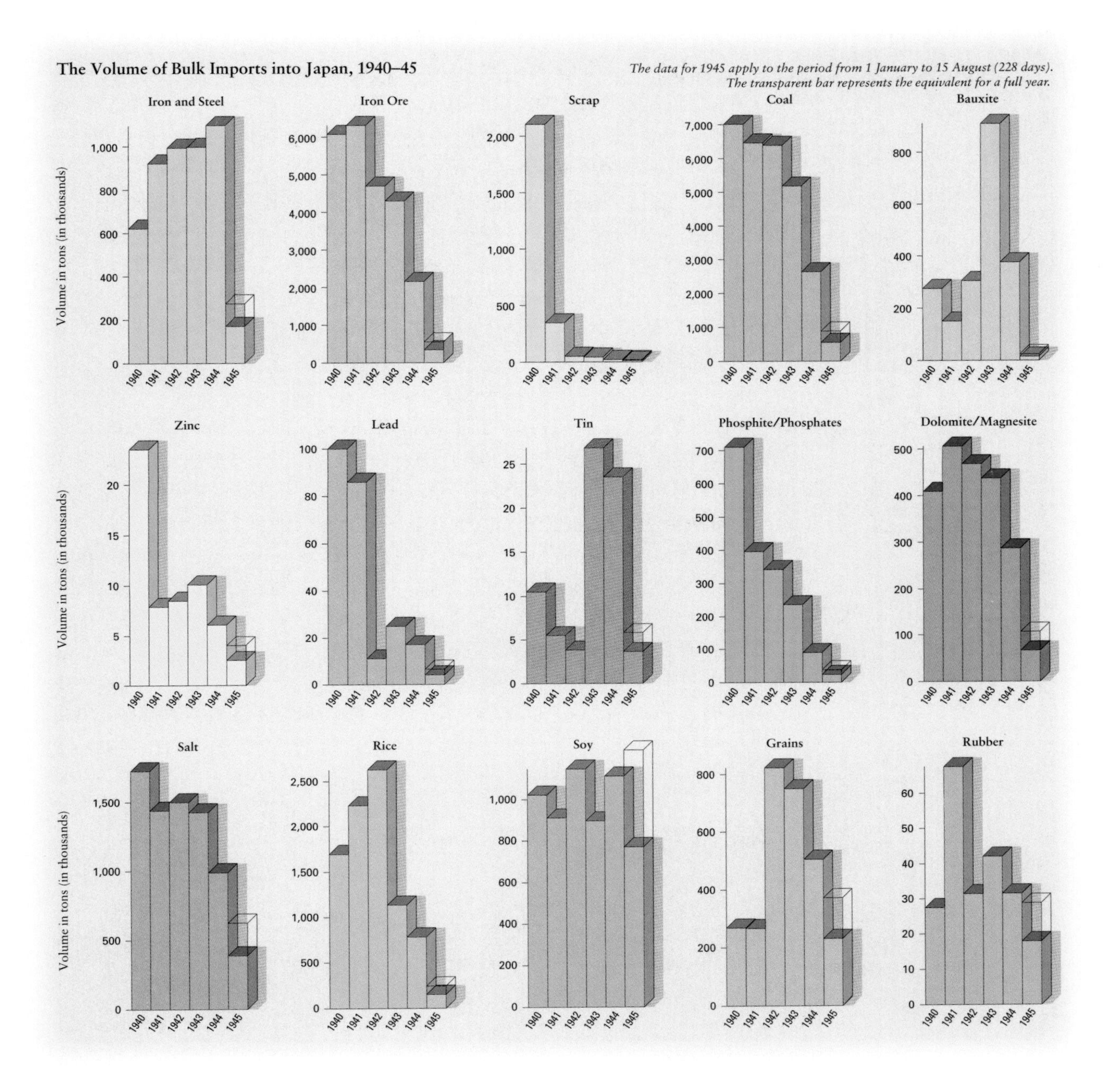

use her as the means of seeking some form of mediation in order to end the war.

Though the Soviet Union did not inform the United States of these efforts, the US interception of Japanese diplomatic signals ensured that the Americans knew of this contact, and in this period there was a growing convergence of American and Japanese wishes. In the last year of the war there was increasing American confidence that the Japanese war could be won without Allied assistance, and with the end of the German war and the first signs of emerging differences between the wartime Allies, the general view of the Truman administration was that Soviet intervention was neither necessary nor desirable. The successful testing of an atomic weapon at Alamogordo on 16 July 1945

VOLUME OF IMPORTS

Japan's economic defeat can be gauged by the fact that in 1945 the volume of imports exceeded that of 1945 only with respect to soy, grains and rubber: only soy showed an increase over 1944 imports. Japan, by summer 1945, was both industrially and in terms of nutritional needs all but finished.

immeasurably strengthened the American belief that Soviet involvement in the Japanese war was unnecessary. The Potsdam Declaration of 26 July 1945 calling upon Japan to surrender immediately and unconditionally on pain of immediate and utter destruction was underwritten in the knowledge that the means of such destruction was available. But the Japanese high command, without knowing what underlay this threat and without any guarantee of the institution of monarchy and the person of the Emperor, believed it had no alternative but to discount the Allied demand, and there was nothing that could be done at this stage to forestall the Soviet determination to play a full part in the war in the Far East.

Surrender

Thus was set the final scene of the Japanese war, namely the use of atomic weapons against Hiroshima (6 August) and Nagasaki (9 August) and the Soviet declaration of war. The Soviets began five military efforts in the last days of the war, and indeed fighting between Soviet and Japanese forces lasted throughout August, despite the announcement of Japan's surrender on 15 August. The main Soviet undertaking was in Manchuria, with a secondary effort directed across the Gobi Desert into northern China: the tertiary efforts were into Korea, against southern Sakhalin and in the Kuriles. In Manchuria the Soviets commanded overwhelming advantages of numbers, position, concentration and, critically important, professional technique. With second-string forces allocated to holding attacks on the main (and obvious) lines of advance, the primary

22 August 1945 and the entry of Soviet armoured forces into Port Arthur. For all the signs of development, the local Manchurian population does not seem too upset by the end of Japanese rule.

The Japanese surrender extended over many months as isolated forces and garrisons were slowly contacted prior to capitulation and repatriation. In the Indies there were local surrenders at Rabaul, on Bougainville and at Balikpapan, Morotai, Labuan, Singapore, Wewak, Kuching, Nauru and Port Blair. Also surrendered, by Colonel Kaida Tatuichi and his chief of staff Major Muiosu Slioji, was the 3,235-strong Japanese garrison in Dutch Timor at the ceremony in the Australian sloop Moresby *at Koepang on 11 September 1945.*

offensive into Manchuria was launched from Mongolia by a tank army that in eleven days advanced a distance that was equivalent of that between Caen and Milan, and across comparable ground. Unless one considers that the Japanese in Manchuria were defeated before this campaign began, the outcome became clear in the first two or three days, with the Japanese outfought on every sector and outmanoeuvred by Soviet armoured forces moving through the passes of the Great Hingan Mountains. With the lavish employment of airborne troops, the Soviets were able to secure all the major cities of Manchoutikuo by the time that the final ceasefires were arranged. On Sakhalin and in the Kuriles the Soviets were no less successful, even though their landings were bitterly resisted on certain of the Kurile islands.

Even after the devastation of Hiroshima and Nagasaki there were senior Japanese officers determined to continue resistance, to seek exoneration from failure in some awesome battle on the sacred soil of Japan that would somehow result in either victory or the redemption of personal, service and national honour via annihilation. Within the Supreme War Council there was a greater realism, although it was hopelessly indecisive: in the absence of any Allied guarantee of the Imperial institution and the person of the Emperor, there was a resistance to acceptance of the terms of the Potsdam Declaration. Soviet

Surrender. Watched by the Supreme Allied Commander General MacArthur and his chief of staff, and by representatives of the United States, China, Britain, the Soviet Union, Australia, Canada, France, the Netherlands and New Zealand, General Umezo Yoshigiro signed the instrument of surrender 'by command and on behalf of the Japanese General Headquarters'.

intervention added to the desperation of the Japanese position because the Council recognized that Japan had to surrender while the power of decision remained with the Americans and if she was to avoid occupation by Soviet forces. But despite such considerations and the fear of social revolution if the war and defeat came to home soil, the Council could not agree on any settled policy: it was to take the personal decision of the Emperor to end the war. The decision provoked mutiny on the part of certain units in the capital that was suppressed, and it was the Emperor's unprecedented broadcast to the nation, plus the dispatch of various members of the Imperial family to major commands to enforce compliance, that ensured that the decision to surrender – 'to bear the unbearable' – was obeyed, the inevitable suicides excepted. On 28 August American and British naval forces entered Tokyo Bay, and thus began a process of formal surrenders that were to extend across the whole of what remained of Japan's overseas empire and lasted into spring 1946.

The main surrender took place in Tokyo Bay on 2 September 1945, and brought an end to a war that, along with its European counterpart, was the most destructive and costly in history. In these few poor pages, the author has attempted to explain rather than describe the unfolding of the Second World War in the Far East, and in so doing would acknowledge one obvious historiographical problem: there are few things more difficult to explain than inevitable defeat. Herein lies the one point of major difference between the European and Far East wars: Germany's defeat was not inevitable, but, surely, Japan's defeat was assured from the very start of hostilities. Yet at the end, one is thrown back upon description because it is through analogy that one can best understand the events of the war as a whole and the events of the last weeks and months of the Pacific struggle.

The coasts of the Pacific, and specifically the Japanese islands, lie exposed to the full force of the *tsunami*, a giant wave of destruction that throws itself ashore, a movement of water sometimes across the vastness of the Pacific from one continent to another triggered by seismic disturbance or the eruption of underwater volcanoes. In both the conflict overall and specifically the last five months of the war, Japan was overwhelmed by a man-made *tsunami* of high-explosive hatred that reached across the whole of the Pacific as a result of a seismic disturbance, within American society and industry, induced at Pearl Harbor on one Sunday morning in December 1941. It was a *tsunami* that was without precedent. At various times in history states have been overpowered by invading armies – Germany in 1945 being the obvious, most pertinent example. But never before had a country been overwhelmed from the sea and across such distances, and this is the evidence of the full range of Japanese failure and American achievement in the Second World War in the Far East. In the *tsunami* that engulfed Japan – state, society, industry, the military and indeed the home islands – is both explanation and description of this conflict.

The arrival of the delegation that was to sign the instrument of their country's surrender: the Missouri, *in Tokyo Bay, on the morning of 2 September 1945. The delegation was led by Foreign Minister Shigemitsu Mamoru and General Umezo Yoshigiro, Chief of the Army General Staff: three officials from the Foreign Ministry, three army and three naval officers were in attendance. The Japanese delegation was piped on board the* Missouri*: on departure it was afforded customary honours. The war was over.*

APPENDICES

APPENDIX A: MAJOR NAVAL ACTIONS OF THE PACIFIC WAR

		Carriers			Battleships	Cruisers		Destroyers
		Fleet	*Light*	*Escort*		*Heavy*	*Light*	
07 Dec 41	Pearl Harbor							
	Imperial Japanese Navy	–/6	–/–	–/–	–/2	–/2	–/1	–/9
	United States Navy	–/–	–/–	–/–	2/8	–/2	3/6	3/31
27 Feb 42	Java Sea							
	Imperial Japanese Navy	–/–	–/–	–/–	–/–	–/2	–/1	–/19
	United States Navy	–/–	–/–	–/–	–/–	–/2	2/3	3/9
07 May 42	Coral Sea							
	Imperial Japanese Navy	–/2	1/1	–/–	–/–	–/6	–/–	–/7
	United States Navy	1/2	–/–	–/–	–/–	–/5	–/–	1/9
04 Jun 42	Midway Islands							
	Imperial Japanese Navy	4/4	1/1	–/–	–/9	1/10	–/4	–/32
	United States Navy	1/3	–/–	–/–	–/–	–/7	–/1	1/15
09 Aug 42	Savo Island							
	Imperial Japanese Navy	–/–	–/–	–/–	–/–	–/6	–/2	–/1
	United States Navy	–/–	–/–	–/–	–/–	4/4	–/–	–/6
24 Aug 42	Eastern Solomons							
	Imperial Japanese Navy	–/2	1/1	–/–	–/3	–/9	–/2	1/22
	United States Navy	–/3	–/–	–/–	–/1	–/5	–/2	–/18
11 Oct 42	Cape Esperance							
	Imperial Japanese Navy	–/–	–/–	–/–	–/–	1/3	–/–	1/2
	United States Navy	–/–	–/–	–/–	–/–	–/2	1/2	–/5
26 Oct 42	Santa Cruz							
	Imperial Japanese Navy	–/3	–/1	–/–	–/2	–/8	1/2	–/30
	United States Navy	1/2	–/–	–/–	–/1	–/3	–/3	1/14
12 Nov 42	First Guadalcanal							
	Imperial Japanese Navy	–/–	–/–	–/–	1/2	–/–	–/1	2/11
	United States Navy	–/–	–/–	–/–	–/–	–/2	–/2	3/8
14 Nov 42	Second Guadalcanal							
	Imperial Japanese Navy	–/–	–/–	–/–	1/1	–/2	–/2	1/8
	United States Navy	–/–	–/–	–/–	–/2	–/–	–/–	3/4
30 Nov 42	Tassafaronga							
	Imperial Japanese Navy	–/–	–/–	–/–	–/–	–/–	–/–	1/8
	United States Navy	–/–	–/–	–/–	–/–	1/4	–/1	–/6
06 Jul 43	Kula Gulf							
	Imperial Japanese Navy	–/–	–/–	–/–	–/–	–/–	–/–	1/10
	United States Navy	/–	–/–	–/–	–/–	–/–	1/3	–/4
13 Jul 43	Kolombangara							
	Imperial Japanese Navy	–/–	–/–	–/–	–/–	–/–	1/1	–/5
	United States Navy	–/–	–/–	–/–	–/–	–/–	–/3	1/10
06 Aug 43	Vella Gulf							
	Imperial Japanese Navy	–/–	–/–	–/–	–/–	–/–	–/–	3/4
	United States Navy	–/–	–/–	–/–	–/–	–/–	–/–	–/6
06 Oct 43	Vella Lavella							
	Imperial Japanese Navy	–/–	–/–	–/–	–/–	–/–	–/–	1/9
	United States Navy	–/–	–/–	–/–	–/–	–/–	–/–	1/6

		Carriers			Battleships	Cruisers		Destroyers
		Fleet	*Light*	*Escort*		*Heavy*	*Light*	
01 Nov 44	Empress Augusta Bay							
	Imperial Japanese Navy	–/–	–/–	–/–	–/–	–/2	1/2	1/6
	United States Navy	–/–	–/–	–/–	–/–	–/–	–/4	–/9
26 Nov 43	Cape St. George							
	Imperial Japanese Navy	–/–	–/–	–/–	–/–	–/–	–/–	3/5
	United States Navy	–/–	–/–	–/–	–/–	–/–	–/–	–/6
20 Jun 44	Philippine Sea							
	Imperial Japanese Navy	3/5	–/4	–/–	–/5	–/11	–/2	–/27
	United States Navy	–/8	–/7	–/–	–/7	–/14	–/18	–/67
23 Oct 44	Leyte Gulf							
	Imperial Japanese Navy	1/1	3/3	–/–	3/9	6/15	4/5	11/35
	United States Navy	–/9	1/8	2/29	–/12	–/5	–/20	4/162
06 Apr 45	Okinawa							
	Imperial Japanese Navy	–/–	–/–	–/–	1/1	–/–	1/1	4/8
	United States Navy	–/5	–/4	–/–	–/4	–/–	–/8	2/26
24 Jul 45	Inland Sea							
	Imperial Japanese Navy	1/na	na	1/na	3/na	2/na	1/na	na
	United States Navy	–/12	–/6	–/–	–/9	–/1	–/21	–/80

The major actions of the Pacific war are listed by date in the form –/–, with the first figure being the losses and the second figure being the number of each type of ship involved in the battle. Submarines are not listed. Damaged units are not listed, and similarly unlisted are ships sunk in related but separate actions: e.g. the loss of the destroyer Nagatsuki *on 6 July 1943 in the aftermath of the battle of Kula Gulf is not included in total of losses of that action. Ships that were damaged in the named action and subsequently lost (e.g. the* Yorktown *at Midway) are included in totals.*

Appendix B: Wartime Commissioning/completion of Major Units

	Dec 1941 IJN / USN	*1942* IJN / USN	*1943* IJN / USN	*1944* IJN / USN	*Jan–Sep 1945* IJN / USN	*Total* IJN / USN
Carriers						
Fleet	–/–	2/1	–/6	5/7	–/4	7/18
Light	–/–	2/–	1/9	1/–	–/–	4/9
Escort	–/–	2/11	2/24	–/33	–/9	4/77
Battleships	–/–	2/4	–/2	–/2	–/–	2/8
Cruisers						
Heavy	–/–	–/–	–/4	–/1	–/8	–/13
Light	–/1	1/8	3/7	3/11	–/6	7/33
Destroyers	–/2	10/84	12/126	7/76	3/61	32/349
Destroyer escorts	–/–	–/–	18/234	20/181	20/5	58/420
Corvettes	–/–	–/–	–/65	72/8	39/–	111/73
Submarines	–/2	20/34	36/56	35/80	20/31	116/203

Appendix C: The Battle of Leyte Gulf

The landings on Leyte and the ensuing battle of Leyte Gulf, 23–26 October 1944, represented something that was unprecedented in the conduct of US operations in the Pacific war, and indeed the precise pattern of operations was never repeated in subsequent operations. To date US landings had been preceded by softening-up operations by carrier forces which were primarily aimed at ensuring air supremacy and the isolation of the objective from outside support. In the course of these operations US carrier forces registered en passant success against local escort forces and shipping, most of the latter being service shipping. In the case of the Leyte, however, American preliminary operations registered very considerable success against merchant shipping on account of the position of the Philippines astride Japan's main trade routes with the southern resources area.

Striking at the Ryukyus and Formosa in addition to the Philippines, US carrier operations for the first time struck directly at the Japanese merchant marine, and in the course of these and subsequent follow-up operations contributed to the prohibitive losses inflicted on Japanese merchantmen obliged to operate without fleet support in waters largely controlled by enemy air power.

During the battle itself American attention to merchant shipping was minimal, seventeen ships of some 90,000 tons being sunk, but in subsequent operations a total of 48 service and merchant ships of 212,476 tons were sunk in Filippine and adjacent waters. Of these only18 ships of 68,913 tons belonged to the merchant fleet, the smallness of such numbers reflecting the relatively small number of merchantmen operating in these waters in the immediate aftermath of the collapse of Japanese sea lines of communications.

The pattern of operations – submarine and carrier operations as a preclude to battle and then the devastating follow-up phase – never repeated itself: the Iwo Jima operation lacked a mercantile dimension: the Okinawa operation sealed off Japan from the south and hence there was no follow-up operations against shipping.

Opposing Forces at the Battle of Leyte Gulf

	Imperial Japanese Navy	**US Navy and Allies**
Carriers		
Fleet	1	9
Light	3	8
Escort	–	29
Aircraft a/c	116	1,561+
Battleships	9	12
Cruisers		
Heavy	15	5
Light	5	20
Destroyers	35	162
Destroyer escorts	–	43
Frigates	–	13
Minelayers	–	3
Mine Sweepers	–	29
Submarines	–	22
Oilers	–	41

Japanese Naval and Shipping Losses September–November 1944

In September/early October 1944 Japanese light forces and service and mercantile shipping, shorn of the distant support of a fleet, suffered very heavy losses as American carrier forces fought for and won air superiority over the Philippines. The Imperial Navy's attempted intervention proved disastrous: in the preliminary, main and mopping-up phases of the battle, between 23 and 28 October, it lost1 fleet and 3 light fleet carriers, 3 battleships, 6 heavy and 4 light cruisers, 11 destroyers, 2 submarines and 2 amphibious units. Thereafter, deprived of both local air cover and fleet support, in the period 29 October/30 November 1944 the Imperial Navy lost1 fleet carrier, 1 escort carrier, 1 battleship, 2 heavy and 2 light cruisers, 11 destroyers, 7 escort destroyers, 8 chasers, 5 submarines, 5 minesweepers, 1 netlayer, 1 minelayer, 6 gunboats, 2 destroyer-transports and 12 assault ships, plus one other unit, either in the Philippines or during the withdrawal of units to the home islands from the south. The decline of shipping losses in theatre in November reflected a reduction of shipping in these waters: the high level of Japanese warship losses outside the theatre reflected the inclusion in these returns of the sinking of the 64,800-ton fleet carrier *Shinano* off central Honshu by the submarine *Archerfish* on 29 November.

Japanese Naval and Shipping Losses September–November 1944

	Warships and Amphibious Units		Naval Shipping		Military Shipping		Civilian Shipping		Overall Shipping Losses	
	No. ships	*tonnage*	*No. ships*	*tonnage*	*No. ships*	*tonnage*	*No. ships*	*tonnage*	*No. ships*	*tonnage*
1 September – 22 October 1944										
Total losses in theatre/related waters	49	29,652	28	133,415	44	190,478	59	179,109	131	503,002
Losses in other theatres	26	37,166	17	53,076	14	48,783	34	113,024	65	214,883
23–28 October 1944										
Leyte Gulf and associated actions	32	324,891	5	33,883	4	12,586	8	45,877	17	92,346
Losses in other theatres	1	950	3	13,760	2	1,526	11	32,478	16	47,764
29 October – 30 November 1944										
Total losses in theatre/related waters	49	119,655	12	52,262	18	91,301	18	68,913	48	212,476
Total losses in other theatres	18	107,346	19	78,664	9	37,366	27	112,665	55	228,695
Overall losses in theatre/related waters	130	474,198	45	219,560	66	294,365	85	293,899	196	807,824
Overall losses in all other waters	45	145,462	39	145,500	25	87,675	72	258,167	136	491,342
Losses on dates or in areas unknown	2	2,328	1	6,067	–	–	2	2,417	3	8,484
TOTAL LOSSES IN ALL THEATRES	177	621,988	85	371,127	91	382,040	159	554,483	335	1,307,650

Biographical details

Brooke, Field Marshal Sir Alan (1883–1963)
Chief of the Imperial General Staff, 1941–6. *De facto* spokesman of the chiefs of staff in dealing with Churchill and the Americans, Brooke commanded widespread respect because of his competence, his determination and his ability to handle (with considerable difficulty) Churchill. Embodiment of Anglo-American trust and understanding: he never understood the Americans, and the Americans never trusted him. With reference to the latter, he deserved better.

Chiang Kai-Shek, Generalissimo (1877–1975)
China's head of state though in effect *primus inter pares* along with various regional warlords over whom he exercised nominal suzerainty. Leader of the Kuomintang (Nationalists) after 1925 and during the civil war with the communists. Detained by dissident Manchurian forces in December 1936 in the Sian Incident and forced to end the civil war: national leader in dealing with Japanese aggression. Wartime Nationalist passivity, military incompetence and corruption exacted its toll: defeated in the resumed civil war after 1945, the Kuomintang was expelled to Formosa in 1949.

Churchill, Winston (1874–1965)
Prime Minister of Britain 1940–45. The personification of British defiance and greatness in 1940–41, matters Pacific were necessarily of lesser consequence to Britain after December 1941: he displayed a penchant for increasingly divisive action as his powers of decision-making diminished and was rightly regarded with considerable suspicion by the US military by the final years of the war.

Cunningham, Admiral of the Fleet Sir Andrew (1883–1963)
First Sea Lord 1942–6. Victor of Matapan and commander of the Mediterranean Fleet in adversity, he served in Washington and then in the Mediterranean under Eisenhower before becoming Chief of Naval Staff. Generally reserved and withdrawn in dealing with Churchill except in his diary entries, he headed a navy that emerged in 1944–5 as the only British service that could arrive in strength in the Pacific before the scheduled end of the Pacific war.

Curtin, John (1885–1945)
Prime Minister of Australia who in the crisis of early 1942 in effect placed his country under American protection and thereafter within the American sphere of influence even at the expense of Australia's traditional relationship with Britain. He was closely associated with MacArthur and was despised by Churchill: Anglo-Australian relations were better 'on the ground' than suggested by often rancorous official exchanges.

Doolittle, Lieutenant General James (1896–1995)
Born in Alaska, Doolittle joined the Army Air Service in 1917 and made his name in the inter-war period with a series of speed and endurance trials. Returning to the Army Air Force in 1941 in a staff post, he commanded the raid of April 1942 before taking command of the 15th Air Force and strategic air forces in north-west Africa. He took command of the 8th Air Force in Britain in 1944 and at the end of the European war was posted to Air Force headquarters in Washington.

Fletcher, Vice Admiral Frank Jack (1885–1973)
Commander of US carrier forces at the Coral Sea, Midway and Eastern Solomons before being side-lined: he ended the war in command of the North Pacific backwater. In period of command lost two carriers sunk and two badly damaged, and Fletcher acquired reputation that wavered between bad luck and ineptitude. If his period of command in the Solomons was less than distinguished, he none the less commanded in the first three carrier battles in history and was never on the losing side.

Fuchida, Commander Mitsuo (1902–76)
One of the Imperial Navy's leading aviators in the pre-war period, Fuchida led the attack on Pearl Harbor and was

heavily involved in the planning of the Midway operation though illness prevent his active involvement in that ill-fated venture. He was assigned to obscurity through a series of staff positions and survived the war. For many years his book *Midway: The Battle that Doomed Japan* (1955) was the standard reference for the Japanese side of the action. After the war he became a convert to Christianity and became an American citizen.

Halsey, Fleet Admiral William J., Jr (1882–1959)
Rough and no nonsense approach, disdain for the Japanese and sheer aggressiveness made him tailor-made for the media. Carrier commander in early operations but missed Midway: appointed to command in southern Pacific at the crisis of Guadalcanal campaign, he drove his forces forward to victory: subsequently side-lined until 1944. Poorly served by his staff, his conduct at battle of Leyte Gulf and handling of Third Fleet off Japan drew much criticism at the time: the sheer scale of operations by 1944–5 was probably too much for him.

King, Fleet Admiral Ernest Joseph (1878–1956)
Chief of Naval Operations 1942–6. By his own admission, an admiral of the son-of-a-bitch variety. Exceptionally able, his virtually unaided insistence on the central Pacific offensive resulted in the collapse of the South West Pacific initiative in 1944. Bitterly anglophobic and inclined to personal indulgence, he commanded respect and fear. Perhaps little realized, the winner and survivor of the Guadalacanal campaign.

Koga, Admiral Mineichi (1885–1943)
Successor of Yamamoto as commander of the Combined Fleet, Koga was dealt a losing hand as the US Navy acquired the means to carry the war into the western Pacific with a strength that was irresistible. Koga presided over the defeat in the northern Solomons and the neutralization of Rabaul, and was obliged to order the abandonment of Truk. With the Palaus neutralized after March 1944, Koga's task of seeking 'the decisive battle' was all but impossible: he was killed in an aircraft accident during the withdrawal from the Palaus.

MacArthur, General of the Army Douglas A. (1880–1964)
Supreme Allied Commander South West Pacific Command. An individual of great complexity and contradictions who has excited extremes of admiration and loathing in roughly equal measures. Very fortunate to have survived an abysmal conduct of the defence of the Philippines characterized by self-advertisement and exacting of great wealth from Commonwealth authorities: he owed his survival to Washington's desire that he remain in the Pacific. Obsessed by own Command and personal interest, and surrounded by an entourage that was generally distrusted, he was to lead South West Pacific Command to a series of victories that culminated in his taking the surrender of Japan on behalf of the Allied Powers. Dismissed by Truman during the Korean War for trying to repeat personal behaviour of the Pacific war.

Marshall, General of the Army George C. (1880–1947)
Chief of Staff, US Army 1939–46. Raised to the pantheon of US heroes and beyond reproach or criticism, Marshall was 'the organizer of victory' in terms of raising ground and air forces. Adept in inter-service in-fighting, his strategic judgement may be questioned, not least in terms of lack of forward planning between 1939 and 1942. Post-war Secretary of State, and architect of the Marshall Plan of American aid that facilitated the recovery of western Europe.

Mitscher, Vice Admiral Marc A. (1887–1947)
Very fortunate to have survived a less than satisfactory performance as captain of the *Hornet* at Midway, Mitscher rose to become the pre-eminent carrier commander, primarily under Spruance as fleet commander. He declined nomination to the post of Chief of Naval Operations after the war and served as commander of the 8th and Atlantic Fleets until his death in 1947.

Nagumo, Vice Admiral Chuichi (1887–1944)
Made his pre-war mark in the surface navy with a specialiation in torpedoes and as one of the more unpleasant hard-liners: he is known to have threatened at

least one colleague with murder. Commanded the First Carrier Striking Force at Pearl Harbor and in subsequent actions until dismissed in the aftermath of Santa Cruz: there is no evidence to suggest that he ever understood carrier warfare and he certainly never left any mark either upon carrier operations or the Imperial Navy's carrier force. Committed suicide as naval commander on Saipan in 1944.

NIMITZ, ADMIRAL CHESTER W. (1885–1966)
Commander-in-Chief US Pacific Fleet and Pacific Ocean Areas. Somewhat overshadowed during the war by his subordinate commanders at sea on the one hand and King on the other, Nimitz possessed (with one exception) sound strategic judgement and an ability to pick the right commanders and work subordinates as a team. Post-war Chief of Naval Operations.

ROOSEVELT, FRANKLIN D. (1882–1945)
Thirty-second and, with Lincoln, greatest president of the United States (1933–45). He provided hope to a nation in the grip of the Depression and led the United States through its defeats to victory in the Second World War and into its inheritance as the greatest power in the world. Often regarded as 'hands-off' in the formulation of military power during the war, his was the critical decision on many episodes: he died on the eve of final victory over Germany.

SLIM, GENERAL SIR WILLIAM (1891–1970)
Not a regular soldier, Slim enlisted in 1914 and served in the Middle East before joining the Indian Army in 1920. He commanded a brigade in Eritrea and a division in Iraq and Syria, and took part in the occupation of Iran in 1941. He assumed forces in the middle of a disastrous retreat in March 1942, and was obliged to sort out the second Arakan débâcle. Army commander in 1943, he commanded at the defence of Imphal and Kohima (1944) and in the campaign that cleared most of Burma (1945). Post-war chief of staff and Governor-General of Australia 1953–60.

SMITH, GENERAL HOLLAND (1882–1967)
One of the inter-war period's pioneers in developing concepts involving the offensive use of sea power in the form of amphibious landings, specifically the opposed landing. He was appointed to command amphibious forces in the Atlantic theatre in 1941 before assuming the same post in the Pacific in 1943. He was amphibious commander in the Marshalls and Marianas before being returned to the United States for a training command after the celebrated Smith v. Smith affair on Saipan. Aggressive, impatient, brusque but used to getting his way through sheer force of argument, the name Howlin' Mad was well earned.

SPRUANCE, ADMIRAL RAYMOND A. (1886–1969)
With a reputation for thinking, Spruance was a surface officer appointed to carrier command at Midway: thereafter he served as Nimitz's chief of staff before taking command of the Fifth Fleet in 1944. His conduct at the battle of the Philippine Sea drew widespread and largely unjustified criticism at the time. He commanded during the gruelling Okinawa campaign. Self-effacing, modest, and possessed of mastery of detail, he became president of the Naval War College after the war.

STILWELL, LIEUTENANT GENERAL JOSEPH (1883–1946)
Ultimately Deputy Supreme Commander South East Asia Command, Chief of Staff to Chiang Kai-shek and commander China–Burma–India theatre with authority over 10th and 14th Army Air Forces. An old China hand, Stilwell was sent to and marched out of Burma with defeated forces: thereafter he collected appointments as Washington slipped into 'the China quagmire' and the morass that was Burma. At the centre of a number of conflicting areas of responsibility, 'Vinegar Joe' was known for his vituperative treatment of most things British and all things Chiang Kai-shek. Dismissed from China in autumn 1944, his removal saw the clearing of a very able China desk that had kept US policy in touch with realities. Commanded in the last stages on Okinawa, and was present, along with suitably acidic comment, in the *Missouri* at the surrender ceremony.

TRUMAN, HARRY S. (1894–1972)
Became thirty-third president of the United States (1945–53) on the death of Roosevelt. There is little doubt that growing difficulties with the Soviet Union and possession of atomic weapons prompted the decision to use

the latter in August 1945. A virtual unknown when he became president though he grew in stature in office, his name will always be associated with the Truman Doctrine and onset of the Cold War.

TOJO, GENERAL HIDEKI (1884–1948)
Prime Minister of Japan 1941–4. Champion of hard-line militarism in the inter-war period, his appointment to office was widely regarded as the prelude to war. In reality the real decisions that were to lead to the Pacific war had been taken before he assumed office, and thereafter he presided over rather than directed national affairs. After a failed suicide attempt, he was tried, convicted and hanged for war crimes, but only after a trial in which he assumed full responsibility for Japan's various actions but displayed a naivety and disingenuousness that was revealing.

TOYODA, ADMIRAL SOEMA (1885–1957)
Toyoda's only real impact as successor to Koga and the last commander of the Combined Fleet was to commit his forces to an offensive at Biak in early June 1944: the American descent on the Marianas provided evidence of the irrelevance of this effort. Under his command, the Imperial Navy fought and suffered overwhelming defeats in the Philippine Sea and off Leyte Gulf: in effect by war's end it had ceased to exist.

TURNER, ADMIRAL RICHMOND KELLY (1885–1961)
Director of the war plans division at the outbreak of war, Turner became naval commander of most American amphibious efforts. An undoubted ability in terms of organization and command was matched by an appalling temper, overbearing egotism, unthinking obstinacy and over-familiarity with the bottle, the latter of which ultimately proved fatal. It has been suggested that Turner more than most bore responsibility for the Pearl Harbor débâcle and sought to blame others for his failure to pass on warnings of Japanese intentions, but the point can never be proved.

UGAKI, VICE ADMIRAL MATOME (1890–1945)
Generally regarded as one of the leading hard-liners of the pre-war Navy, Ugaki was chief of staff of the carrier forces in the opening phase of the war. Thereafter he became commander of battleship forces, but his prominence lay in two matters. He was one of the founders of the kamikazes and committed suicide on the day of Japan's surrender, and he left a diary which is enlightening: an inability to contemplate anything but victory before the Philippine Sea and the statement after Hiroshima that Japan had to prolong the war in order to develop atomic weapons of her own indicate an utter lack of appreciation of the power of Japan's enemies.

YAMAMOTO, FLEET ADMIRAL ISOROKU (1884–1943)
Commander of the Combined Fleet 1943–5. Best known of Japanese commanders, whether military or naval, and generally regarded as an influence of moderation when that commodity was in short supply. He initiated the Pearl Harbor strike and was the decisive factor in enforcing both this operation and the Midway endeavour on a reluctant naval staff. He presided over the defeat in the Guadalcanal campaign, and was responsible for the singularly unsuccessful air campaign in the south-west Pacific in April 1943. Deliberately murdered by the Americans when his aircraft was shot down, he was fortunate to die before the real defeats began. Refused posthumous ennoblement.

YAMASHITA, GENERAL TOMOYUKI HOBUN (1885–1946)
Commander of the 25th Army which conducted the campaign that resulted in the singularly impressive conquest of Malaya and Singapore in 1941–2. He was personally and politically *persona non grata* with Tokyo, and after having been side-lined was appointed commander in the Philippines where he was responsible for conducting a protracted defence of Luzon: his forces were still in the field at the end of the war. Specifically blamed for the devastation of Manila, for which his forces were not responsible, he was subsequently hanged for war crimes: his real offence would seem to have been competence though his forces were responsible for the massacre of allegedly more than 120,000 people in the aftermath of the fall of Singapore.

FURTHER READING

The task of providing a reading list is fraught with peril, and for obvious reason: what is omitted can be as contentious as what is included, and the order in which works are cited to some people may indicate precedence and usefulness. One cannot make provision on the first score: one would deny the second, though on this point I would note one work as special and cite it as worthy of opening this section. David C. Evans and Mark R. Peattie, *Kaigun. Strategy, Tactics and Technology in the Imperial Navy 1887–1941* (Annapolis, Naval Institute Press, 1997), invites two comments. The first, simply, is to ask how historians managed before its publication, and such a question invites an answer to the effect: not as well as they will do in future. The second is to state that one has only ever read one text superior to it on this subject. That text was the original manuscript, not the one that was published. One would express the hope that Mark will be able to produce from what was deleted from the original manuscript a companion volume that will do justice to that manuscript, to *Kaigun*, to David's memory and to his own lifetime of scholarship and achievement.

To note the basic standbys: the US Army, Air Force and Marine Corps official histories, some now in their fifth decade and many reprinted in the last ten years, still stand critical examination and present themselves as the best available introductions to their various subjects. Less aged, and infinitely more valuable, is Grace Pearson Hayes, *The History of the Joint Chiefs of Staff in World War II. The War against Japan* (Annapolis, Maryland, Naval Institute Press, 1982): it is to the formulation of American (and to a lesser extent Allied) policy as *Kaigun* is to the inter-war Japanese Navy. The thought, however, was to set out a further reading list concentrating upon the renderings of more recent years, until one realized that E. B. Potter's *Nimitz* (Annapolis, Maryland, Naval Institute Press) was published as long ago as 1976 and *The Quiet Warrior: A Biography of Admiral Raymond A. Spruance* (Boston, Little, Brown), in 1974. That autobiography none the less does commend itself, rather more than the same author's biography of Halsey which somehow managed to avoid a real judgement on Halsey's conduct at the battle of Leyte Gulf. Martha Byrd's interesting *Chennault. Giving Wings to the Tiger* (Tuscaloosa, University of Alabama Press, 1987), deserves consideration on several counts, not least an examination of dimensions of the war – air power *per se* and the China theatre – seldom afforded much consideration in most western accounts of the war against Japan.

In terms of battles one notes that in the last two decades only two books would seem to commend themselves, namely William T. Y'Blood's final word, *Red Sun Setting. The Battle of the Philippine Sea,* and Denis and Peggy Warner's *Disaster in the Pacific. New Light on the Battle of Savo Island* (both Annapolis, Maryland, Naval Institute Press, 1981 and 1992 respectively), though with respect to the latter one is not fully convinced that content quite equalled claim. While on such matters one would note, for all the wrong reasons, James Rusbridger and Eric Nave, *Betrayal at Pearl Harbor. How Churchill Lured Roosevelt into World War II* (New York, Touchstone, 1991), as a book in which claim most definitely is not proven. Various works on intelligence matters must also be noted, and this writer leaves it to the reader to decide upon respective merits, suffice to note (in alphabetical order) Edward J. Drea, *MacArthur's ULTRA. Codebreaking and the*

War against Japan, 1942–1945 (University Press of Kansas, 1992), W.J. Holmes, *Double-Edged Secrets. US Naval Intelligence Operations in the Pacific during World War II*, Rear-Admiral Edwin T. Layton, USN (Ret) with Captain Roger Pineau USNR (Ret) and John Costello, *'And I Was There.' Pearl Harbor and Midway - Breaking the Secrets* (New York, Morrow, 1985), John Prados, *Combined Fleet Decoded. The Secret History of American Intelligence and the Japanese Navy in World War II* (New York, Random House, 1995), and Alan Stripp, *Code Breaker in the Far East* (London, Cass, 1989).

Among the general interest books one would commend four books for what they bring that is new. Meirion and Susie Harries, *Soldiers of the Sun. The Rise and Fall of the Imperial Japanese Army* (New York, Random House, 1991), is full of interesting detail: Jerry E. Strahan, *Andrew Jackson Higgins and the Boats that won World War II* (Baton Rouge, Louisiana State University Press, 1994) may have overstated the case but none the less provide a perspective that is seldom afforded due consideration, and on kindred matters one would commend John B. Lundstrom's *The First South Pacific Campaign: Pacific Fleet Strategy, December 1941 – June 1942* and *The First Team. Pacific Naval Air Combat from Pearl Harbor to Midway* (Annapolis, Maryland, Naval Institute Press, 1976 and 1984 respectively) for the opening phase of the war. John J. Stephan, *Hawaii under the Rising Sun. Japan's Plans for Conquest after Pearl Harbor* (Honolulu, University of Hawaii, 1984), provides a fascinating account of what might have been.

In the same vein Thomas B. Allen and Norman Polmar, *Code-name Downfall. The Secret Plan to Invade Japan and why Truman Dropped the Bomb* (New York, Simon and Schuster, 1995) invites attention though one would state one's own preference for John Ray Skates' masterly *The Invasion of Japan. The Alternative to the Bomb* (University of South Carolina Press, 1994). Likewise, Lieutenant Colonel Merrill L. Bartlett, USMC (Ret), (Editor), *Assault from the Sea. Essays on the History of Amphibious Warfare* (Annapolis, Maryland, Naval Institute Press, 1983), provides in its relevant sections valuable insights into its subject, while on this subject one cannot but note Richard Frank, *Guadalcanal. The Definitive Account of the Landmark Battle* (New York, Random House, 1990), which, if not the final word on the subject, comes perilously close to being so, even if the distinction between a battle and a campaign is not necessarily very clear.

Finally I acknowledge two favourites. The subjects are desperately neglected but Rear Admiral Worrall Reed Carter, USN (Ret), *Beans, Bullets and Black Oil. The Story of Fleet Logistics afloat in the Pacific during World War II*, (Washington DC, GPO, 1953) provides a basis of understanding of naval operations that has not lost its relevance, and to which I return all too frequently. And last of all, and perhaps least, I would ask the reader's indulgence in commending my own *Grave of a Dozen Schemes. British Naval Planning and the War against Japan, 1943–1945* (Annapolis, Maryland, Naval Institute Press, 1996) as perhaps one of the better books dealing with the British dimension of this conflict. I would note, however, that it should come with a health warning: the subject is most complicated, and perhaps the work too accurately recreates these complexities: indeed one reviewer perceptively if accidentally referred to it as *Grave of a Thousand Schemes*. It most definitely is not light reading on a pleasant autumnal evening, but, as always in such matters, this recommendation is made on the normal basis: for what it is worth, if anything.

INDEX

Figures in *italic* refer to captions

PICTURE CREDITS

Every effort has been made to contact the copyright holders for images reproduced in this book. The publishers would welcome any errors or omissions being brought to their attention.

AKG: endpaper, and pp. 20, 24–5, 26–7, 28, 31, 34–5, 37, 38, 39, 53, 101, 117, 119, 135, 167, 179, 190, 194, 196, 206, 207, 208; Corbis-Bettman/UPI: pp. 6, 16, 43, 68 (centre), 80–81, 91 (centre), 97, 111, 124, 126, 131, 155, 157, 166; ET Archive: pp. 48, 58, 74–5, 82, 86–7, 99, 108, 123, 130, 136–7, 154 (top), 176, 186, 187, 188–9, 191, 195, 200–1, 209; Imperial Japanese Navy: pp. 44 (left), 51, 95, 141 (right); Imperial War Museum: pp. 44 (right), 45, 62, 66, 67, 68 (bottom), 104–5, 115, 128, 129, 142, 143, 149, 152, 153, 154 (bottom), 164–5, 170, 177, 178, 188–9, 192, 193, 197, 200; Philip Jarrett: pp. 57, 73; National Archives, Navy Department: pp. 60–61; US Army Air Force: pp. 81, 112, 138, 139, 182, 199; USMC: pp. 107, 133; US Navy: pp. 84, 88, 89, 91 (top), 118, 122, 127, 140, 141 (left), 147, 148, 160–61, 173, 174, 175, 184; US Naval Historical Centre: pp. 77, 106

Drawings on the title page and on pages 50, 56–7, 64, 104, 108, 110, 168–9, 172–3, 184–5, and charts on pp. 120, 121, 158–9, 202–3, 204, and 205 are by Peter Smith and Malcolm Swanston of Arcadia Editions Ltd.

ENDPAPER: *At 9.25 on the morning of 2 September 1945: Tokyo Bay. As the Japanese delegation left the Missouri on board the destroyer Lansdown the sun broke through the overcast as 450 U.S. carrier aircraft flew over the Allied warships. That evening all Allied delegations were invited to Beating the Retreat on board the flagship Duke of York by the massed bands of units of the British Pacific Fleet. As was the tradition, proceedings were brought to a close with the sunset hymn. During the singing of the verse: 'So be it, Lord, thy throne shall never Like earth's proud empires pass away; Thy kingdom stands, and grows for ever, Till all thy creatures own thy sway' the flags of all delegations were lowered in unison. Symbolism was complete.*